A PRESIDENCY UPSTAGED

Joseph V. Hughes Jr. and Holly O. Hughes
Series on the Presidency and Leadership

James P. Pfiffner, General Editor

A list of titles in this series is available
at the end of the book.

A Presidency Upstaged

THE PUBLIC LEADERSHIP OF GEORGE H. W. BUSH

LORI COX HAN

Texas A&M University Press COLLEGE STATION

First edition

This paper meets the requirements of
ANSI/NISO, Z39.48-1992
(Permanence of Paper).
Binding materials have been
chosen for durability.

Library of Congress Cataloging-in-Publication Data

Han, Lori Cox.
A presidency upstaged : the public leadership of George H. W. Bush / Lori Cox Han.
— 1st ed.
p. cm. — (Joseph V. Hughes Jr. and Holly O. Hughes series
on the presidency and leadership)
Includes bibliographical references and index.
ISBN-13: 978-1-60344-220-6 (cloth : alk. paper)
ISBN-10: 1-60344-220-0 (cloth : alk. paper)
1. Bush, George, 1924– —Public opinion. 2. Bush, George, 1924–
—Relations with journalists. 3. Press and politics—United States—History—20th
century. 4. Political leadership—United States—History—20th century.
5. Public relations and politics—United States—History—20th century.
6. Public opinion—United States—History—20th century.
7. Mass media—Political aspects—United States—History—
20th century. 8. Presidents—United States—Messages.
9. United States—Politics and government—1989–1993.
I. Title. II. Series: Joseph V. Hughes, Jr. and Holly O. Hughes series
on the presidency and leadership.

E881.H347 2011
973.928092—dc22
2010022911

For my son and native Texan,

Davis Anthony Han

Contents

Acknowledgments

My interest in this topic, as well as the research and writing for this book, has spanned several years. I first began working on this project in 2001 while still an assistant professor at Austin College. My goal was to take a closer look at the public aspects of the George H. W. Bush presidency to gain a better understanding of the role that public leadership plays in the modern presidency. Despite the fact that Bush was a one-term president who was known for wanting to distance himself from the stagecraft of the Reagan years, I suspected that the Bush communication strategy would nonetheless make an excellent case study. Looking back at the Bush years can leave one with a sense of disconnect: How could a president who oversaw the fall of the Berlin Wall and the end of the Cold War, and who saw record-breaking approval ratings for his job performance during Operation Desert Storm, see his political fortunes change so dramatically by 1992 and not win reelection? While many factors, such as the economy, played a role in the outcome of the 1992 presidential election, simply dismissing Bush as an unsuccessful communicator, which many had done, left too many unanswered questions about the complexities of the public aspects of the presidency.

In addition, the Bush years also represent a time of dramatic changes within the news media industry. Having been a newspaper reporter in California during most of the Bush presidency, I had experienced first-hand the trends of the newspaper industry, including downsizing, hiring and salary freezes, the consolidation of daily newspapers, and the coming of the Internet age, all of which contributed to increased competition and a shifting tone to more negative and sensational news coverage. As I transitioned from a full-time journalist to a full-time graduate student in the early 1990s, and thus developed my scholarly interest in the public presidency, the question of Bush as a communicator continued to intrigue me, with particular interest in how the changes in the news industry had shaped Bush's communication strategy and public style. The ideal opportunity to begin the analysis came nearly a decade later when I was an assistant professor at Austin College, only about a three-hour drive from the Bush Presidential Library in College Station.

Thus, my scholarly journey with Bush 41 had begun. I presented the first draft of chapter 1 at APSA in 2002, thinking that the book would be done within two years (and in time for my tenure decision). In 2005, I presented the first draft of what would become chapters 2 and 3 at APSA, two months after accepting my current position at Chapman University, a move that took me back home to California (with tenure long behind me). Yet my motivation for and interest in the project never waned, and each subsequent trip to the Bush Library continued to yield relevant documents to support my research. Nearly every year, when seeing colleagues at conferences, I would be asked, "How is the Bush book coming?" My standard response became, "If I don't finish it soon, it may just become my retirement project." Happily, that did not occur, as I was able to finish the first draft of the manuscript during the 2008–2009 academic year once I put nearly five years of administrative responsibilities as department chair (on two campuses) behind me. In hindsight, I am glad that the final draft of the book was not completed until late 2009, which allowed me to include important documents released at the Bush Library in the fall of 2009 under a Freedom of Information Act request that I submitted more than six years earlier in the spring of 2003. I take it as a sign that things worked out how they were meant to be.

Given that writing this book became a rather long journey, I have many people to thank. First, I am deeply appreciative of the continued support and patience of Mary Lenn Dixon, editor-in-chief of Texas A&M University Press, while this manuscript reached its conclusion. I also appreciate Jim Pfiffner's early enthusiasm for the project and his desire to include the book in the Presidency and Leadership series. I am also grateful for the amazing knowledge and professionalism of the entire staff at the Bush Library. Having conducted research at nearly every presidential library, I have spent more time at the Bush Library than any other. As a result, I can say without a doubt that the archivists at the Bush Library exemplify the very best within their profession, and their shared enthusiasm for helping me find the documents that I needed was always appreciated.

I received funding from various sources for travel to the Bush Library while working on this project. First, I thank the Bush Foundation for providing me with two O'Donnell Research Grants, in December 2002 and December 2008, which helped tremendously at both the beginning and the end stages of the project. The latter grant was particularly beneficial as it allowed me to travel to College Station in November 2009 to access my FOIA documents (just in time to include the documents in the final draft of the manuscript). I also thank my colleagues at Chapman University on the Research and Development Council who approved my requests for travel funds to College Station during the summers of 2006 and 2008. And most importantly, I would like to acknowledge the early support for this project that I received while still a faculty member at Austin College through the Richardson Fund for faculty development. I would especially like to thank Mike Imhoff, vice president of academic affairs at Austin College, for his continued support of all of my research endeavors while I was a faculty member there. Whenever the social science travel budget had been depleted, I could always count on Mike to find some extra funding for me, whether for a research trip to a presidential library (including two to the Bush Library) or to present a paper at a conference. I also appreciated how he always took the time to read whatever I had presented or published and for the support he provided in many other ways during my seven years at Austin College.

I have too many friends within the Presidency Research Group to list here, but I remain humbled to be part of such a collegial group of scholars who have added so much to my professional life and scholarship over these last several years. However, two friends in particular deserve mention here—Diane Heith and Victoria Farrar-Myers—whom I have known since we all met way back in November 1996 at the Neustadt Conference at Columbia University as soon-to-be newly minted PhDs looking for our first tenure-track jobs. Both Diane and Victoria have provided invaluable support both professionally and personally, and they always patiently listened and gave feedback when the subject of "my Bush book" would inevitably come up in conversation. Finally, I am forever and most grateful for the love and support of my family. My husband, Tom, read several drafts of various chapters, and he remains my most insightful and helpful critic. My daughter, Taylor, and my son, Davis, as always, showed tremendous patience as I worked to finish this manuscript. Whenever I spend quality time with Tom and the kids, even if it keeps me from getting a few more pages written, I am always reminded of the most important things in life.

CHAPTER 1

Introduction

George H. W. Bush and the Public Presidency

When Pres. George H. W. Bush left office in January 1993, much was left to be determined about his legacy. Presidential legacies are often built not only on issues of substance, such as domestic, economic, and foreign policy achievements, but also on issues of style, such as a president's approval ratings and ability to connect with the American public. As Ronald Reagan's successor, Bush is remembered as a president who sought to "stay the course" in terms of policy while distancing himself from the stagecraft and public relations strategies of the Reagan years. But, as Bush discovered during his one-term presidency, continuity coupled with mediocre communication skills does not make for a strong public image as an effective and active leader in the White House. As it continues to evolve, the Bush legacy in terms of his style and public leadership skills has already and will continue to be heavily influenced by the fact that Bush, a one-term president, held office following Reagan and preceding Bill Clinton, both two-term presidents who were dynamic and skilled communicators. On issues of substance, the Bush legacy has benefitted from time and distance from his years in office as he has crafted a strong image as an elder statesman in his post–White House years. His prudence and caution as president, particularly in regard to foreign policy issues, is also remembered more longingly when contrasted with the worldview of son George W. Bush's two-term administration. This suggests that the long-term view of even a president who loses his reelection effort and is not immediately considered a success can be rehabilitated through both hindsight and the missteps of his successors in office.

While many facets of the Bush years provide much for presidency scholars to assess and analyze, it is the role of the public presidency that is considered here. Much can be learned from studying the public presidency of Bush, including his relationship with the press, the communication strategies employed by his advisors, the role of public opinion polling within the Bush White House, and how these issues shaped and defined his image as a leader. Understanding Bush's public leadership is essential in order to fully comprehend the significance of the Bush years during an age when the mass media played, and has since continued to play, such a crucial role in governance. Many presidency scholars have already weighed in with their opinions about Bush's successes and failures (mostly the latter) in the area of presidential leadership. However, a better understanding of Bush's public leadership is necessary to place his years in the White House within their proper political perspective. Two important volumes have been written on specific aspects of the Bush public presidency—*The Press and the Bush Presidency* by Mark J. Rozell and *The Rhetorical Presidency of George H. W. Bush* edited by Martin J. Medhurst. Further study in these areas, as well as others related to White House communication strategies, can provide a wealth of data and knowledge regarding Bush's presidency.

A consensus among scholars and political commentators alike seems to exist that Bush was, at best, a mediocre communicator. While he brought a strong resume to the Oval Office, which included his experience as vice president, CIA director, U.S. ambassador to the United Nations, ambassador to China, head of the Republican National Committee, and two terms in the House of Representatives, he lacked the public connection that Reagan had so skillfully used to his governing advantage. Given the general agreement on this topic—that Bush was not a strong communicator—why bother to take a closer look at the public aspects of his administration? It is important to understand the public aspects of the presidency, particularly within the context of our media-driven political environment, whether or not the president is seen as a successful communicator. Presidents and their advisors have been implementing public strategies as part of the day-to-day governing process now for decades, and understanding the role that this plays in presidential decision-making, governance, and leadership helps to explain one of the crucial ways in which presidents are, rightly or wrongly, judged. In the broader sense, this book discusses the importance of the public presidency and its impact on presidential leadership. The specific purpose is to place the Bush years in the proper context of how presidential leadership has been defined through the public lens and how this can shape a president's ability to govern effectively. As the title, *A Presidency Upstaged*, implies, the timing of the Bush presidency in terms of his historical placement as well as the role of the news media in the overall political environment often left Bush at a strategic disadvantage.

No one disputes that Ronald Reagan, for example, knew how to give a great speech and could easily connect with the U.S. public; understanding his success in that regard tells us much about Reagan the man and the inner workings of his administration. The same type of analysis for Bush, then, can provide similar insights into his administration; the rapid and dramatic changes that occurred in the news industry during the late 1980s and early 1990s while Bush was in office make the issue even more compelling as to the evolving relationship between the president and the press.

This introductory chapter provides a review of the emerging literature on the Bush presidency and a discussion of the strengths and weaknesses of Bush's public leadership. The structure of the book includes an in-depth analysis of various public aspects of the day-to-day operation of the Bush White House in an attempt to answer several questions. First and perhaps most importantly: Can a president and his administration learn the skill and strategy necessary to implement a successful communication strategy, or was Bush's failure in the area of public leadership part of a larger, systemic problem? Bush provides an excellent case study for several reasons. A general assumption exists that Reagan succeeded as president while Bush failed. If that is the case, then was it simply a matter of style versus substance—was Reagan a great communicator with a hollow message while Bush provided a depth and breadth of political knowledge but lacked public skills? While that certainly may be oversimplifying the comparison between the two administrations, understanding the distinction between style and substance—and the importance of being an effective communicator—is now crucial in defining presidential leadership and what that means for determining presidential success or failure. Bush certainly enjoyed successes during his four years in office. For example, during the Gulf War, his governing style of behind-the-scenes negotiating and consensus building, coupled with his substantive knowledge of international affairs, proved successful in building an international coalition with strong support at home for military action. Unfortunately for Bush, while those types of skills are often essential for successful presidential leadership, they are often not the skills on full public display and thus cannot sustain an image of successful *public* leadership. An irony of the Bush years comes from the fact that his strengths as president—experience and knowledge at the national and international level—did not automatically meet the public expectations left in the wake of the Reagan years and the increasing demands of the 24-hour news cycle.

Other questions must follow to better understand the Bush presidency within the public realm. Beginning with Jimmy Carter's election in 1976, four out of the last six presidents selected by U.S. voters have been former state governors and, more importantly, Washington outsiders. Bush stands out among the six most recent presidents as the only one with an impressive national and international political resume prior to assuming the presidency. Given that Bush was a Washington insider with nearly twenty-five years of political experience, culminating in his eight years as Reagan's vice president, did Bush not see the road map? That is, why did he not learn from Reagan's success and instead distance himself from a proven public strategy? There was no shortage of White House advisors working on the overall communications strategy, and the number of public events increased while Bush was in office. A strategy more focused on substance than style might have been a good fit for Bush and his view of the presidency, but it turned out to not be a good fit for Bush given the political environment in which he attempted to govern. As a result, despite all of his political experience, Bush struggled to implement an effective day-to-day communication strategy amid the public expectations that had been created by his successor in the White House.

Presidential Leadership and the Public Presidency

Leadership, particularly in the political context, has a variety of definitions and is often viewed as a malleable term, but in general it is considered a process that involves influence, occurs in groups, and includes attention to goals.[1] The definition of leadership can also include "individual traits, leader behavior, patterns of interacting, role relationships, relations with followers, and follower perceptions." The job of the president, then, obviously encompasses both governance and leadership—occurring through "formal aspects of government and in a multitude of ways surrounding formal governing."[2] Based mostly on the scholarship of political scientists, the definition of presidential leadership that emerged in 1960 was Richard Neustadt's view that modern presidential power equates the ability to bargain and persuade.[3] Since then, other important works have redefined, modified, or expanded the notion of presidential leadership to encompass various views of presidents and the presidency, including the president as a transformational leader as well as the state of the postmodern presidency.[4] Other important topics shaping the definition of presidential leadership have included changes in the political environment, the institutionalization of and leadership within the executive branch, policy making and the president's relationship with Congress, and the public presidency and changes in White House communication strategies.[5] As Bert Rockman states, the study of presidential leadership is both fascinating and complex in that presidents may vary in temperaments, but all are confronted with similar pressures while in office—"it is the manipulable factor in a sea of largely nonmanipulable forces."[6]

Public leadership—that is, the art and skill of communication on the public stage—has gained increasing significance in terms of understanding the more general notion of presidential leadership. Specifically, and in its political context, public leadership can be defined simply as the ability of a public official to use the public component of a political office to accomplish a specific task, goal, or agenda item. As such, the end result of public leadership can be something as specific and tangible as the passage of a new law or the start of a government initiative, or something as broad-based and intangible as rhetoric that motivates, inspires, or comforts the masses. However, at either extreme, public leadership skills matter and play a large role in allowing a public official to accomplish his or her political goals.[7] The importance of public leadership to effective governance is perhaps most pronounced when viewing that of a president.

The president's proficiency as a public communicator, what Fred Greenstein refers to as the "outer face of leadership," is an important determinant in understanding the strengths and weaknesses of individual presidents.[8] As defined by George C. Edwards III in the early 1980s, during the time when Ronald Reagan was raising the bar in terms of presidential communications in the television age, the "public presidency" encompasses a president's understanding and leadership of public opinion; a president's influence of the press; press portrayals of the president; and the public's expectations and evaluation of the president.[9] Utilizing the public aspects of leadership has led modern presidents to seek public support by what Samuel Kernell refers to as "going public," a style of presidential leadership that includes "a class of activities that presidents engage in as they promote themselves and their policies before the American public." Addresses to the nation, press conferences, and other public appearances are examples of how a president attempts to sell his agenda or other presidential actions to not only the public but other political actors as well. This activity has been made easier in recent years with the technological developments of the mass media.[10] Developing an effective White House communication strategy, which considers the president's leadership style and policy agenda within the context of press relations, speechwriting, and public activities, is now more important than ever in an attempt to control the political environment in which presidents operate: "communication strategies emerge for every president, and can shape, to varying degrees, the relationship that the president has with both the press and the public, which in turn can help determine the overall success of the administration and its policies."[11]

As presidential scholar Clinton Rossiter observed in 1963, the president "is not one kind of leader one part of the day, another kind in another part—leader of the bureaucracy in the morning, of the armed forces at lunch, of Congress in the afternoon, of the people in the evening. He exerts every kind of leadership every moment of the day, and every kind feeds upon and into all the others."[12] The importance of Rossiter's observation has gained more credibility over the years, as the media age has continued to infiltrate the parameters of presidential leadership. Public expectations have been raised during the past four decades for what is now defined as strong presidential leadership—a concept that has changed greatly since the days of the administrations of Abraham Lincoln, Woodrow Wilson, or even both Roosevelts (Theodore and Franklin). Beginning with John F. Kennedy's skill at using television and other means of communication to effectively present an image of strong leadership emanating from the White House, the public responsibilities of a president are now on a strategic par with other policy-related day-to-day functions within an administration.

However, as more recent studies have shown, even politicians who are skilled communicators do not have an easy time of influencing the public through their rhetoric or the symbolism of their offices. Several impediments still exist that make the task of leading the public difficult. The growing number of media technologies, outlets, and channels make it difficult for even the president to have his voice heard among the cacophony of news anchors, political pundits, and other entertainment options. In addition, the current divide among the electorate in which the voters are firmly grounded in their beliefs and cannot be persuaded otherwise can make attempts at presidential rhetoric futile; even those presidents who are charismatic face many obstacles and are frustrated in their attempts to lead the public, even though the "American political system provides presidents with strong incentives to increase their persuasive resources by seeking public support."[13]

Other recent studies have also begun to question the "going public" model in terms of its effectiveness and usefulness for governance, as it is often Congress and the bureaucracy, and not the public, to which presidents direct their public speeches in an attempt to influence legislation and implement public policy. In addition to "going public," presidents also "signal" members of Congress and the bureaucracy to gain support for their policy initiatives.[14] Presidents have also received much criticism of late for their willingness to "pander" to public opinion in terms of choosing which public policies to support and for adopting a model of governing that resembles a "permanent campaign."[15] While presidents do appear sometimes to pander to public opinion, they do so to maximize their influence over Congress and the public (who can be motivated to influence Congress to support the president) to push through legislation that is already generally supported by the public.[16] Presidential rhetoric can also have an important moral message and "send signals to Congress, contribute vital public support to a burgeoning social movement, make important connections between policy decisions and ethical concerns, enhance their constitutional role, oppose political adversaries, or engage in party leadership."[17]

These studies, of course, shift the debate of the "going public" model. The technological developments of the mass media in recent years have allowed presidents to go public more often and with much greater ease. Yet going public does not necessarily translate into greater success with efforts at public leadership. Strategy matters in this regard, and only in some cases does a president have success at gaining the support of both the public and other relevant actors in the policymaking process to enact some sort of tangible change. Those who hold public office do not have the luxury of acting unilaterally in accomplishing their goals and, depending on the circumstances and the mood of the public, must appeal to other politicians, the public, the news media, or any combination of those three to succeed in their public leadership efforts.

Between the years of 1961 and 2001, three presidents are usually categorized as "successful" communicators—Kennedy, Reagan, and Clinton—while the remaining five—Lyndon Johnson, Richard Nixon, Gerald Ford, Jimmy Carter, and Bush—are categorized as generally "unsuccessful." An assessment of George W. Bush as a communicator is somewhat complex; the younger Bush was certainly not known for his "polished and inspiring public performances," but he did nonetheless win reelection (as did Nixon) and seemed to connect well with certain voters.[18] And while it is certainly not methodologically sound to so easily place presidencies into generalized categories of "successful" or "unsuccessful" based on communication skills, this is now among the standard measurements many scholars use when assessing presidential skill and effectiveness while in office, as well as determining presidential legacies. Just as good communication skills can negate other presidential shortcomings, bad communication skills can cloud public perceptions of positive aspects (whether policy related or ceremonial) of the presidency. The ability to effectively communicate can highlight positive elements of an administration to the public, which can have obvious benefits (public approval ratings and relations with Congress, for example), while a poor communicator cannot adequately "sell" substantive and important policy matters to the public. Right or wrong, the public cannot appreciate what it does not clearly see or is not being told in an effective (and sometimes entertaining) manner.

How Americans view the president as an individual leader and the presidency as an institution helps to define presidential leadership. Americans have high expectations of their presidents, even though achieving the status of presidential "greatness" remains elusive for most occupants of the Oval Office. The symbolic powers of the office, however, can go a long way toward providing a president with firmer ground on which to maneuver, at least within the public realm of the office. The U.S. presidency is "the focus of intense emotions. . . . Presidents are the nation's number one celebrity; most everything they do is news. . . . by their actions presidents can arouse a sense of hope or despair, honor or dishonor."[19] So while these informal and symbolic powers of the office can enhance presidential leadership if used effectively, they can also detract from the president's ability to govern in other areas. Popular presidents also have much greater success at influencing public opinion than do unpopular presidents. Public opinion about the president, and whether or not the public approves of the president's actions, does matter in the day-to-day operation of the White House—"mass evaluations of the president weigh in the balance of power between governmental units and make political life easier or more difficult for the president than it would otherwise be."[20] Public opinion can also play an important role in a president's effectiveness as a leader or success as a policymaker. The White House is now obsessed with popularity and how the president rates in public opinion polls, since high approval ratings can translate into more successful dealings with Congress.[21]

Ronald Reagan set a new standard for his use of the symbolic powers of the presidency during the 1980s. No president had ever fit into the role of national leader quite so easily, especially via the medium of television. The Reagan administration enjoyed unqualified success in its management of news generated by the White House as well as the image portrayed of the man in charge. As a communicator, Reagan was "devastatingly simple and viscerally seductive," which translated into one of the greatest achievements of his presidency.[22] As Reagan's legacy continues to evolve, it has already been well documented that his brand of *public* leadership changed an important aspect of *presidential* leadership, not only in how the White House now manages the public aspect of the office but how the public views the presidency as well. During the Reagan years, the president was "literally 'produced' as never before; he had never been orchestrated before in the same way. There is no great mystery about this, it could easily be studied, and any new president could decide whether or not he wished to adopt the same techniques."[23]

The emphasis on style, image, and symbolism so prevalent during the Reagan administration is not necessarily a positive change to presidential leadership. Style over substance can also pose dangers for the notion of a "deliberative democracy," inherent in the U.S. system of republican government. In many aspects, the Constitution provides for a "government by discussion" and requires broad-based public discussion of matters of public concern. Not only must adequate information be provided to the public at large, but there needs to be "an absence of strategic manipulation of information, perspective, processes, or outcomes in general."[24] While this is not an attempt to indict the Reagan administration for harms done to the U.S. public through successful image manipulation of the presidency, it does raise the point, as other scholars have done, that the powers available through the rhetorical aspects of the presidency have not only greatly deviated from the original constitutional intentions of the Founders but have harmed the constitutional balance of power among the branches as well.[25]

Leadership and the Bush Presidency—Substance over Style?

Several presidential scholars have provided definitions, explanations, and assessments of George Bush's style of presidential leadership. Most are in agreement that Bush was a cautious and prudent president who saw his role as the manager and caretaker of the federal government, as opposed to a visionary leader. And while his presidency is not considered one of great innovation, from either a policy or leadership perspective, Bush is viewed as a capable and intelligent man who, through his vast party and government experience, was qualified for the job. Bush had a strong commitment to public service, instilled in him from an early age. According to Fred Greenstein, "It is necessary to go back to Franklin Roosevelt to find a chief executive with the rich governmental experience of George Bush."[26] Based on contemporary standards of "successful" presidential leadership, however, Bush came up short in many categories. Bush was viewed as "a president for some seasons, not all. He [was] Mr. Inside."[27] Bush has been called the "semi-sovereign president" with a strategy based on a "lesser scale of policymaking so long as he could work his will through internal and unaccountable channels"; a not-so-public president with a style different from the very public approach to governing through the use of mandates, public opinion, and legislative activism.[28] The Bush years have also been called the "status-quo presidency" and the "guardianship presidency."[29] Bush was an insider with a limited agenda, and since academics tend to have a scholarly bias for "activist" presidents, which Bush was not, assessments of the Bush years have been mostly negative.[30] According to Michael Genovese, Bush's presidency focused on procedure, not ideas. Bush was "more cautious, more moderate, more pragmatic than Reagan. Bush was a manager at a time when the nation needed a leader, a status quo president in a time of change, a minimalist in a momentous time. . . . [he] often seemed a passive observer in a dramatically changing world."[31] Stephen Skowronek also provides an instructive observation, in that "the historic significance of [Bush's] leadership effort lies in its dismal confirmation of what all presidents should know by now: that the political premise of affiliated leadership is utterly exhausted."[32]

Understanding Bush's style of leadership also demands the inevitable comparisons to Reagan, his immediate predecessor and former boss. In this regard, Bush was challenged from the start to define his own presidency separate from that of Reagan. The negativity that had permeated the 1988 presidential campaign, in which he defeated Massachusetts Gov. Michael Dukakis, did not allow Bush to get off to a quick start in building a strong image of presidential leadership. As Timothy Naftali states, "the election campaign of 1988, so long on patriotic symbols and so short on substance, had left only a vague impression of the incoming president, certainly nothing as powerful as the public image of Ronald Reagan, who despite Iran-Contra appeared to be departing directly from 1600 Pennsylvania Avenue for Mount Rushmore."[33] Bush talked of creating a "new world order" but also had to contend with the long shadow being cast on his presidency by the conservative policy agenda and skilled rhetoric of the Reagan presidency. The Bush presidency, however, was not merely a "redux" or "interregnum" of the Reagan years; his attempts at governing were just as complex but for different reasons: "The heart of the Bush presidency lay in its attempts to deal with the economic instability and cultural anxiety" created by the Reagan years.[34]

Bush admittedly had difficulty in developing his own "vision" for the country and based his policy prioritizations on reviving commitments to federal programs that Reagan had "sought to bury" like environmental regulations, Medicaid, and Head Start. According to Skowronek, the policy "reconstruction" of the Reagan years had turned out to be "largely rhetorical," which made articulating a vision difficult for Bush: "During his four years in the presidency, [Bush] was continually tripping over the question of who he really was."[35] Many of Reagan's policies may have had substance, but many, like his economic policies and the uncontrollable national debt, "unleashed a host of demons that plagued his successor."[36] Bush constantly struggled with his political identity as he tried to stake out a more mainstream political position within the Republican Party, as well as keeping his distance from the symbolic imagery and public relations tactics used by Reagan to govern. According to Neustadt, one of Reagan's greatest legacies was that of imagery and his skillful use of public leadership, which was unfortunate for Bush: "Mr. Reagan leaves, in terms of imagery, a pretty big screen for Mr. Bush to fill. The image includes Reagan, the chief of state, almost always striking the right note. The image includes Reagan as tough tactician in congressional relations during 1981. . . . The media report presidential-congressional relations as a spectator sport, and the White House understood that fact in the Reagan administration. They may not have understood substance, but they surely understood *that*."[37]

Plan of the Book

Understanding the public presidency of George H. W. Bush, and assessing its impact on his years in the White House, requires a better understanding of several distinct yet interrelated topics. Key among those topics include a consideration of Bush's overall communication strategy, especially his use of the presidential bully pulpit and his attempts to step back from the imagery of the Reagan years to focus more on substance. Also, his open access to the White House press corps, and his attempts to provide more information and less image manipulation, backfired in that his administration still received negative news coverage (as had previous presidents in the television age). For Bush, two ironies stand out regarding the public aspects of his presidency. First, despite efforts to minimize the public aspects of the office, Bush increased his public appearances and relied on an extensive public strategy in doing so. Second, at least until the economic recession in 1992, Bush enjoyed relatively high approval ratings yet was unable to translate his public support into a second term in office.

From the start of the Bush administration in 1989, the heir apparent to the Reagan legacy of public leadership worked hard to distance himself from the stagecraft of the previous eight years. In doing so, he seemed to be, as pointed out by the *Los Angeles Times* in early 1989, "posing a basic question: Can the President of the United States really lead simply by trying to develop popular policies—without slick television packaging and elaborate schemes to manipulate the news media? As a political consultant might put it, is substance enough?"[38] During his first three years in office, Bush's approval ratings seemed to vindicate his anti-Reagan communication strategy. But according to Mark Rozell, by late 1991, with the nation dealing with an economic recession, Bush's failure to cultivate "a positive image of his own impressive background and accomplishments—and to have developed a coherent message of what his administration stood for—doomed his presidency when the public begged for a sense of direction to lead the country out of its problems. Lacking a coherent message, Bush was popular during good times, and then people blamed him for the perceived bad times."[39]

Bush came to office with high expectations in some areas and low expectations in others. He was the first Washington insider since Gerald Ford; having been vice president for eight years meant that compared to "outsiders" like Carter or Reagan, he did not need extensive on-the-job training. Bush had "considerable experiences in government, and had served a long apprenticeship for the presidency."[40] Many of the difficulties that Bush experienced in office had little to do with him personally but more to do with the changes to the political environment during the Reagan years, specifically the "gap between expectations and capability that may reflect a more fundamental crisis of identity and purpose" for the presidency.[41] But the low expectations in the area of public leadership, after Reagan had raised the bar so effectively, were unfortunately accurate. This became an insurmountable aspect to governing for Bush; "While the perception of a president as effective reinforces his power, a perception of him as ineffective is difficult to dispel and undermines his ability to provide leadership."[42]

Bush may have not always succeeded in his style as a communicator, but his years in the White House, and the content of his messages while president, did have many substantive aspects. A more in-depth analysis of those messages, and the strategy behind them, is necessary to see past the lack of imagery to better appreciate the effort. As such, the chapters that follow are organized around various aspects of the Bush public presidency. Chapter 2 considers the internal factors within the White House that contributed to the Bush public presidency, including his governing style, the communication strategies developed and employed, and the internal operations of the speech and press offices. These elements combine to make the "output" of the public presidency; that is, the message and image presented to the American public (along with the news media and other political actors). Chapter 3 will then consider the external factors that helped to shape the Bush public presidency, including the state of the news industry and the political environment in which Bush attempted to govern. The post-Reagan years were not always easy to navigate for the Bush White House, and it was through the "feedback" from news media coverage, public opinion, and policy and electoral outcomes that provided the impetus for how the administration governed and strategized on a day-to-day basis.

Chapters 4 and 5, through a case-study approach, provide the analysis that brings together the internal and external factors of the Bush public presidency to provide an in-depth look at the public strategies employed and the subsequent end result. In doing so, the "output" is assessed through the lens of the "feedback;" or, to put it more simply, how did Bush rate as a public leader? Traditional public venues for presidents—state of the union addresses and major policy addresses—are analyzed in terms of White House strategy for key events, followed by an analysis of several news sources to assess media coverage and public perception. Documents from the Bush Presidential Library, including internal White House memos, also help to illuminate and explain the Bush public strategy. The concluding chapter reconsiders the importance of the public presidency and further analyzes the Bush legacy in that regard and whether or not the prevalent assumptions of Bush as a communicator are accurate and fair.

CHAPTER 2

Internal Factors

Process and Strategy in the Bush White House

The public strategy of the George H. W. Bush administration, particularly that with the press, can be summed up as more access, more information, less image manipulation. Bush wanted to develop a strong and substantive relationship with the press, especially in providing more real interaction between him and the White House press corps than during the previous administration. As a result, he moved away from various communication strategies that had been employed by Ronald Reagan's advisors and instead afforded the press extensive access to the entire administration. For example, he hoped to gain favorable coverage by holding many informal discussions with reporters, and he courted the press as members of the political elite. However, while Bush held many more press conferences than Reagan and met with reporters regularly on an informal basis, he did not use these events as a means to advance his policy agenda. Instead, he simply allowed reporters to ask him questions, which meant that he often talked to the press but did not do a good job of framing public perceptions of his vision for the United States. Wanting numerous informal, last-minute press sessions in an attempt to create an open and friendly presidency suggests that Bush's strategy reflected what he considered to be his greatest asset, which was face-to-face, personal contact with reporters.[1] What the strategy lacked, however, was an overall message to the U.S. public about his policy agenda, as well as a consistently clear understanding of the dramatic changes occurring within the news industry during his four years in office.

The attempt to de-emphasize and move away from what was considered to be stagecraft during the Reagan years can be seen in the strategy, process, and procedures involving communications within the Bush White House. This chapter offers an assessment of the internal factors affecting the Bush public presidency, including the overall communication strategy and attempts to develop Bush's public image; press strategies and the operation of the press office under the guidance of Press Secretary Marlin Fitzwater; the public strategy, including the work of the Office of Communications in developing public events for the president; and the speechwriting process and Bush as an orator. These elements combine to make up the many components of Bush's attempts at public leadership and how the heir-apparent to the Reagan administration sought to take a different approach in managing communications and the presidential image. The "output" from this strategy—Bush's actual speeches and public events—usually reflected the administration's attempt to favor substance over style, as well as to favor more behind-the-scenes access over staged press events. However, the overt attempts not to be Reagan at times hampered the efforts of the president to sound presidential, at least compared to the "Great Communicator," Ronald Reagan.

Communication Strategy Meets Public Image

In spite of Bush's professional experience in both national and international political circles, as well as his knowledge of relevant policy issues, Bush never mastered the role of "communicator-in-chief." The overall communication strategy within the Bush White House often relied on an anti-Reagan approach—the president sought to distance himself from the staged photo opportunities and line-of-the-day news management style that the Reagan administration had used so effectively. Bush wanted his administration to focus on substantive issues by avoiding the reputation of being a "symbolic presidency" that relied on the "stagecraft" developed during the Reagan years. Throughout his four years in office, Bush maintained a high level of public discussion of issues but did so through an overall lower public profile.[2] The problem for Bush came in the area of his public image—how to portray himself as an active leader on issues of substance (policy matters and running the federal government) without overexposure to the public and press in the area of public relations. It is important to remember, however, that Reagan was not infallible as a communicator. As Stephen Skowronek points out, "The difficulty comes not in explaining Reagan's fame as a master of rhetoric and a communicator of ideas but in trying to square that with his other reputation for wandering into incoherence, misstatement of fact, and fantasy during his more extemporaneous remarks."[3] In spite of that, Reagan's strengths in the area of communication not only overshadowed those types of incidents but also often masked his weaknesses in the area of policy specifics. The image seen by Americans was that of an active leader with a skill for communicating his message and vision for the country.

Much of Bush's communication strategy focused on his use of press conferences, with the goal of meeting the needs of newspapers, and not the network news, hence the focus on informal question-and-answer sessions as opposed to primetime press conferences. Press Secretary Marlin Fitzwater recognized Bush's strengths and weaknesses in this area and advised the president accordingly not to "try to compete with former movie star Reagan at prime-time news conferences in the awesome setting of the East Room." Instead, Bush heeded the advice and met with reporters in the briefing room.[4] Bush relied on "almost unceasing news conferences" where he could show his "command of facts and his ease in fielding reporters' questions." This became a much more subtle approach to image manipulation to reduce reporters' preparation time and generally keep them behind the camera. What the public saw was a confident, informed president who knew how to answer "faceless journalists."[5]

From the start, Bush's communication team was at a disadvantage in their efforts to develop an effective communication strategy. Not only did the new president want to do things much differently than his predecessor, in spite of Reagan's success with the public aspects of the job, but Bush also had an image problem to live down as soon as he entered the White House. During the 1988 presidential campaign, Bush earned the reputation as a "mud-slinging, whining, nasty man who had used negative advertising to downgrade his opponent." Bush's advisors had developed this aggressive campaign strategy to tear down the "wimp" image that had manifested itself in the press. Bush also sought to convince Americans that he could provide strong leadership at both the national and international level, despite the public's view that he had been the "invisible man" of the Reagan administration and the loyal vice president who had escaped public scrutiny over Iran-Contra.[6] The *New York Times* put it this way: "First the press portrayed him as a wimp, a preppy, a tinny-voiced lap dog who stood for nothing in the Reagan White House and could never win an election on his own. Then he was a pit bull who would do anything, say anything on the campaign trail to become President. Now he is the buoyant winner, the sportsman, the regular guy going to the White House."[7]

While Bush had also promised to continue the Reagan policy legacy, he also talked of a "kinder and gentler America," endorsed "a thousand points of light" regarding public service, and distanced himself from the core conservative agenda. As a result, he had difficulty maintaining his public connection to the strong values of many of his conservative backers. He also made his infamous "read my lips, no new taxes" promise during the campaign, which would be broken with the tax compromise bill in 1990.[8] Many scholars and political observers now look back on that decision as not only necessary but the right political thing to do; it nonetheless served as a reminder to voters in 1992 of Bush's broken promise on the tax pledge, an issue especially salient to conservative members of his own party.

Throughout his four years in office, Bush was often criticized in the press for "either lacking such a vision, failing to articulate one effectively, or both."[9] Bush's trouble with "the vision thing" and failure to articulate a clear message to the American people "raised the art of empty rhetoric to new heights."[10] Behind-the-scenes substance—the political knowledge and skill of the Bush administration—did not automatically translate into the public image of an active and effective president. Bush had an "insular management style" resulting not "from a phobia about leaks but from his thinking on how to get things done," which only served to contradict the image held by those who knew Bush as "open, warm, and inclusive."[11] By 1992, Bush was viewed as out of touch with average Americans, especially those affected by the recession that had begun in 1991, which hurt him in his reelection bid. The image of a strong, competent leader (which is what emerged during the Gulf War) never seemed to consistently appear during the Bush years. And this made for repeated criticisms by the press, as noted by *New York Times* columnist James Reston: "I had thought I knew George Bush fairly well, but I didn't recognize his warrior pose. I longed for years that some gentleman president would come along and set an example of calm thinking and honest talking, and I felt that George Bush was precisely that sort of man. . . . But something happened to him on his way to the White House. He campaigned like Richard Nixon and talked like Lyndon Johnson, saying publicly that Saddam Hussein was worse than Hitler, and vowing publicly to 'kick him in the ass.' And when it was said that maybe he was a bit of a wimp, he disproved it by plunging into two wars in his first two years in office."[12]

Press Strategies

In general, the Bush press strategy sought to downplay the importance of presidential image that had been so important to the Reagan administration. From the start, Fitzwater crafted a strategy that would highlight the differences between Bush and Reagan "both stylistically and substantively," one that relied on Bush's vast knowledge of policies and his ability to communicate effectively with reporters in a more personal, less formal format.[13] The role of the press office in helping to implement the press strategy involved responding to the day-to-day needs of the press, whether answering questions about the president's position on a particular issue or the more managerial role of issuing press credentials, preparing the president's daily news summary, or conducting press conferences.[14] Fitzwater was uniquely qualified to shape this new strategy since he had served as Reagan's assistant to the president for press relations beginning in 1987 and had participated in the implementation of the Reagan strategy. (Fitzwater was in effect the press secretary, but James Brady maintained the official title throughout the Reagan years despite his inability to return to the job after being shot in the assassination attempt against Reagan in March 1981). In December 1988, just weeks prior to Bush's inauguration, Fitzwater declared the need for a new press strategy (in a discussion paper written for the president-elect) that would "[throw] out all the old ways of doing things, and [suggest] an entirely new scheme of press relations." The major premise of this new press "scheme" placed a much greater emphasis on pulling the president back from time on the national stage and replacing the staged events with more informal press access (that is, emphasizing substance over style). According to Fitzwater:

> The press takes the irrational position that the President is a public entity, and that reporters must keep watch over every move and utterance on behalf of the American people. To this end they have constructed elaborate schemes, committed millions of dollars and untold walkie-talkies and helicopters to pursue you to the ends of the earth. Thus, our basic task is to introduce them to a new kind of President—the private man. The lessons of history in this regard regale us with stories of Lyndon Johnson careening through the Texas countryside with mad-cap reporters giving chase; Jimmy Carter sneaking away from Camp David for an afternoon of fishing in the Shenandoahs; and Ronald Reagan having the quietest of dinners at the Jockey Club. The conclusion one reaches from these episodes is that there is no answer to this problem which will satisfy all parties. Thus, our task should be to satisfy you first, and the press as much as possible. We are therefore considering the following: An edict that says: The President of the United States has a right to an uninterrupted and unintruded visit to the ice cream store. It's not

> news. It's unpredictable. It's personal. And security is enhanced by its very unpredictability.[15]

The detailed discussion paper continued to highlight specific strategies that Fitzwater wanted to implement in dealing with the press. First, in relation to press pools, Fitzwater wanted to develop a new method of covering personal or impromptu movements by the president: a press office staff person and a White House photographer would accompany the president to provide photos and information, if "news" should occur. The press travel pool would still be allowed to travel in the presidential motorcade, however, for a scheduled event or movement. Fitzwater seemed willing to endure the wrath of the White House press corps in return for providing a bit of a privacy buffer for the president:

> This approach won't satisfy the press, but it will provide a source of information on the trip for the 50 or so phone calls that will develop at any moment. . . . The press will demand a full travel pool on every movement. If no pool is provided, they threaten to have chase cars and motorcycle couriers stake out the White House on evenings and weekends. Susan Zirinsky, Chief CBS field producer and the model for *Broadcast News* producer, says she staked out Jimmy Carter in Plains, Georgia, with chase cars every morning at 4:30 to catch him jogging. On the other hand, the networks will probably do this even if a pool is in the motorcade. When President Reagan had dinner at the Cafritz's recently, a pool went along. The nets all went anyway and staked out the home. Recommendation: Use a standard travel pool whenever possible; go alone on occasional impromptu occasions; be prepared to take some heat. We would have to establish a record that demonstrates no abuse of the "no pool" trips. Even so, the chase will be on![16]

Fitzwater also wanted to eliminate having reporters shouting questions at the president, what he considered to be a "bad idea" from the Reagan administration that should not continue: "Answering questions on the way to the helicopter is no way to communicate. Trying to shout over the engines of Air Force One is impossible. Answering shouted questions in the Rose Garden is impolite. With due respect to President Reagan, we believe that Presidential dignity and stature would be enhanced by avoiding these opportunities to talk to the press." Fitzwater's suggested solution to the problem included either eliminating all correspondents from photo opportunities or having Bush stick to the rule of "no questions" during these events since expecting reporters to abide by the rule would mean "asking a reporter not to be a reporter." This issue within the discussion paper provided the segue for Fitzwater to elaborate on the rationale behind having Bush provide more access to the press as the main way to distance himself from Reagan's communication strategy: "It should be noted that the press shouted some questions at President Carter during photo opportunities, but far fewer than they did under President Reagan. This is probably because President Carter was continually accessible to the press on a formal and informal basis. Thus there is some precedent for suggesting that your general accessibility would be enough to at least reduce the amount of shouted questions at photo opportunities."

The remaining points of the discussion paper are worth listing here, as it gives an invaluable insight into the mindset on the issue of press relations as the Bush transition team prepared to take office:

> Press Conferences: We recommend that you hold informal press conferences during the day in Room 450, much as you have done recently in announcing new Cabinet positions. These can be announced the same day they are held, and last for 20 minutes to a half-hour, to get credit for having held a full-scale press conference. A minimum of preparation is required, and you are the focus of the news, rather than the reporters.
>
> East Room Press Conferences: We recommend holding these dinosauras-showus-maximus extravaganzas only on special occasions—perhaps two or three times a year. The East Room press conference has developed in a way that gives more of a forum to the press than it does to the President. The cutaway cameras focus on the questions, often which are prosecutorial and inflammatory. In terms of viewer impact, the question is just as important as the answer. . . . In addition, we want to develop press conferences that you will get credit for. It always galled me that the press would not give President Reagan credit for holding a press conference unless it was prime-time, 30 minutes, East Room. We should reverse this so that all forums in which you openly address questions, whether in the briefing room or Room 450, are considered press conferences. The way to do that is to immediately establish the nature of your press conferences.[17]

> Frequent Appearances in the Briefing Room: These could be held for 10–15 minutes duration, on an impromptu, irregular basis. We would recommend doing them without prior notification, so that they are limited to the regular working White House press, and require a minimum of preparation on your part. Again, these have to be frequent enough so that the press views them as routine accessibility, rather than signaling any special announcement.
>
> Pool Briefings: A new idea would be to establish a rotation among regular White House press corps to form a pool of 3–5 reporters who would be taken into the Oval Office once or twice a week for a 10-minute session with the President. The pool would do a report on the interview, and a transcript could be provided to all members of the press corps.
>
> Ad Hoc Access: Perhaps the most effective means of establishing your accessibility to the press is through ad hoc visits to the press working area, hallway discussions, motorcade interviews, etc. You have maintained press relationships of this nature throughout the campaign and the transition. These kinds of events are in stark contrast to President Reagan's style, and make a considerable impression on press attitudes. We recommend you maintain these informal contacts.

The overall theme of this discussion paper suggested how Bush could build "a reputation for accessibility and willingness to deal with the press" in a way that Reagan had not by relying on the daily management of presidential news through limited access to the president himself. In effect, if less was more in the Reagan years regarding press access to the president, the Bush strategy turned that idea on its head by hoping that more would be more. Fitzwater was also looking for a way to appease the press to "lead to better behavior at photo opportunities, less hostility in the press generally, and fewer leaks. The most effective way to put down leaks is for you to be on the record discussing the issues at hand." Clearly, Bush had wanted to develop a strong relationship with the press, especially in providing more real interaction between him and White House reporters.

The initial change in press strategy from Reagan to Bush was obvious in the first weeks of the new administration: Bush held firm to the decision to break away from taking shouted questions from the press corps, invited two newspaper reporters into the Oval Office for a brief question-and-answer session, and even asked reporters their opinion on how to allow follow-up questions during news conferences.[18] The new strategy also seemed to work, what an editorial in the *Washington Post* referred to as "the contrast between [Bush's] performance, in terms of knowledgeability, and that of his predecessor" following an informal press conference during his first week in office (on January 27, 1989).[19] The *Los Angeles Times* reported that during Bush's first meeting with the press, "aides looked on, relaxed, smiling, as Bush easily fielded dozens of questions. During the [Reagan] years, press conferences were anxious times for staff members, who stood by worrying about possible presidential misstatements."[20] A *Los Angeles Times* editorial on the same day praised the new president for his performance while encouraging him to continue the new accessibility to the press: "[Bush] fielded questions with dispatch and evident confidence. . . . The hastily summoned 11 a.m. meeting may have denied Bush the kind of mass audience that an evening session with live coverage by all the television networks would have offered, but that choice doesn't mean that the President isn't ready for prime time. Bush appeared relaxed, well-briefed and on easy terms with the White House press corps. Ronald Reagan, working from a polished text, may have been a great communicator, but George Bush, vamping it, gives an early impression of someone who's on top of his job."[21]

* * *

Many in the press, however, were also quick to acknowledge that while they might appreciate the change in strategy, op-ed writers also began to question whether this new, more informal style with the press was "presidential." Richard Cohen of the *Washington Post* wrote on January 31 that "[Bush] is quickly squandering that special aura of mystery that veils the presidency. Like Carter, he appears both ordinary and indecisive, a man of good intentions whose foremost intention is to be liked. On a whim, he transformed a routine White House briefing into a presidential press conference in which the entire message, really, was that he is not Ronald Reagan. True. But so far, he's not presidential either."[22]

Nonetheless, Fitzwater and the communications team believed that Bush was off to a good start in terms of press relations.[23] In an April 14, 1989, memo to Bush (through Chief of Staff John Sununu), Fitzwater wrote, "As we approach the end of the first three months of the Administration, I believe the press strategy laid out in January has been successful. But, it appears to be time to add a couple of dimensions to our press plan. We have established your accessibility. The demeanor of the press corps has changed for the better. You have established your own presence and personal style. I believe it is now time to present a Presidential posture that shows you directing the decision-making process, and laying out new directions for the Nation. These objectives will require more use of television and radio appearances in which you are allowed to make a full and direct presentation to the American people."[24] The specifics of the press strategy included the following points:

> Bush's first prime-time press conference, which, according to Fitzwater, was expected to be "tougher than any of your press conferences so far" due to the "televised attacks of one kind or another on your Administration."
>
> Cooperation with a *New York Times* story on the presidential decision-making process "to show the strong methodological approach to decisions that you conduct."
>
> The first network interview with Peter Jennings, Brit Hume, or both of ABC News because "their coverage has been the fairest, and they are the most reliable to deal with" even though such interviews "represent talk show appearances . . . [since] competitive advantage is their number one priority; and in my discussions with the networks, it is clear that each cares about having the 'first Bush interview' more than they care about substance or format."
>
> A satellite interview with CBS News during their affiliate meeting in Los Angeles: "The audience would be nearly a thousand station owners and managers. This has questionable direct mass audience value, but it would send a signal to the television industry that you are interested in their media and that you feel comfortable with televised appearances."
>
> A televised speech to the nation from the Oval Office following the NATO Summit "for America to see you as their President in the Oval Office. . . . This speech should discuss the solidarity of the Alliance, your views on US-Soviet relations, and the 'vision thing' as it relates to foreign policy."
>
> A radio roundtable from Camp David: "you would achieve a kind of national radio dialogue, through the six correspondents, and the American people. The Camp David angle just gives it a showbiz twist, and allows you to do it in a relaxed setting. Also, it would not violate our rules on 'no cameras or pictures' from Camp David."

The memo concludes: "In summary, I believe we have received very good press in the first three months of your Administration. The press will never admit to positive news coverage, because it offends their sense of purpose as a government watchdog. It also draws peer criticism of being co-optive. Thus, we are now seeing some articles that say our press coverage isn't massive enough, or well-staged. We can mitigate this problem by broadening the kind of media events in which you participate."

As this initial strategy set out to do, Bush would continue to court members of the press throughout his four years in office to seek a "mutually beneficial relationship" with several journalists. He thought that by making himself accessible and "drawing journalists into his network of personal relationships and speaking frankly to them, Bush hoped in the early days of his presidency to neutralize potential media hostility and to enhance thereby his governing capability."[25] But in his many conversations with reporters, he would often simply allow reporters to ask him questions, which meant that he made "little connection between his public relations and his policy initiatives. . . . He talked to the press, not over it."[26] His access to reporters may have provided an advantage to provide reporters with more substantive information directly from the president, but "in leaning over backward to avoid Reaganesque oratory, he deprived his presidency of the teaching function that enabled presidents such as Roosevelt, Kennedy, and Reagan to frame public perceptions, place their administrations in a favorable light, and buffer themselves from negative developments."[27]

Bush also struggled with appearances on television and could not capitalize on the medium's power to connect with Americans in the way that Reagan had. During the Bush transition in late 1988, there was no push to develop a television strategy for the new president; as the transition team reported, "there is no slot on Bush's staff for a TV adviser." This despite the fact that Roger Ailes, a former television producer who had helped to develop the "new" Richard Nixon television image in 1968, had served as Bush's chief media adviser during the 1988 campaign.[28] As political observers have witnessed during the past five decades, television has changed political life tremendously by "personalizing" the process and providing a "front-row seat" for U.S. citizens while watching political events unfold. However, the intimacy factor that television provides for politicians did not help Bush. In their early study of television and its impact on U.S. politics, Kurt Lang and Gladys Engel Lang argue that "the ordinary viewer and the professional TV critic appear to agree on one point: television exposes the charlatan and celebrates the real article."[29]

Unfortunately for Bush, he may have been the "real article" in terms of substance, but television certainly did not "celebrate" the image that he projected. According to Tom Griscom, a communications advisor in the Reagan administration, presidents in the post-Reagan era would need to ask themselves important questions when developing their communication strategy: "Is television a friend or enemy? Are you a good manipulator? Do you have a visual image, or is it better for one to find other ways to get a message to the American people? It is important for each president to know their communication strengths and how to incorporate them into their administration."[30] Bush never performed well on television, appearing to be "too 'hot' for a medium that seemed to favor a calm and cool persona. Bush had trouble sitting still. He waved his hands and arms too much. He was given to awkward gestures and ill-timed smiles. His tortured syntax, charming perhaps in conversation, was baffling on the tube. The combination made him seem more like a loopy, distracted, jargon-mad creature than the leader of the free world."[31]

Knowing that their president was not a master of television appearances like Reagan, the Bush administration found alternative means to get its message out. For example, Bush increased the number of press conferences immediately after taking office, but since his advisors believed that he did not perform well on television, they became informal and often impromptu early morning events with little news value. This meant that many news organizations did not provide coverage, yet the press could not complain about Bush being inaccessible.[32] While a primary goal of the Reagan administration was to get their president on the evening news, Bush emphasized "continuity, conciliation and compromise," which did not make for exciting pictures on television: "There was to be no equivalent of Michael Deaver to take charge of Bush's image; there would not be a theme of the week and presidential trips would not be tailored to meet the requirements of nightly television news broadcasts."[33]

As this discussion shows, the Bush administration viewed the press differently than the Reagan administration had, and this affected the relationship. While the news media was a vehicle through which Reagan excelled at communicating, Bush's advisors considered the press more of a hindrance. This view is evident in Fitzwater's description of the press in his memoirs: "The press corps is an unwanted appendage, like a cocklebur that attaches to your pants leg. For the White House staff, it's a problem to be managed, a block of people to be moved around like a checker—brought into the Oval Office at the top of each meeting, ushered into the Rose

Garden to witness a bill signing, and wedged into a maze of hallways that can't be freely entered."[34] Not surprisingly, other members of the administration have also stated their opinions about how unfairly they believe Bush was treated by the press. According to former Agriculture Secretary and Republican National Committee Chairman Clayton Yeutter, Bush may never receive the recognition he deserves for his accomplishments while in the White House: "the Bush administration accomplished much more than most people realize, but the media never focused on anything positive related to the President. The media biases in recent years were the worst I have ever seen, as some of the polls indicate. History, too, may well overlook the positive accomplishment and focus on President Bush's mistakes."[35]

Public Strategies

According to David Demarest, the Bush White House communications director from January 1989 until June 1992, to understand Bush's public strategy, "one had to start from the standpoint that President Bush did not like the message managed." This provided an extra challenge for White House staffers responsible for communications and press relations, since the media scrutinized how the Bush team would manage this aspect of governing following the Reagan years. Demarest and his team tried to create a more businesslike relationship with the news media, not wanting to "play the press" as the Reagan administration had done. Demarest recalled that he "wanted to avoid primetime, glitzy, East Room press conferences that had become a show time for reporters." Instead, the decision was made to hold daytime press briefings, since "'breaking news' was not the goal—having a businesslike relationship with reporters was."[36] That view permeated among some of the top advisors in the Bush White House. Bush "had little experience as a performer, was ambivalent about public relations, and invested low resources in developing communications plans for his programs. . . . John Sununu, Bush's chief of staff, was equally uninterested in communications. So it was difficult for other members of the White House staff to develop and implement public relations initiatives." With some major policy announcements, Sununu was so determined to avoid leaks to the press that he would not allow any advance work, whether with the news media or with other political actors who might be supportive of the particular policy initiative. As a result, the Bush White House often received "lackluster stories in the press."[37]

The job of communications director within the Bush White House Office of Communications consisted of speechwriting and research, public liaison, media relations, and intergovernmental affairs. In general, the office coordinated regional media coverage, coordinated information coming out of the executive branch, and engaged in long-term strategies to help shape the public image of the president and his administration.[38] Demarest initially had a job that was "greatly reduced" from his predecessors in the Reagan administration, since Bush had decided to have Fitzwater initially handle communications strategy as well as press relations. Fitzwater did so "despite his own misgivings over combining the two jobs"; this ended before the end of Bush's first year in office, as it had been a "total failure" according to Fitzwater. Perhaps the biggest challenge to the communications strategy was Bush himself; since he had "little interest in communications, his communications operation was not a priority at any time during his administration."[39] Chief of Staff John Sununu also presented an impediment to the implementation of the communications strategy, which often needed to be coordinated with legislative strategy. Sununu wanted control over both, and as a result, Demarest had to "maneuver around Sununu" by setting up weekly event meetings to coordinate communications efforts with groups outside of the White House such as cabinet or other executive offices.[40]

The Bush administration continued to rely on the Office of Communications in relating information to members of the press from around the country in the form of press releases, background information, radio actualities, and satellite feeds, recognizing that one of the overall goals of the office was to assist reporters on the White House beat. The news media had come to rely on the information and assistance provided over the years in helping them do their job, and the "mutually beneficial aspects of the office helped to ensure the office's institutionalization."[41] As with the press office and press strategy, Demarest wanted strategy within the communications office to move away from the image manipulation and public relations emphasis of the Reagan years in part because he "felt that such heavy-handed tactics were degrading to both the White House and the press corps." Ironically, the press would ultimately complain about the openness and accessibility along with the lack of public relations manipulation.[42] In his initial expanded role, Fitzwater was influential in devising strategies within the communications office in the early months of the administration. For example, in a February 2, 1989, memo to the president (through Sununu), Fitzwater explained to Bush, in response to the president's inquiry, why they needed a press aide at Camp David:

> 1) To provide staff liaison for your activities at the Camp which create public inquiries. For example, phone calls you make from the Camp are often relayed to the Press by the recipient of the call. Dignitaries die and special messages of condolence are required to be written. Crises around the world will require special statements from Camp David. All of these situations require a Press Aide at the Camp to coordinate these responses. . . . 2) To provide a source of information concerning any guests you have at the Camp or any departures from the Camp. The Press will take to staking-out Camp David once they discover that you have guests coming and going during the weekend. A sizable group was prepared to go last weekend to stake-out Speaker [Jim] Wright. An on-site Press Aide gives the Secret Service and the Camp Commander assurance that someone is available to manage these situations. 3) To coordinate your arrival departure with the Washington Press Corps. The Press will cover your arrivals and departures every weekend. A Camp David Press Aide is needed to coordinate these events. In summary, there is a general agreement with the Press Corps that one Press Aide will accompany the President at all times to ensure that some source of information is available about the President. To abandon that agreement would mean a barrage of Press maintaining stake-outs at Camp David. . . . No one in the Press Corps has ever suggested that too many staff people go to Camp David. Indeed, the only criticism we have ever received was not having enough people at the Camp to respond in various crisis situations.[43]

Other initial strategies reflected the overall move away from the types of public strategies used by Reagan, exemplified by Fitzwater's recommendation one week prior to Bush's inauguration to discontinue the practice of Saturday weekly radio addresses that Reagan had begun in 1982. His reasons, outlined in a memo to Sununu, included: "1. It was President Reagan's 'thing' because of his radio background. 2. After eight years, people are tired of it. President-elect Bush needs something new. 3. It gives the Democrats an equal time forum that the radio networks would like to drop anyway. 4. The only real advantage—capturing Saturday night TV and Sunday AM papers—can be realized in other ways. Other ideas include: 1. Occasional Saturday AM coffees with selected press. 2. Special radio addresses on special subjects. 3. Saturday press announcements. 4. Written messages."[44] Bush would give a handful of radio addresses later in his administration, five in 1991 and thirteen in 1992 (all but three delivered on a Saturday morning).[45] Despite Fitzwater's decision to eliminate what had been a standard form of communication for Reagan, the practice of weekly radio addresses was reinstituted during Bill Clinton's administration and has remained a standard presidential communication tool ever since.[46]

Other communications procedures would continue. For example, the Office of Communications continued to rely on the coverage provided by non-Washington members of the press as a means to communicate, a tradition that had begun during the Kennedy years and a strategy upon which every president since has relied to get his message out to the American public.[47] In general, regional press briefings were seen as an important component of this strategy. In 1989, the Office of Communications "coordinated briefings with the local media every three months (or so). Our goal is to do at least that many this year, if not more. These briefings give us good local ink and go a long way towards nurturing relations with our beyond-the-Beltway media."[48] By early 1990, more attention was given to developing a more extensive regional media strategy. Kristin Clark Taylor, director of media relations (a sub-unit of the communications office; by 1991, the offices of media relations and public affairs had been combined and renamed the Office of Media Affairs), developed a strategy for "on-the-road regional media coverage" for review by John Sununu and deputy chief of staff Andy Card:

> There is a strong need to better accommodate the local media when the President travels. Local media outlets are obviously eager to cover the President when he visits their home state; providing them with increased access to the President and Senior Staff would serve to enhance this coverage. We have already laid the foundation for a positive relationship with the regional media with our own outreach efforts (i.e., inviting local editorial page editors, newspaper publishers, newspaper editors, editorial cartoonists, and specialty media into the White House for briefings with the President). Including them in on-the-road interviews would only serve to bolster this relationship. In a recent meeting with Dave Demarest we discussed the following options that I now submit to you for review and feedback:

Senior Staff/Surrogate Interviews with Regional Media: Surrogates are often untapped resources of information when on the road. MR (Media Relations) would like to schedule radio or newspaper interviews with the local media and appropriate senior staff *in addition to or in place of* the President. Surrogates can include Senior Staff, Cabinet Members and/or accompanying dignitaries. Because most local media would be glad to obtain such interviews, this would be an effective way to get the Administration's message even further into the "heartland."

Specialty Media: When appropriate, specialty media could accompany the President on a trip and MR could coordinate roundtable interviews with the President and senior staff on the road. Example: Crime/Law enforcement and/or Hispanic media during the upcoming California trip. This kind of "on location" interview makes for good copy and sometimes dramatic backdrops. Such interviews would work best when the trip is issue-oriented.

Radio Talk Shows: Before each trip, MR could do a quick survey of the highest-density radio markets in the host state and arrange for Presidential/senior staff interviews. If we did telephone interviews rather than face-to-face, it would mean a minimum amount of prep and travel time. A package of four or five five-minute telephone interviews during morning or afternoon drive time could easily reach millions throughout the host state.

"Quickie" Press Availabilities: To allow the local media markets at least a few minutes of an "exclusive" with the President, MR could arrange brief five-minute interviews, back-to-back, with the largest markets in both the print and electronic industry—thereby reaching hundreds of thousands (if not millions in the large markets of readers and listeners).

Regional Roundtable Interviews: These would be roundtable interviews with local newspaper executives (editorial page editors, publishers, etc.). Rather than inviting the beat reporter for a straight news story, we would focus on the newspaper executive to both establish a good rapport and provide the opportunity for more in-depth, reflective interviews, about 25 to 30 minutes. A similar but shorter format could be used for TV station managers and news directors.

MR Preparation Before Each Trip: Before each big trip, MR would research the media in the host state: find out the largest radio, TV

> and newspaper markets, contact the media outlets and arrange the interviews.[49]

Demarest added his handwritten endorsement of the strategy at the bottom of the memo: "Governor/Andy—I see this as a menu to review a week or two before each trip so that we can pick which (if any) local media opportunity to pursue. The locals give us invariably better coverage than the nationals as you are well aware of."[50] Card responded to Demarest with the following note: "Why don't you, Kristin, and others in your operation get together with Sig, Marlin, and me to talk about this. Marlin has reservations about the concept. The ball is in your court."[51] Fitzwater, however, believed that only certain regional media coverage, such as surrogate interviews, were helpful, while he disagreed with having Bush participate in radio talk show appearances, regional roundtable interviews, and local individual media:

> 1) All of these local or regional media are already "reached" by the Presidential event itself. Thousands of dollars and hundreds of man-hours are put into Presidential trips so that a specific message can be delivered in a specific way. Local press interviews either dilute or divert that message. It buys us little, if any, additional coverage. And it runs the risk of destroying the entire Presidential event if the President answers an interview question in a controversial way. 2) It causes problems of competitive fairness to grant one or two local outfits an exclusive interview with the President. The result is that we antagonize all of the other media in that location. We also generate hundreds of requests for interviews, which have to be denied, and which also create ill will. In summary, some of these ideas are typical campaign techniques. But we are not in a campaign, and I believe most of these techniques are not only inappropriate but destructive of our basic reasons for making the trips in the first place.[52]

While elements of the "on-the-road" regional press strategy were implemented for certain events, most of the regional news media events with the president took place in Washington and at the White House. For example, Bush's first interview with regional newspapers occurred on March 15, 1989, a twenty-minute session in the Oval Office with reporters from the *Chicago Sun-Times, Hartford Courant, Baltimore Sun, Fort Worth Star-Telegram,* Hearst Newspapers, and the Copley News Service.

The purpose of the meeting was billed as "an opportunity for the President to meet with correspondents of newspapers representing different areas of the county."[53] Two weeks later, Bush would also hold a ninety-minute regional press luncheon (including brief remarks and a question-and-answer session) for seventy regional print, television, and radio reporters. The background memo to Bush suggested that the president expect the following:

> Although these reporters are from across the country and many of their questions will be only of regional significance, you should also be prepared to field questions on broader matters of national interest. Please note also that a White House press pool will cover your remarks. You should be aware that many of the newspapers at the luncheon endorsed you during the campaign and have given you fair, even favorable, coverage in the past. You will recognize many of the correspondents (Dave Silverbrand of WGME-TV in Portland, Maine; Burl Osborne of the *Dallas Morning News*; David Beeder of the *Omaha World-Herald*) from your campaign days. Although no recording equipment will be allowed while the actual meal is being served, please consider everything you say during lunch to be on-the-record. Your remarks at the podium and the resulting question and answer session will, of course, be on-the-record.[54]

The Bush communications team also provided regular press access to the president to specific groups within the news media as well as specialty press. For example, in March 1990, Bush participated in a group interview with the seven news services that regularly covered the White House—Copley, Cox, Hearst, Knight Ridder, McClatchy, Newhouse, and Scripps-Howard. According to Fitzwater, the importance of the event stemmed from the fact that "this group's newspapers cover virtually the entire country in their readership."[55] Similarly, in February 1990, Bush held a luncheon for black newspaper publishers and editors:

> In response to a specific request . . . you agreed to meet with a group of black newspaper executives. . . . During this luncheon meeting, the obvious issues are bound to surface: the freeing of Nelson Mandela and your prediction of when you'll meet with Mandela and/or De Klerk; your assessment of the country's racial climate, the current

> state of the Civil Rights Commission, and the Party's attempt to bring more blacks into the Republican fold. The Willie Horton ad might also be discussed. This is the first such meeting with black newspaper executives in more than a decade, and for this reason you might be asked about the black media's access to the White House. This is an opportunity for you to mention your earlier interview with Black Entertainment Television and with *Ebony* and *Jet* magazines. The questions are expected to be hard-hitting but not combative. You should also note that a few of these papers (*Cleveland Call and Post, Atlanta Daily World* and the *Jacksonville Advocate Free Press*) endorsed you during the campaign. You will be seated beside Portia Scott and Jake Oliver of the *Afro-American*, a black newspaper out of Baltimore that has identified your willingness to interview and meet with black media as a positive, forward-looking pattern.[56]

A luncheon was also scheduled in June 1989 for Bush to meet with editorial cartoonists. The purpose, as explained to Bush:

> You will join approximately ten Editorial Cartoonists for a one-hour luncheon in the Roosevelt Room. This meeting is designed to establish an easy, comfortable rapport with many of the nation's top cartoonists. The atmosphere is expected to be friendly and informal. It is important to remember that, although the artists themselves are rarely seen or heard from, their work reaches many millions and has a tremendous influence on public perception. As you are no doubt aware, they also have a keen political sense. Most are full members of their newspaper's Editorial Boards and are very vocal in editorial discussions. Their cartoons sometimes even counter the newspaper's written editorial policy. Their bent is mostly liberal, and their cartoons—if only for the sole reason of capturing attention—are usually biting and critical. By definition, a cartoon's success is through ridicule. In other words, complimentary cartoons don't work. This luncheon is more of an attempt to provide a personal glimpse into your personality than to persuade them into making their artwork more complimentary. After lunch, there will be an informal question and answer session and, hopefully, a broad-based discussion on a variety of topics. A flip chart will be in the corner of the room in case you or any of the cartoonists want to try your hand at a few drawings.[57]

Other specialty media were also given access to the president as part of the overall communication strategy. On May 1, 1990, Bush held a roundtable interview with disabled journalists. Taylor reported back to Bush that the "overall response from the participants was very positive; they were genuinely enthusiastic about being afforded the access."[58] Similarly, an interview with Bush on May 8, 1990, with health and fitness writers received positive press coverage, as well as an "overwhelmingly positive" response from the participants.[59] A luncheon for Hispanic media executives was held in February 1991, which contributed to a future cover story on the Bush administration in *Hispanic Business Magazine*; the magazine devoted nearly an entire issue to the Bush administration with photos of Bush from the luncheon surrounding questions and answers "on issues of importance to the Hispanic community."[60] In addition, the communications team would prepare bylined articles from the president to appear in specific publications. For example, an article with Bush's byline appeared on page one in *BusinessWeek's* 1990 Special Edition, published annually on a single issue (with this particular issue devoted to the environment).[61] And in the fall of 1990, a brief editorial with Bush's byline appeared in magazines published by Times Mirror. As reported to Bush by Taylor in Media Relations: "In May, you participated in a photo opportunity with Francis Pandolfi, President and CEO of Times Mirror Magazines, to commend the company for its conservation efforts and partnership agreements with the Department of the Interior. The attached editorial is a result of your support for such programs as Times Mirror Magazines' Conservation Council. This piece and your photo will be published in *Field and Stream, Outdoor Life, Golf Magazine, Popular Science*, and several other magazines (combined circulation is 33 million). This recognition of their effort helps to highlight your concern for the environment as well as your support for increased cooperation of the public and private sectors in environmental awareness."[62]

The communications team believed that the outreach to specialty media provided positive coverage of Bush in publications with significant circulation and those outside of the standard political coverage provided through the White House press corps. According to Taylor in a memo to Bush in August 1990:

> The following is a sampling of press coverage you've received as a result of our outreach to specialty media:
>
> The *Santa Fe New Mexican* devoted their entire front page to the

Hispanic roundtable interview, printing excerpts in both English and Spanish.

Mainstream Magazine is one of the largest-circulation publications reaching the disabled community. Cyndi Jones wrote this story (marked with paper clip) as a result of the disabled roundtable interview. Wheelchair-bound, she also came in from California to cover the ADA ceremony. (Most of our disabled media who participated in the roundtable interview flew in to cover the ADA event as well).

McCall's excerpts Q&A from the magazine editors roundtable, where the President spoke of the prospect of a female President. This interview, to be published in the September issue, will reach *McCalls'* 5,000,000 women readers.

Outdoor Life writes about the roundtable interview with outdoor writers in their August issue (circulation: 1,500,000).

Prevention, the nation's foremost health magazine with a circulation of 3,200,000, focuses on our *health and fitness roundtable,* promising to help promote the President's efforts to improve our physical well-being.

CBN, in addition to airing their exclusive interview with the President during the regional radio roundtable to their 1,500 Christian radio stations, ran a story on the interview in their monthly publication, *Flame.*

Good Housekeeping sent us an advance text (rough copy) on their September issue. This piece details the magazine editors roundtable and will reach the magazine's 24 million readers in September.

This is just a sampling of the kinds of clips we regularly receive as a result of our roundtable interviews and briefings.[63]

Taylor also reported that Bush's June 1990 interview with economic writers provided immediate positive press coverage: "Although many of the participants in your June 21 interview with economic writers were monthly or weekly publications, we received immediate coverage from several of the networks present. Steve Aug, ABC's economic correspondent at the interview, ran a piece on *Good Morning America* this morning (along with a photo of the meeting), which highlighted the session and focused on your comments about U.S. aid to the Soviet Union. NBC's Irving R. Levine, also present at the interview, ran a story on the interview session which ran on this morning's *Sunrise Show.* Both were very positive pieces."[64] The same month, Taylor also reported that a story stemming from an earlier press conference with regional reporters had run on the Cox News Service wire and had run "in over 500 newspapers, [which] underscores the vital impact this kind of accessibility has on members of the local and regional media."[65] The White House press corps did not always take a positive view of being left out of such events. In response to the same regional press conference, *Washington Times* correspondent Frank Murray wrote an article in which he characterized the event as "as valuable as a news blackout."[66]

Foreign press opportunities were also considered a good use of the president's time. In March 1990, advisor Roman Popadiuk sent a memo to Fitzwater detailing many options with members of the foreign press:

> You have expressed an interest in setting up some foreign press interviews for the President. As you may recall, the two round tables we held in October and November of last year were extremely successful. I would suggest that we keep with this format. Following are some suggestions from which you can choose: 1. A regional round table, as mentioned above. We have already done Europe and Latin America. We had planned one for Asia in January but never pursued it. 2. We can hold a press conference in Room 450 to which a White House pool can also be invited. Remember, we did one last year and the foreign press was quite happy. 3. We can do a "world interview" by having either one or two key newspapers from each of the five major geographic regions or—and this may be a better alternative—we can have the major wire service from each continent in a group session with the President. 4. We can append a foreign correspondent to any one domestic group of journalists that we bring in to see the President. This has the disadvantage of pleasing only one correspondent/country so it really doesn't do much for us with the foreign press. 5. We can set up a WORLDNET by which foreign correspondents can ask the President questions. This is just suggested as a possibility but not one that I would favor. 6. We can have one-on-one personal interviews with the major newspaper correspondents from the country of the current state/official visitor. The disadvantage here, as you well know, is that we would be doing one every other day.[67]

* * *

In addition, the strategy for foreign press coverage included written interviews, which were viewed as "easily done and get the President's views out to the respective countries"; other coverage tied to specific foreign developments such as an upcoming economic summit; interviews with foreign press tied to the U.S.-Soviet Union summit; and foreign television interviews.[68]

The use of radio actualities, handled by the public liaison division of the Office of Communications, also continued as a way to reach out to specific audiences important to both Bush and the Republican Party by providing ready-made quotes by the president or other information that could be easily inserted into radio news programming. As news industry budgets began to shrink during the late 1980s, radio actualities became even more influential as a cost-efficient way for radio news shows to fill airtime without the cost of reporter manpower. A radio actuality in November 1990, in which Bush recorded a two-and-a-half-minute message to recognize troops and hostages in the Middle East for the National Day of Prayer, provides an example of how the Bush communications team used actualities to court particular constituencies. In a November 5, 1990, memo to Sununu, Leigh Ann Metzger, a special assistant to the president for public liaison, reported on another actuality that had been requested by evangelical leaders who met with Bush in the Roosevelt Room on October 30:

> According to the Press Office, approximately 1,500 calls were received during the two-day period that the message was available. This is a very high response rate, particularly given the short notification. In fact, several important constituent groups, including the National Religious Broadcasters and the Coral Ridge Presbyterian Church, called our office complaining the lines had been continually busy! My office informed all participants at the evangelical meeting of the President's message as soon as it became available. In addition, National Religious Broadcasters and other conservative media outlets contacted their members regarding the actuality. The actuality was a success with the evangelical community, and is needed proof of our desire for a renewed working relationship.[69]

Other targeted messages by the president or other White House surrogates were also used as part of the overall communications strategy. For example, in October 1989 Demarest developed guidelines for "Assistants to the President" for the use of targeted video messages featuring Bush:

> In recognition of the popularity of presidential video messages, it has become necessary to outline a few parameters which can guide your recommendation of these requests. If your office is interested in securing a video message there are several considerations. First, is appropriateness. In general, we are interested in messages that are directed toward a national audience. This would include meetings or conventions of large national organizations, network public service announcements, and inserts in nationally televised programs. Requests that are more difficult to approve are for state-specific programs or individual chapters of national organizations. Second is cost. The White House does not have the resources to pay for video messages. We hire an outside production company which charges the host organization to produce the message. A message can cost the host organization anywhere between $300 and $1,500, depending on the number of video messages we can produce in one sitting. Third is time. A three week minimum lead time is necessary. This ensures reasonable time for legal approval, scripting, scheduling and post production work.[70]

Satellite interviews with Bush or surrogates were also used on occasion to "get the President's word out more creatively and aggressively" and to "enhance the President's message." For example, in May 1990, Arnold Schwarzenegger participated in a series of satellite interviews to promote the President's Council on Physical Fitness and Sports that were broadcast on ESPN, the syndicated show *Inside Edition*, and by the largest television station in Philadelphia.[71] Similarly, public service announcements were considered an effective part of the communications strategy. In April 1990, Bush, along with wife Barbara, appeared in a public service announcement for the *Cartoon All-Stars to the Rescue* program, an animated drug prevention television special featuring many of the most popular characters from Saturday morning television. In a memo to Bush from Deputy Director of Media Relations Maria Eitel Sheehan, the taped message was viewed by an extensive audience: "The messages . . . were seen on the ABC, CBS and NBC networks during programs like *Good Morning America, Days of Our Lives, Golden Girls, Entertainment Tonight, Wheel of Fortune*, and *48 Hours*, for a total of 32 airings. Your message was also seen immediately prior to the airing of the Cartoon. According to audience research: 'More people watched the special than watched any other entertainment program in the history of America's Saturday morning television.' The program was seen by 30 million people including 40% of children in the United States ages 2–11."[72]

While much of the communications strategy was handled for Bush by both the press and communications offices, it was the public events with Bush that were perhaps the most essential ingredient. Despite the fact that it was well recognized within the White House that Bush was "more comfortable building consensus one-on-one, behind closed doors," he could not escape the increased expectation by the public and the press that the president must regularly appear on center stage.[73] Given Bush's dislike of many of the public aspects of the presidency, he nevertheless participated in more total public activities than Reagan had during his first term.[74] Bush relied extensively on press conferences, and by 1991, he also began to hold formal press conferences with foreign dignitaries (a trend that would continue in the Bill Clinton, George W. Bush, and Barack Obama presidencies). Bush also gave more routine (including policy) addresses, as opposed to national (including addresses to the nation) addresses than Reagan, with a sizable (and not surprising) increase in these appearances during his reelection campaign in 1992. Also during the 1992 campaign, Bush began to rely more on the use of town meetings and roundtable discussions. Bush engaged in a total of 1,972 public activities during his four years in office (which includes all public remarks as chronicled in the *Public Papers of the Presidents*). This is an increase of nearly 500 public activities compared to Reagan's first term, during which Reagan participated in a total of 1,496 public activities. Most, if not all, of that increase came from appearances outside Washington, D.C. For example, during his four years in office, Bush made 721 U.S. public appearances compared to 380 for Reagan and 182 foreign public appearances compared to 89 for Reagan.[75]

Bush as Orator

The speechwriting process provides a good example of how Bush sought to "dismantle" some of the strengths of the Reagan presidency in an attempt to distance himself from the strategy of stagecraft. Ever the anti-Reagan in this area, Bush "abhorred soaring rhetoric and emotional speeches. . . . [he] instead chose a more pedestrian style that was almost deliberately flat, characterized by broken, incomplete sentences and steadfast avoidance of the word 'I.'"[76] According to Demarest, Bush "was not interested in being an orator. In fact, he would write notes rather regularly at the bottom of speeches saying that the speech was too flowery or 'too much.' He was much more interested in a just-the-facts kind of delivery."[77] Bush also intentionally understaffed the Office of Public Liaison and isolated his speechwriters from the decision-making process in the Oval Office.[78] A prominent speechwriter during the Reagan years, Peggy Noonan observed of Bush after working on his 1989 inauguration speech that "No dramatic or portentous statements, neither John Kennedy nor John Wayne. A man who does not choose to talk like that is here. He will be low-key, direct, domestic."[79] And while many people, both inside and outside of the beltway, liked Bush personally, he never mastered the bully pulpit as a means to govern. Scholarly assessments to date have not been overwhelmingly positive. According to John Robert Greene, "in the area of the public presidency—that part of leadership that requires the president to connect with the citizenry at large—historians will find Bush wanting. George Bush was, to put it charitably, an uninspiring speaker."[80] Additionally, Carol Gelderman observes, "Bush's speeches were mediocre at best. Their shapelessness symptomized the president's policy drift. He seemed unable to figure out what he wanted his administration to accomplish and repeatedly acknowledged his difficulty with the 'vision-thing.' . . . He hopscotched from one issue to another—drugs one day, the deficit the next, education the third day. Because he appeared to stand for nothing, he offended those who cared deeply about something, especially the Reaganites."[81]

As Martin Medhurst points out, while Bush may not be remembered for his eloquence as a public speaker, he was nonetheless a "rhetorical president in the sense that he, like all of his predecessors and successors, made choices about what to say, how to say it, where and to whom to say it. A president cannot escape rhetoric—as much as some would like to do so. For good or ill, all presidents are rhetorical presidents."[82] Medhurst also argues, however, that the Bush administration was infected with "an antirhetorical virus" that stemmed from three interlocking components: Bush's step back from the communication strategy of Reagan instead of working harder to attempt to reach Reagan's level as an orator; Bush's own attitude about communicating with the public (that he disliked public speaking); and his belief that governance could be separated from politics. Bush believed in a "fundamental difference between politics and government, between what one needed to do to win the presidency and what one should do once in office, in short, a difference between politics and principles." As a result, Bush left himself at a distinct disadvantage vis-à-vis the public and the presidential image he was expected to project."[83]

Since it was not a high strategic priority in the Bush White House, turnover was high in the speechwriting office until the arrival of Tony Snow, a former journalist for the conservative newspaper the *Washington Times.* (Snow would also serve as George W. Bush's third press secretary.) Snow became one of Bush's favorite writers, an important point since other writers had rarely impressed the president. According to Snow, "Bush regarded speechmaking as 'a necessary evil.' He didn't like giving speeches." Bush also had difficulty giving speeches that called for emotion (such as Reagan's June 1984 speech in Normandy, France, to commemorate the fortieth anniversary of the D-Day invasion, viewed by many as one of Reagan's best speeches). In addition, Snow recalled that Bush "did not have any sense of how language worked, and I think that's a reflection, ironically, of his both commendable and damnable humility." Bush chose to show his emotions offstage, not in front of the cameras, so he did not capitalize on emotional moments of a speech in the same way that Reagan had been able to do.[84] After the fall of the Berlin Wall in 1989, Bush was accused of being too unemotional; as recalled by journalist Tom Wicker, Bush "chose to 'play it cool,' not wishing to either appear as an instigator of revolt or to raise the likelihood of a violent reaction from Moscow." During an Oval Office press conference, Lesley Stahl of CBS questioned Bush about why he was not more elated, to which Bush responded, "I'm not an emotional kind of guy."[85] The irony of this, however, is that Bush would often get emotional during speeches, as he did in April 1989 when addressing three thousand mourners at the Norfolk Naval Station after forty-seven men had been killed on the USS *Iowa* from an accidental explosion. As Bush recalled in his diary, despite much rehearsal of the remarks, he nonetheless choked up and had to end the speech abruptly.[86]

Humor also did not come easily to Bush during his public speeches, an element that had become a trademark for Reagan in his speeches, often through the use of self-deprecating remarks. As a result, the Bush White House would sometimes rely on outside writers to provide humorous content for speeches. As Bush wrote to Demarest and the speechwriting team in June 1991: "It seems to me that in our speeches, though you all are generally doing a very, very good job on them, we are sometimes a quart low on humor. I know you have some contract with another, but every time I ask Ray Siller to send me a line or two, I find that I am very comfortable with his humor. A lot of it is inside Hollywood (á la Johnny Carson) that might not fit, but that's not the point. All we need is a good line every once in awhile to lighten things up. Please call Ray. He tells me he is very willing to help. And be sure if he does send in material, that I personally see it. Humor is something that I have to feel very comfortable with. Thanks. Keep up the good work."[87] The "contract with another" that Bush mentions referred to Doug Gamble, a writer in California who supplied humorous material to Bush while in the White House, as well as during the 1988 presidential campaign, for a monthly fee. Gamble had also provided material to Reagan beginning in 1984.[88]

The speechwriting process in the Bush White House included five full-time writers, a dozen researchers, and several outside consultants. While Bush usually provided substantive speeches and was knowledgeable and conversant on policy specifics, he lacked a smooth style of delivery, due in part to his reluctance to practice his public speaking. And in spite of Bush's knowledge of policy matters, his off-the-cuff remarks were no better. "Bush had little training in public speaking . . . [and] when he spoke extemporaneously, he often mangled syntax and used incredibly cryptic phrases obviously assuming the audience could read his mind or that they possessed the same special knowledge he did."[89] At various points throughout his presidency, his public performances were "worthy of a Saturday Night Live parody by comedian Dana Carvey"; many speaking events by Bush could be described as "a series of awkward poses, thoughts cascading, hands flailing, syntax garbled, eyes wandering. . . . His grammar was [often] so jumbled that a seventh-grade teacher could spend weeks diagramming a George Bush sentence."[90] As Demarest recalled,

> The Bush administration was not a rhetorical presidency. Even though my bio states that I supervised 1,300 speeches from Rose Garden remarks to State of the Union address, speeches were not the vehicle through which the President attempted to galvanize the country. Many of his speeches were only heard by a select few. These speeches were given for the benefit of those people who were present. Some groups were important to him, and he wanted to make a personal connection with them. Network coverage was not essential. Hence, President Bush gave an incredible number of speeches that were not covered by the press. Bush now admits that communications was not one of his strong suits. I disagree with that assertion. Oratory, on the other hand, was not one of his strong suits, unless he was speaking about certain topics. If he spoke about the military or foreign policy, for instance, the speech was powerful. If he spoke about "points of light," the speech was powerful. When he

> discussed home ownership and Project Hope from HUD, however, the President did not deliver an invigorating speech. Unfortunately, the predominant speeches were often focused on domestic issues. He did not have the zeal for those issues as he did foreign policy issues. When discussing them, President Bush would tailor the speech for the particular audience to whom he was speaking, not for the larger national audience.[91]

Not only did Bush's style as an orator shape his speeches and other public remarks, so too did the political circumstances in which he governed. Like many other presidents before him, Bush's public agenda—that is, the prioritization of some policy topics over others in public remarks—focused more often on international issues than any other. Given Bush's experience in the international arena prior to winning the presidency, as well as the major international events while Bush was president (pro-democracy events in Tiananmen Square in China, the fall of the Berlin Wall, the U.S. invasion of Panama, the collapse of the Soviet Union, and the Gulf War), the fact that he talked about foreign policy or defense issues more often than domestic or economic issues is not surprising. While campaigning in 1988, candidate Bush had promised an extensive domestic agenda, including initiatives and programs for education, the environment, crime control, and banking reform. However, he had little opportunity to pursue these policies due to limited federal spending opportunities given the size of the national budget deficit when he took office in 1989 (and his initial promise of no new taxes), as well as the difficulty that he encountered working with a Democratic Congress. The Bush administration also believed that major changes to policies were not necessary, since the president sought only incremental changes to policies that had already been changed during the Reagan years. As a result, the Bush "policy agenda in its first year seemed to be reactive rather than strategic. It reflected the president's style, which was to be a problem solver rather than a visionary, a doer rather than a dreamer."[92]

As a result, by May 1991, top advisors on the communications team were still grappling with the "vision thing." According to Dorrance Smith, a former television network executive who served as an assistant to the president for media affairs from 1991 to 1993, the goal of the administration should be to "put to rest any debate about whether or not the President has a vision. The debate should begin to center on the vision itself." In a memo to Demarest, Fitzwater, Deputy Chief of Staff Andrew

Card, and Director of the Office of National Service Gregg Petersmeyer, Smith recommended the following points for a future speech to develop Bush's vision in preparation for the upcoming 1992 election:

> A unifying phrase that becomes his trademark for his domestic vision—like "New World Order" or "Thousand Points of Light."
>
> Explain why the President does not propose a program as a manifestation of the vision. Why we do not federalize the solutions to the domestic problems?
>
> Set the political agenda around the domestic themes that he will run on.
>
> Use the audience as the tool to display that he has been describing this vision all along. Only when you see all the parts together do you see that he really has a methodical approach to governing.
>
> Challenge Americans to join in the responsibility. The President's vision is a "shared concern." He must be the rallying point for new thinking which is steeped in the realities of the day, and challenge Americans to view the process differently.
>
> Deride cynicism. The effectiveness of the President's vision is that it is a pragmatic look at the nation, and focuses on realistic solutions, solutions that define roles for the individual, the community, and the state. Deride the cynics. Promote the problem solvers.
>
> Use the Persian Gulf analogy to show how he is attacking domestic problems with the same cooperative spirit.[93]

Throughout his four years in office, however, Bush's public addresses did not reflect any particular emphasis on domestic or economic issues. When examining his public remarks in major presidential addresses, the yearly breakdown of the frequency with which Bush discussed policy issues for each major policy category (international issues, domestic issues, and economic issues) in major addresses can be seen in table 1.[94] The fluctuations in Bush's emphasis in his major addresses are due mostly to the priority of certain issues at distinct times during his time in office. For example, the highest yearly totals for international policy issues can be found in 1990 and 1991, with a significant part of both years focused on the Gulf War. Domestic policies were discussed most often in 1989 as Bush initially began to pursue a few key issues as promised during the 1988 campaign (such as education), while the overall increased focus on both domestic and economic issues in 1992 stemmed from the extent to

Table 1. Policy Prioritization in Bush's Major Public Addresses

	1989	1990	1991	1992
International	48%	77%	65%	48%
Domestic	38%	11%	27%	31%
Economic	14%	12%	8%	21%

which the recession was driving the focus during Bush's reelection campaign (particularly given the Clinton campaign's emphasis on the mantra "It's the Economy, Stupid").

Conclusion

While more accessible to the press and public than Reagan, Bush was reluctant to speak directly to the public as often as Reagan did, yet he nonetheless engaged in more public activities. Bush never seemed to capture the aura nor did he have the stage presence that Reagan had while delivering a major address. His insistence on moving past the theatrical emphasis of the Reagan years, along with his perceived inability to effectively articulate a "vision" for the United States, hurt his ability to lead the public in a way that presidents are now expected to do. The irony is that unlike Reagan, Bush was more nuanced and had the ability to see the complexity of many issues, particularly those involving the intricacies of domestic policies and how they impacted the day-to-day operation of the federal government. Reagan had viewed things as more black and white, and right or wrong (certainly evident in Reagan's anti-communist rhetoric during the early 1980s). The ability to connect to citizens turned out to be a great advantage to Reagan in terms of public leadership, but it set perhaps too high a bar for Bush in this regard. The comparisons to Reagan's public leadership were inevitable, and Bush was never able to live up to that standard, no matter how good his public performances. Even his closest advisors admitted that Bush "could be a very good speaker, but he was no Ronald Reagan. Very few people are, will be, or have been as effective as Reagan."[95] And while Reagan understood the importance of speeches for effective public leadership, that they were its "heart and soul," Bush was determined to chart a different course for his public strategy: "By his own admission, George Bush was a fox, seeing speeches as only one piece among many—press conferences, trips, presidential appearances, personal diplomacy, written statements, and the like—to create a mosaic of a presidency. In that mosaic, speechmaking was a low priority."[96]

The disadvantages that Bush suffered in the area of press and communication strategies included "the inevitable comparisons to Reagan," the fact that the administration "downplayed public and press relations," and the fact that with a Democratic Congress Bush had few opportunities to be an "activist domestic policy president."[97] As this chapter shows, however, the Bush administration was not lacking in terms of public strategies, and the press and communications offices continued to play an important role in the day-to-day operation of the White House. Fitzwater developed a fairly strategy-intense approach to press relations, as did Demarest with communications, but it was often a recalibrated approach that occurred during the Reagan administration. The attempts to manipulate press coverage to provide a favorable view of the president, along with a governing advantage, were still present in the Bush White House, but the attempts to manipulate the press often came from a different angle (that being an emphasis on accessibility and more decorum in press relations to provide a more substantive and professional environment). Unfortunately for Bush, the press corps more often than not did not appreciate this new approach, due not only to the patterns that had been developed during the Reagan years, but also due to the changing news media environment that was causing even more competition among the long-standing national major media outlets as well as the newer news outlets that began to emerge during the Bush years.

In an interview after Bush left office, he stated that the thing that he missed least about Washington was dealing with the press: "By that I mean the Washington, inside-the-Beltway press. I don't say that bitterly, just as a matter of fact. They do their thing, now I'm free to do mine. I have no desire to get back into the media game, to interact with the press. And I don't miss the political infighting, either. Not one bit." Bush also discussed his biggest disappointments as president, which related in part to his style of communicating:

> There were several, foreign and domestic. But I think my biggest was that I wasn't articulate enough to overcome the politically-driven, press-driven perception that the economy in 1992 was in a deep recession. In the third quarter of '92, and indeed the beginning of the fourth quarter, during the campaign, things were going better. But when I tried to point that out, the perception was that I was

> totally out of touch. I just wasn't a good enough communicator. If [Reagan] had been in my place, he'd have cut through the opposition fog that everything was going to hell. He'd say, "Wait a minute, here are the facts, the reality." And the reality was that the recession had bottomed out in 1991, and the economy had grown not just by the 2.7 percent I claimed for the third quarter, but by 3.4 percent. And in the fourth quarter, it grew at a very robust 5.8 percent—not exactly a recession . . . but I failed as a communicator.[98]

As the Bush legacy continues to unfold, one question that remains is whether or not a different approach or strategy would have helped Bush to have better success in the area of public leadership—if perhaps a more Reaganesque approach would have helped Bush secure a second term in office. But the Bush strategy seemed to fit the president and what he wanted to accomplish in the public aspects of his presidency. Instead, it may have been the public expectation left behind by Reagan that created the greatest obstacle for the Bush White House in regards to communications.

CHAPTER 3

External Factors

The News Media and Public Opinion

By the time he left the White House in January 1993, George H. W. Bush seemed happy to leave the national press behind as he embarked on his post-presidential years. Having followed the "Great Communicator" in the White House, and then having lost his reelection bid to the first president born in the television age, the public aspects of the Bush presidency had not left a positive lasting impression. Bush had believed that providing more informal access to the Washington press corps and talking policy specifics in a way that Reagan had not done would have earned him positive news coverage. However, a president who was more interested in substance than style combined with an increasingly competitive news media focusing on personalized and negative political coverage left Bush at a disadvantage to engage in a substantive dialogue on policy issues. Bush's public style (or perhaps lack of interest in developing a public style and image) would have been better suited for the news media environment of an earlier time like the 1960s, when the national news cycle was still driven more by words than by images (through top newspapers, news magazines, and substantive network news shows on ABC, CBS, and NBC). By the time Bush became president in 1989, the 24-hour news cycle had clearly emerged, and the president's relationship with the press had changed forever. Given that Bush was not a made-for-television president, it is not surprising that his view of the national press was less than laudatory when he left the White House. Nearly ten years later, while giving a talk at Austin College in Sherman, Texas, in 2002, Bush shared his views about the national press, continuing a regular theme articulated during his post-presidency public events: "I joined press-bashers anonymous, until the [2000] election recount. I gave a talk in St. Louis a while back and received a standing ovation from 14,000 people for railing against the national press—the people I used to have to say thank you to. . . . I make the distinction between the national and the local press. The one thing I don't miss [as president] is national press conferences."[1]

This chapter considers the external factors with which the Bush administration had to contend in regards to the public presidency, including vast changes within the news industry (shrinking budgets and resources, increased competition, and a shift to more entertainment-driven programming in news divisions) and how that shaped political news coverage, particularly from the White House, and ultimately Bush's standing in public opinion polls. This is significant, since the Bush White House and the news media covering it never seemed to fully understand the wants and needs of the other, which by 1992 hurt the president's chance for reelection and perhaps left the press and its viewers and readers looking for a more enticing and exciting story emanating from the White House (which they received, for better or worse, with Bill Clinton). This poses interesting questions as to how the news media as an industry contributes to the public opinion of political leaders, communication strategies employed by those same political leaders, and the tone found within public debate and how the electorate responds accordingly. The proliferation of "soft" news, talking heads, and instant analysis now dominates the 24-hour news cycle, and much of this current media environment got its start at the end of the 1980s, just as Bush came into office. As such, this chapter will assess the news media as an industry during the Bush years to provide a better insight into Bush's legacy in the area of presidential-press relationships and consider how Bush's public strategy was hindered by the circumstances within the news industry between 1989 and 1993. Also, Bush's connection to public opinion will be examined, including the rise and fall of his approval numbers along with the use of internal polling by the White House as an attempt to lead public opinion on the president's policy initiatives.

The State of the News Industry, 1989–93

By January 1989, when Bush first took office, major changes were underway within the news industry at large, as well as structural changes in how major news outlets were covering the White House. A general shift had begun in the presidential-press relationship in the late 1970s, as what had been known as the broadcasting age (or the "golden age of television") transformed into the new media age of the 1980s and 1990s.[2] With the dramatic technological changes during this time period came a change in how presidents were covered by the news media, as presidents began to receive less substantive coverage as well as a shift in coverage that was more negative and critical. These changes also began to diminish the president's ability to lead the public.[3] While the Bush team had sought a more traditional press strategy—one that moved away from the stagecraft of the Reagan years and back to a more formal, information-driven (as opposed to image-driven) relationship—the news industry itself was changing in ways that would complicate and at times thwart that strategy. Not only were budgets and profits of news organizations shrinking, but rapid technological changes and the start of the mega-merger trend among media-related corporations were reshaping the industry between 1989 and 1993. This created a rather untenable environment at times for a president convinced that his greatest strength would be to emphasize substance over style in the public arena.

First and foremost, by 1989, the industry began to feel the effects of the oncoming economic recession, coupled with the need to remain competitive in an industry requiring newer and more expensive high-tech equipment like computers, color presses, and satellite dishes, among other innovations, in order to appeal to the "new media" appetites of its audience. This was especially challenging for print news sources, such as major daily newspapers and weekly newsmagazines, which were hurt by the "immediacy of television news." Newspapers began to add more features, along with interpretation and analysis of news with the assumption that many readers had already seen something about the story the night before on television. Similarly, the major newsweeklies—*Time, Newsweek,* and *U.S. News and World Report*—had to "rethink and reformulate" their magazines to address declining readership by adding more color photos and graphics, shortening articles, and recruiting "big-name columnists."[4] In effect, both mediums were forced to compete head-on with television for their survival at a time when fewer Americans seemed interested in reading, as opposed to viewing, their news.

Within industry and other business-oriented publications, which track trends within the media industry, gloomy reports abounded during the late 1980s and early 1990s about dramatic—and not so pleasant—changes that were on the horizon due to budget cuts and shrinking advertising revenues. This is also the time period when mega-media mergers really began. Time, Inc., and Warner Communications first merged in 1990, a decade before the even bigger (and largest ever) merger of AOL and Time-Warner in

2000. At the time, media analysts were unsure of the exact implications but reported that "whatever eventually happens to Time-Warner, the industry will not be the same again."[5] Media critic Ben Bagdikian, in the fourth edition of *The Media Monopoly*, published in 1992, reported that media ownership had consolidated from fifty national and multinational corporations in 1983 to just twenty by 1992. (That number, as Bagdikian reported in the seventh edition of his book, had dropped to merely five "global-dimension firms," which operate like a cartel, by 2003. They were Time-Warner, the Walt Disney Company, Rupert Murdoch's News Corporation, Viacom, and Bertelsmann.) Bagdikian also wrote that the high debt incurred by major media corporations in the 1980s had "increased the tendency of sameness in all media." Followed by the recession that hit the industry by 1991, and the decline in value of media stocks, a panic ensued within the industry that led to drastic cost-cutting in news operations and an increase in advertising rates. As a result, "objective reporting" had become "too narrowly defined, so that information given out by leaders in the most powerful positions is reported to the exclusion of that from alternative sources."[6]

At the same time, newspapers were having an "identity crisis," struggling to compete with the ever-expanding cable television and Internet options for news. By 1992, the "coming of the information age" had forced newspapers to begin the reinvention of the daily newspaper, as they were faced with "circulation problems, by setbacks in their fight to keep the Bell companies out of the information delivery business, and by the depth of the recession, which has sped the collapse of the industry's retail advertising base."[7] Newspapers were being hit with an "economic malaise," including structural changes within the newsroom from downsizing of editorial staffs and hiring and salary freezes. Entry-level jobs at the time were hit particularly hard—what some referred to as a "lost generation" of journalists—as journalism schools continued to send more graduates out into the job market even though many entry-level jobs no longer existed.[8] Newspapers were also dying off quite rapidly during this time period. In 1909, there were 2,600 newspapers, down to 1,556 in 1994. Also important to note is the decline in the number of cities with competing daily newspapers—181 in 1940, down to 33 by 1994—also indicative of the consolidations going on within the newspaper industry.[9]

Not only were circulations declining and newspapers closing, particularly in larger markets with more than one major daily, but Sunday publications were merging to cut costs. In addition, many major dailies were dropping the once-popular Sunday magazines. In 1983, a total of sixty newspapers included a Sunday magazine, and by 1992 a third had ended publication (including *Michigan Magazine* in the *Detroit News*, the *Sacramento Bee Magazine* in the *Sacramento Bee*, the *Atlanta Weekly* in the *Atlanta Journal* and *Constitution*, and the *Nevadan Today* in the *Las Vegas Review Journal*) due to the recession and the waning commitment of publishers in the face of increasing competition from newer and more high-tech media outlets.[10]

During this time period, salaries for many broadcast and print reporters were stagnant or they declined. One study showed no raises in the average salaries for television producers and reporters from 1990 to 1991, an industry that had once been known for steadily increasing salaries. All broadcast news programs, regardless of market size, were hurt from the "sagging economy" along with the increasing competition from CNN and other cable news outlets. Newspaper reporters and lower-level editors fared even worse during this time period. One study showed that base pay for reporters with one to four years' experience decreased an average of 6.4 percent by 1992. Many newspaper jobs also disappeared at that time, with the industry losing more than twenty thousand jobs from 1990 to 1992 due to the economic recession and low demand for advertising.[11]

Broadcast journalists were also struggling to compete within the new confines of the marketplace, discovering that the traditional ways of putting together a newscast could not compete with all of the new options for viewers. For both networks and local affiliates, broadcast news was "struggling to survive in its native habitat," and, "battered by recession, defecting youth, cable and VCR competition, and tabloid telecasts," they had little relief in sight. The mega mergers and other changes within the news industry represented "a new culture of information, profoundly reshaping the leisure time and information habits of tens of millions of Americans." For example, even MTV (often credited, or blamed, depending on one's perspective, for many changes in television viewing habits) had jumped into the news game, with daily and weekend news broadcasts and a growing staff of reporters. In addition to music news, political news on the presidential campaign, and global issues such as AIDS and human rights were now being covered by the youth-targeted music network.[12]

Other newer news outlets continued to emerge as well, particularly as cable began to dominate the marketplace for consumers. While CNN had been around since 1980, the once-fledgling cable network seemed to come into its own by the late 1980s, forcing the networks to compete with its 24-

hour news format. Following CNN's successful round-the-clock coverage of the Gulf War in 1991, its place among the leading news organizations in the country had been secured. A new media environment had been born, providing new challenges for President Bush and all those to follow in the White House. Earlier presidents during the television age, and for the most part including Reagan as well, only had the three networks with which to contend, in addition to the traditional newspaper and magazine print sources. Bush became the first recipient of the "proliferation and development of information technology" in this new media age, with new worries about "control of [his] message on CNN with its real-time news dissemination capability," as well as many other outlets such as MTV news, talk radio, and the Internet.[13]

In 1992, MTV's interest in providing political coverage to younger voters provides an excellent example of how the Bush White House would be forced to change its press strategy in this new media environment. Throughout the year, MTV had covered the Democratic and Republican conventions, promoted its "Choose or Lose" campaign to encourage young people to vote, and conducted live interviews with the Democratic nominee Bill Clinton and running mate Al Gore. MTV had also requested a similar appearance by President Bush. Initially, Bush declined to appear on the network for an interview with MTV political reporter Tabitha Soren. But after MTV complained that it had been snubbed by the White House, and fearing that Bush was losing the youth vote to the baby boomer ticket of Clinton and Gore, Bush relented, and allowed Soren to interview him while on a whistle-stop train trip across the country (reminiscent of Harry Truman in 1948) in the waning days of the campaign.

This generational influence played an important role in changes within the news industry at large that began to emerge during this time period. During the late 1980s, Generation Xers (categorized as the generation after the baby boomers—those born after 1964 and throughout the 1970s) were beginning to come of age and represented media consumers who had been "immersed in televised information from infancy onward." As their consumer power in the marketplace began to increase, more programming was geared to attract their attention in the ever-increasingly competitive media market, including news programming. According to media scholar Doris Graber, "GenXers have spent more time watching the world unfold on audiovisual monitors than in any other waking-hours activity. They have learned from infancy on to prize the creation of virtual reality that visual presentations make possible. . . . But, above all, GenXers are niche viewers. They want to limit their news consumption, including news about politics, to the information that interests them most. They resist being told what information they ought to consume."[14]

• • •

The content of that information, along with the style of reporting, also began to change at the start of the 1990s. Following Watergate, many journalists during the 1970s and 1980s seemed to relish their role as government watchdogs, keeping an eye out for political corruption or scandals. That trend, coupled with declining profits, tended to increase the sensational and cynical nature of political news reporting, as well as a move to less objective reporting and more news analysis. Many media critics blame this shift in reporting style on smaller reporting staffs, and less quality news, as part of the overall attempt to increase profits. For example, newspapers in the past two decades have tried to attract readers and increase circulation, thereby increasing advertising revenue, with light feature stories and less serious reporting on national and international issues. By focusing on the bottom line, according to Leonard Downie Jr. and Robert G. Kaiser, "too much of what has been offered as news in recent years has been untrustworthy, irresponsible, misleading or incomplete.... But the most alarming weaknesses of the news media have been systemic, and they have seriously undermined good journalism. Too many of those who own and lead the nation's news media have cynically underestimated or ignored America's need for good journalism, and evaded their responsibility to provide it."[15] And while cable news channels, led by CNN and later joined by MSNBC and Fox (both of which debuted in 1996), changed the face of broadcast news in the early 1990s by providing live, real-time coverage of important events as they were unfolding (like the Gulf War), that strength in technological capability had begun to erode by the end of the decade as the focus shifted to "less important but emotionally charged events, usually crime and tragedy." No formula for success in the news industry remains static for long, as more and more changes in technology continually dictate newer strategies for remaining competitive in the marketplace. Like the other sectors of the industry, which underwent many systemic and permanent changes due to the economic downturn at the start of the 1990s, cable news channels now "fill many of their hours as cheaply as possible with repetitive, bare-bones news summaries and talk shows that present biased opinions and argument as though they were news. This coverage was frequently marred by misleading reporting and talking-head analysis that distorted the facts, meaning and importance of events like school shootings or freak accidents, projecting sideshows into the center ring of national life."[16]

A Traditional President in a New Media World

The tone and content of news coverage can greatly influence a president's public image. Timing can also affect presidential leadership by dictating the circumstances under which a president must govern. Bush, unwilling to actively pursue a public relations strategy to promote his presidency and policy initiatives, instead ended up "blending into the landscape, reacting to events, and allowing Congress or others to set the national agenda."[17] At a time when the news industry was looking for something new and fresh to fit within its newer and more competitive formats, a World War II generation president with traditional views of the press did not make for a good match with an industry in transition. And while many members of the White House press corps may have favored the old media game (dominance by the networks, major daily papers, and weekly news magazines in driving the news content and agenda), the editors to whom they answered and the publishers from whom they received their paychecks had already begun to play the new media game in an attempt to increase profits and remain viable in a dramatically changing industry.

The trend of shrinking newsroom staffs, while the number of news outlets continued to increase thanks to technological advances in cable and Internet options, had an impact on the style and tone of news coverage. And those same changes shaped political news coverage, particularly that of the White House, in a variety of ways. With the push toward globalization and streamlined operations that was occurring within most industries, including the news industry, White House reporters had to operate in an environment where "there was much more of a tendency to look at the bottom line and to judge their operations by their profits." The costs of covering the president were also increasing at a time when news budgets were being slashed, and that affected the number of people who could travel with the president, because not all news organizations were willing to spend their precious resources on providing their reporters with the technical conveniences necessary to compete. And with the expanding presence of cable network news at the time, there was a definite increase in the amount of news analysis due to "an assumption that with the existence of cable everybody has seen what a president has said, so then a newspaper doesn't have the same need to tell exactly what the president said or what some of the responses were because that would have already been on the network news."[18]

This became one of the major flaws of the Bush White House in the area of communication in that "it often did not act strategically," and it "rarely held strategy sessions to map out a long-term strategy of how to communicate Bush's goals."[19] As a result, many speeches were given with only the audience in attendance in mind, and not the broader news coverage, since network coverage was not viewed as essential like it had been for Reagan. A lack of a strategy in this area did not benefit Bush's coverage, since the industry at the time relied on basic news coverage to come from broadcast outlets. So without that supply of information, newspapers and other print sources would then analyze Bush's overall leadership rather than report on what he had said during a speech, which often led to a more critical assessment of the Bush White House. In addition, the view of the Bush communications office was that reporters were "smart enough to cover issues that [were] important" and that it was not the communications division's job to "spoonfeed the press artificially constructed themes," a pattern that many reporters had relied upon during the Reagan years.[20]

The Bush team did develop what they considered to be an effective press strategy that relied on the president's strengths, including knowledge of the policymaking process and accessibility to reporters, yet rarely if ever did Bush's advisors consider newer or more innovative ways to keep up with changes within the news industry. As a result, the press-communications strategy was often more optimistic than practical. For example, in an April 1989 memo that Fitzwater presented to Bush and Sununu with a plan to continue what he believed had been a successful press strategy during the first few months of the administration, the suggested activities within the memo all related to standard presidential press activities, such as a primetime news conference and interview opportunities for network news and the *New York Times*.[21] As discussed in chapter 2, other White House memos suggest that throughout the Bush term, Fitzwater and other senior advisors were reluctant to pursue strategies that seemed gimmicky, unpresidential, or too much like the Reagan PR machine, like Fitzwater's opposition to increasing regional and local press coverage in February 1990 during a presidential trip because such activities were too campaign-like.[22] Similarly, for example, Fitzwater argued against a joint appearance by Bush and Soviet President Mikhail Gorbachev on the *Phil Donahue Show*:

> Shows of this kind have been proposed by *Reader's Digest*, ABC's *Capital-to-Capital* and NBC-TV. There are a number of important reasons why this show, and others like it, present serious drawbacks for the President and for United States foreign policy. I therefore recommend against this project on the following grounds: 1. It is unfair to President Bush and President Gorbachev to be put in some kind of televised beauty contest. Neither President Gorbachev nor President Bush should have to perform on television in a context in which the philosophies and policies of the two countries are at stake. 2. The foreign policy of the United States, with regard to the Soviet Union, is too important to be determined in a television production. It doesn't really matter who is interviewing the two Presidents, or how the production is staged. The fact remains that the leaders of the superpowers should not be giving answers, in this spontaneous setting, that have such an enormous impact on world affairs. 3. Even if this type of forum were acceptable, Phil Donahue and Vladimir Posner are the last two personalities on the face of the earth that any president would want to engage in a serious foreign policy discussion.[23]

The Bush White House, however, was not above attempting to control the news cycle with less-than-substantive presidential actions. For example, Fitzwater wrote in a memo to Sununu on July 21, 1989, about a two-month press plan that would include the president's vacation to Kennebunkport, Maine: "This plan follows your guidance to provide media activities for the President during his stay in Kennebunkport. The purpose would be to give the President a national presence during this period. . . . Remember also that President Bush will provide pictures from Kennebunkport for the news everyday via jogging, golfing, fishing, and other movement. These are all covered by pools. Therefore, the President will have a daily media presence which can be exploited at any time by the simple action of addressing the pool."[24]

The overall goal of Bush's public appearances was to promote an image based on presidential dignity. In response to a request for Bush to be a guest on the Voice of America *Live International Call-In* in July 1989, Fitzwater claimed that "Presidents don't do call in shows."[25] The White House declined an invitation for Bush to speak at a 1989 *Time Magazine* Executive Forum because it was "a 'pay to attend' symposium which would have the effect of marketing the presidency."[26] Other speaking invitations for Bush that were declined included the 1989 Annual Convention of the National Association of Broadcasters in Las Vegas, since according to Fitzwater, "These are fat cat owners, etc. Little real press value. Vegas is wrong location," and taping an introduction for a PBS series on business ethics, since "We have no control over content. Pres intro amounts to endorsement. No telling what kind of unethical behavior is described on film."[27] In contrast, in November 1990 Bush did a live Oval Office interview with CNN to allow him "to discuss with the American people, in a calm and dignified setting, [his] thoughts and reassurances concerning the Gulf War."[28]

While the news media as an industry may have been experiencing shrinking budgets and resources during the late 1980s and early 1990s, there was nonetheless an expansion of newer media outlets which meant more news organizations to request interviews with the president. While no president can or should accommodate every request for an interview or media appearance, the management of such requests, particularly the delicate balance between those accepted and declined, is instructive to gain insight into how certain news organizations or specific reporters were viewed by the White House. With the Bush White House, while there seemed to be a preference for more traditional news outlets in an attempt to showcase the president's command of substantive policy matters, there also seemed to be a preference for some journalists over others (which is not an uncommon occurrence in any administration). While nothing in the Bush years could compare to the enemies lists, which included prominent journalists, during the Richard Nixon administration, internal White House memos show that Bush, along with Fitzwater and other staffers, had a preference for some media personalities and outlets more than others.

Dan Rather, the anchor of *CBS Evening News*, was perhaps the most notable among the big names in journalism that was not viewed favorably by the Bush White House. Bush and Rather had become "mortal enemies" during a live interview in 1988 when Bush countered Rather's attack about Iran-Contra by asking the anchor if he would like his entire career to be judged by the time he walked off the set during a newscast and caused seven minutes of dead airtime for his network. As a result, Rather's relationship with the White House remained strained throughout the Bush years, which ultimately posed a challenge for CBS in its White House coverage. According to Fitzwater, "During the Bush presidency, we offered many interviews to CBS correspondents Bob Schieffer, Charles

Kuralt, Randall Pinkston, Harry Smith, and others. All we wanted was someone who would be civil. But CBS management always said, 'No, only Dan Rather interviews the president.'"[29] A note from Bush to Fitzwater in March 1990 gives some insight into how Rather was viewed by the White House: "Marlin: Re: Your favorite Newscaster strikes again: Please register with someone at some level some kind of exception to this comment—Rather, whom I have defended, cannot resist the gratuitous dig. What Praise is my question? Rise to my defense. Do not take this anymore . . . Shout from the roof tops . . . we will not take it any more . . . Bomb Leslie . . . Cajole Wyatt . . . Call Burke . . . Tell Larry—I shalt not taketh it any more . . . A stick in the eye of CBS . . . May the prophets crap in their tents ever more . . . put down at this moment as undecided, but I will get off this neutral position unless there is marked improvement. It is your fault . . . fumed the leader of all the people. [signed] GB."[30]

That same day, Fitzwater drafted a letter to Barbara Cohen, Washington Bureau Chief of CBS News: "This is to complain that Dan Rather's reporting, especially his introductions to stories and his cross-talk interviews, is distorted, biased, and generally full of kow [*sic*] manure. I offer the example of last night's report on China. Transcript is enclosed. President Bush does not have a policy of praising China's old-line Communist leaders. This is pure Dan Rather baloney. Dan's characterization of a "policy of kowtowing" is pure Dan Rather gratuitous insult. The final irony of this story is that being No. 1 on China's enemy list clearly demonstrates that we do have a tough policy with regard to human rights in China, and they don't like it. Only Dan Rather could allow his hatred for George Bush to so obscure this obvious situation."[31]

While the copy of the letter is marked "unsent," and even taking the comments of both Bush and Fitzwater slightly tongue-in-cheek, a general attitude about Rather emanates from this exchange.

In another example of the general attitude about Rather within the communications and press teams, a staffer wrote the following to Fitzwater: "While our friends in the press room find this ridiculous, the attached *USA Today* story by Benedetto and the Cincinnati paper which has a circulation of 2 million exemplify the importance of travelling without necessarily getting on Dan Rather's *Evening News*."[32] In addition, in 1991, the White House was attempting to obtain transcript copies of Rather's radio commentaries for CBS News to monitor comments about the administration. As communications staffer Roman Popadiuk informed Chief of Staff John Sununu:

> Barbara Cohen, CBS Bureau Chief in Washington, informs us that due to cost-saving measures CBS has not been making transcripts of Dan Rather's Radio Commentary spots for over three years, or any other transcripts. They do have available a majority of the tapes for the past year which we requested. She claims it would cost the White House $3,500 to have these tapes transcribed. However, she says that CBS is interested in knowing why the White House wants these and it appears to us that they are leaving this as a loophole to possibly deny us transcripts if they don't like our explanation. Our options are as follows: 1) That you elevate this to the highest levels by calling Eric Ober, who is President of CBS News in New York City. Ms. Cohen claims she already discussed the issue with Ober; 2) We pay the $3,500 for the transcripts to be provided to us; 3) We ask for dubs of the tapes and ask our own White House stenographers to transcribe them. There is no guarantee that options 2 or 3 would work; or, 4) We are checking with numerous data base systems to see if they have those transcripts. We will have the answer tomorrow.[33]

While the Bush White House may have taken a particular interest in Rather's comments, monitoring news media coverage of the president was certainly not a new trend during the Bush years. A formalized "daily news summary" had been developed by the Nixon White House and has been used in one form or another ever since, a practice that has been institutionalized within the press or communications offices.[34] The Bush White House relied on several information sources to keep up with coverage of the president and his policy initiatives, including an extensive daily news summary of major print and broadcast sources, as well as weekly "editorial round-ups" that summarized editorials and op-ed pieces in major newspapers.[35] In addition, coverage of the president in roughly thirty regional newspapers, including larger regional daily newspapers such as the *Seattle Times, Dallas Morning News, Minneapolis Star Tribune, Phoenix Republic, San Diego Union*, and *Denver Post*, were tracked by staffers in the communications office.[36] By 1991, the Office of Media Relations had developed an extensive tracking system and content analysis of news coverage of presidential events, including which news organizations covered the event, the placement of the story about the event, and whether or not the coverage was considered "favorable" or "unfavorable."[37]

In general, Fitzwater had a good professional relationship with most reporters, which proved to be an asset to the Bush White House. He was also well respected among the White House press corps and was respectful in return. That mutual respect is evident in his relationship with Helen Thomas, the longtime UPI correspondent and grand dame of the White House press corps. In a personal note to an associate in 1992, Fitzwater wrote, "Great to hear from you. I am some kind of important muckety muck now. I only bow once a day to Helen Thomas."[38] In his memoir, he wrote of Thomas, "Few reporters in the White House can create news the way Helen Thomas does. There is no other reporter like her."[39] Thomas returned the compliment in her memoir: "Fitzwater was a real professional who was respected because he played it straight with us since he had access to the White House inner circle. Marlin understood the needs of the press, and when he continued in the job under President Bush, we knew we could count on him. . . . Of course we tangled from time to time because Marlin hated to brief and we constantly reminded him that was his job, to brief us. . . . But he did it, through six years and 850 briefings. And I think I detected a look of total relief each time one ended."[40]

Memos and correspondence from Fitzwater's files show numerous examples of a positive working relationship with many reporters and an ability to remain diplomatic even when turning down interview requests. In April 1991, Maureen Dowd and Andrew Rosenthal of the *New York Times* requested an interview with Bush: "Marlin: We have run out of room on our wall for the hashmarks that count the days since we last talked to the President. Having waited patiently in line behind the news magazines, the religious writers, sporting journals, C.N.N. and what-have-you, we'd like to renew our request for an interview. It is the perfect time for a thoughtful discussion of the Middle East, Bush's new domestic initiatives and other issues, especially with two of his favorite reporters. We mean it. Really. Gonna do it. It would be crass, of course, to remind you that when Bush didn't let Andy talk at the Dowd-[Tom] Friedman [3/28/90] interview, the President and you both promised another chance. Your obd't servants, Andy and Mo." To which Fitzwater responded: "Mo/ Andy: Thank God you're never crass. Otherwise you might mention the farm editors coming next week. As much as the President would like to contribute to your 'women' story, it may take awhile. Your Humble Slave, Marlin F."[41] In a response to Juan Williams of the *Washington Post*, who also requested an interview in March 1991, Fitzwater tried to explain the difficulty in meeting all such requests: "Dear Juan: Thank you for your patience in continuing to seek an interview with the President.

Unfortunately, half the world's news media is standing in line for an interview. I'm afraid we won't be able to do it for a while. The President is trying to do as many press conferences as possible, which are open to everyone. It is just going to be impossible to grant individual requests in the near-term. You might consider interviewing Governor Sununu, who is shepherding our domestic program through the Congress. Please let me know if you have any interest in talking to him. Thanks again."[42]

Bush also occasionally responded to interview requests, sometimes typing the responses himself. Regarding Bernard Shaw of CNN, Bush wrote in January 1990 in a memo to Fitzwater: "Bernard Shaw, whom I consider friendly, asked me at movie about coming by for a cup of coffee. You may recall that early on in admin. I talked to him about getting his wife involved in admin. He asked if he could come by for a private, no agenda—no Panama for example, chat. I told him O.K. but to talk to you. Let's set it up unless there is a compelling reason to stall."[43] The meeting occurred four days later. Just two months prior to the 1992 election, Bush sent the following memo: "To Jim Baker, Marlin, Kathy Super, Re: Phone call from my friend David Frost. He called this AM. Wants to do an interview to be aired Friday before election. 'Will come anywhere to do it.' I did not commit. I did tell him I'm interested. He is the best as far as I am concerned personally. I told him to contact Marlin. [signed] GB."[44] Bush also responded personally to a request from Peter Jennings at ABC about Bush's participation in a documentary on presidential leadership in a time of war, which Jennings called a "special project, something different from the ordinary news gathering we do each day. I would like to make a portrait of your Presidency in this time of crisis and great national resolve, to create a record for the nation of your leadership of the war, to write history's second draft." Bush's response: "Dear Peter, I am asking Marlin to take a look at your interesting proposal. I do see some obvious problems. Keeping this kind of history would be great, but I worry about some of the conflicts. In any event thanks for the letter, and we will get back to you. Sincerely, George Bush."[45]

Given the competition for the president's time, some reporters were not afraid to provide Fitzwater with a hard sell about the importance of their publication or news show or how their organization could provide positive or unbiased treatment in their coverage of Bush. Al Hunt of the *Wall Street Journal* wrote the following to Fitzwater in January 1992: "The *Wall Street Journal* would love to take its place alongside *People* magazine in the journalistic hall of fame and interview the President! Our pictures aren't quite as dazzling but our six million readers not only read—they vote. Seriously, we would love to do an interview with the President right after he submits the budget next week. Clearly, the focus these days is on the economy and the *Wall Street Journal* really is the best place for him to ventilate his views. Michel McQueen, John Harwood and I would do the interview. Of course, it would be any time at your convenience but naturally we would like to avoid Fridays since we don't have a weekend paper."[46] A similar pitch was made the following month by Douglas Harbrecht of *Business Week*:

> Just a reminder that our request still stands. If the President wants to talk in depth about his economic policies for short and long term growth, he can do so in *Business Week.* I know our 1 million readers would find a Q&A with President Bush at this important time very compelling reading. I was surprised to see the CBS-*Washington Post* poll show that 69 percent of those polled believed the economic policies outlined in the President's State of the Union address still don't go far enough. I was in New Hampshire watching the address with 800 business executives. The President's address was well received there, but even among that group, there was a certain tepidness, and a hunger for more details. As you might know, Treasury Secretary Nicholas Brady visited Friday with our editorial board in New York. The Secretary wanted to provide the Administration's view. But if the President wants to get his message out, without the filter of interpretation, in the country's number one economic news magazine, here's your forum. As you know, with Q&As, you could review the transcript in advance. Still hope we can do it, Marlin.[47]

When considering media requests, Fitzwater, Demarest, and other communication staffers always weighed the pros and cons of a particular interview or appearance, with strong consideration to the potential audience for the president's message as well as whether or not Bush would appear "presidential." In early 1989, Fitzwater considered a presidential visit to the Washington bureau of Hearst Newspapers worth the time and effort: "Hearst is GOP oriented, generally supports the Pres. Different kind of outreach—unexpected. Could be done in 30 minutes." However, a request from the *Boston Herald* for a "day in the life" story about Bush was not considered a valuable use of time: "Everybody does 'day in the life' story. . . . But it's too intrusive, and competitively unfair, to give an exclusive on this." Regarding Bush's participation in a *Frontline* documentary on PBS in 1992, Fitzwater told other staffers: "I have resisted this due to *Frontline's* historic antagonism toward the President." Regarding an interview request from the American Association of Retired Person's (AARP) magazine, Demarest urged acceptance: "You may have already heard directly from AARP. They have requested an interview with the President. This is an opportunity that we should not pass up. Their magazine has a circulation of 24 million. They have already done an interview with Clinton. The deadline, I understand, is September 8th." Fitzwater responded by writing "OK" on the memo.[48]

In his relationships with reporters, Fitzwater offered praise when he thought it was warranted but was also not afraid to complain about coverage he and the White House perceived to be unfair. In a response to a controversial 1989 story on ABC's *World News Tonight*, in which a suspected American spy was seen passing a briefcase full of top-secret information to a Soviet spy (the people in the video were actors and the tape had been doctored to look like a surveillance tape), Fitzwater wrote a personal note to ABC's national security correspondent John McWethy: "Jack: I realize reporters are hesitant to receive praise from flacks. But I just wanted to privately say, 'We're proud of you,' for demanding honesty in the 'briefcase' film clip."[49] However, Fitzwater offered no praise to CNN for their primary coverage in early 1992. In a letter to CNN President Tom Johnson, he wrote:

> I am compelled to raise an important subject related to the fairness of your election news coverage the evening of Tuesday, March 17, 1992. On all of Cable News Network's newscasts from 6 P.M. to 11:00 P.M., your editors and producers interviewed 20 citizens in the states of Michigan and Illinois. Only one comment in 20 was even remotely favorable to President Bush. Attached are the verbatim quotes from all the "bumper" interviews during this period. Out of all the votes cast in these two states, 1.2 million were Republican and 1.9 million were Democrats. Of all the Republican votes cast, 935,000 went to President Bush. Imagine the President's astonishment to find that almost none of those Bush voters found their way in front of your cameras. It is inconceivable to me that out of 20 interviews, only one would have anything favorable to say about the President of the United States. Experience would suggest that your correspondents interviewed many more people than the 20

> selected for broadcast. Thus, it's even harder to believe that your selection does not represent a political bias. Whether it be on the basis of voting patterns, or the percentage of votes cast, it's hard to believe only one person in 20 would say something good about the President. It's equally difficult to believe that this unfair coverage is accidental and not intentional editing. I would hope for a higher standard of journalistic integrity at CNN. Historically, CNN has exhibited higher standards. And, I ask you to look into this matter in terms of your future election coverage.[50]

Some responses by Fitzwater, however, were much more lighthearted, such as this 1989 letter to Lorne Michaels at NBC's *Saturday Night Live*: "President Bush has asked me to respond to your request for his appearance on 'Saturday Night Live.' While my advice to the President is that he would be falling down crazy not to want to join Chevy Chase for a night of foolishness on *Saturday Night Live*, he seems to feel he can resist. And while you are right that there is no Soviet or Chinese *Saturday Night Live*, this may mean totalitarianism has more good sense than we thought. In any case, the President respectfully declines the opportunity to appear on the anniversary show."[51] However, the relationship with the news division at NBC was not always as jovial. A series of correspondence between Fitzwater and Tim Russert, who became NBC News Washington Bureau Chief in 1989 and moderator of *Meet the Press* in 1991, show Russert's persistence in attempts to interview Bush. In 1989, Russert received this response from Fitzwater:

> Thank you for your letter of August 4, raising questions about your interview request. First, I want to point out that your request is still under consideration, and is reviewed at regular intervals by our Scheduling Committee. Secondly, life is not fair, but we try to be as fair as possible in granting interview requests. Normally, we do not offer explanations for staff decisions. Nevertheless, all of us in the White House feel NBC has indeed tried to cover the Administration fairly and objectively. Tom Brokaw, yourself and all of the NBC correspondents who cover the White House are held in high esteem by the President, the Chief of Staff, myself, and other members of the White House staff. I assure you there is no personal slight intended in terms of the granting of interview requests. It's only because of our personal and professional feelings for you and NBC that I

offer the following explanations on the specific points you raised: 1. President Bush promised David Frost an interview for PBS during the Presidential campaign. The President intends to keep that promise. 2. ABC-TV presented the White House with an innovative and imaginative television opportunity in terms of their *Prime Time Live* show. We felt it was worth accepting in terms of audience, production, programming commitment, and personal commitments. 3. The "pool report" reference to Jim Miklaszewski has to deal considerably with the internal workings of the White House Press Corps, including the prejudices and habits of press "pools" roaming the corridors of the West Wing. I have the highest regard for Jim: I have worked with him many years. This unfortunate, minor incident received no public attention and will certainly cast no reflection on NBC News. 4. No Administration officials appeared on weekend talk shows the weekend of August 5 and 6 because of a policy decision that appearances at that time would not be helpful to our discussions about hostage-taking in the Middle East. Secretary Baker did appear on the ABC premiere of *Prime Time Live* on Thursday, August 3 because it was the premiere show, because of a prior commitment to Sam Donaldson, and because Secretary Baker wanted to do it. In conclusion, NBC has received, and will continue to receive, fair treatment in terms of White House interview requests.[52]

Beginning in late 1991, Russert remained persistent in his requests to have Bush appear on *Meet the Press*. The following is an example of the back-and-forth correspondence between Russert, Fitzwater, and others within the White House, which highlights a level of professionalism on both sides even in an environment where top Washington journalists were competing to get access to the president:

December 2, 1991—Russert Letter to Fitzwater: Dear Marlin: It was good talking to you. After watching the President on *This Week with David Brinkley* yesterday, I had a thought. On Sunday, December 15th from 6:30 to 8:00 P.M., the six announced Democratic candidates will have their first televised debate on NBC. Would the President like to have the opportunity to set the agenda for that debate by taping a special edition of *Meet the Press* which would air Sunday morning the 15th at 10:30 A.M.? The panel would be Tom Brokaw, John Cochran and myself. His presence would guarantee balance in the Sunday and Monday political news coverage. Many thanks for your assistance.

December 11, 1991—Fitzwater Letter to Russert: Dear Tim: Thanks for the opportunity for the President to appear on *Meet the Press*. Unfortunately, we will not be able to accept your invitation this time. Maybe something will work out after the State of the Union. Thanks for your interest.

December 19, 1991—Russert Letter to Fitzwater: Dear Marlin: Thanks for your note of December 11, 1991. Always the optimist, I will hold February 2, 9 and 16th as possible dates for a *Meet the Press* interview with the President. As you suggested they are after the State of the Union. I note they are also before New Hampshire. Thanks again for your consideration.

January 9, 1992—Russert Letter to Fitzwater: Dear Marlin: Welcome home. I hope the President continues to feel fine. I just wanted to renew our invitation for the President to be our guest on *Meet the Press* before the New Hampshire primary. I watched with great interest his interviews on *This Week with David Brinkley* and on PBS with David Frost. I can assure you the same objectivity and fairness. I hope he will take this opportunity to share his views with the people of the United States—and New Hampshire. Thank you for your consideration.

January 9, 1992—Russert Letter to Sam Skinner, Chief of Staff: Dear Sam: Attached is my correspondence with Marlin Fitzwater extending an invitation to the President to appear on *Meet the Press*. As you can see, Marlin indicates there may be a possibility of doing something after the State of the Union. As you know, the President has recently done interviews on *This Week with David Brinkley* on ABC and with David Frost on PBS. I am holding February 2, 9, and 16th as possible dates. Note these are before the New Hampshire primary. As always, I can assure you *Meet the Press* is a fair, objective and balanced interview program. I would appreciate your support of this request.

January 21, 1992—Personal note from Russert to Fitzwater: Dear Marlin, I hear the President may travel to New Hampshire the weekend before the primary—February 15th and 16th. We could broadcast *Meet the Press* live from New Hampshire on the 16th—a nice touch. Also holding Feb. 2 and 9. Hope all else goes well. Tim.

January 23, 1992—Fitzwater Letter to Russert: Dear Tim: You get high marks for persistence. Everyone here appreciates your "Meet the Press" offer, but the feeling seems to be that the President will not be able to accept until later in the year. Nevertheless, with the campaign organization now coming together, this situation could break at any time. So thanks for staying in touch.

June 29, 1992—Russert Letter to Bush: Dear Mr. President: I read in Thursday's *New York Times* that you sat for an extended period of time with their reporters to discuss your platform and plans for America. You will recall last May I invited you to appear as the sole guest on a special one-hour edition of *Meet the Press* any Sunday this summer (except August 2 or August 9 when we are pre-empted by the Barcelona Summer Olympics). Tom Brokaw and John Chancellor will join me on the panel. I have enjoyed your appearances on 20/20 and *CNN International Hour.* I realize you may view *Meet the Press* as a more traditional format, but nonetheless we think it is an important one. I hope you will now take advantage of this opportunity to spend one hour on national television discussing with knowledgeable reporters your views on the issues and challenges facing our country. It would be an interesting and widely-viewed morning. I can assure you it will be a fair, civil and substantive discussion. We want to talk issues not process. I hope you will accept.

June 30, 1992—Copy of Bush letter with handwritten remarks from Fitzwater to Russert: Tim: Thanks for your request. We'll consider it. Schedule tight before the convention. [signed] Marlin.

July 30, 1992—Russert Letter to Fitzwater: Dear Marlin: As you may have read, beginning Sunday, September 20, 1992, Meet the Press will be expanded to one hour every week. We would very much like to have both President Bush and Vice President Quayle as our premiere guests on September 20. I would give them the full hour. The panel would be Tom Brokaw and John Chancellor. If you would prefer to have just President Bush, we will, of course, accommodate your wish. I hope you will take advantage of this opportunity to have a serious and substantive discussion on the issues confronting the nation.

August 21, 1992—Russert Letter to Bush: Dear Mr. President: Congratulations on your convention. As you may have read, beginning Sunday, September 20, 1992, *Meet the Press* will be expanded to one hour every week. We would very much like to have you as our premiere guest for the full hour. The panel would be Tom Brokaw and John Chancellor. We are confident this debut of *Meet the Press* in its new one-hour format will receive considerable attention. I hope you will take advantage of this opportunity to have a serious and substantive discussion on the issues confronting the nation.

August 21, 1992—Handwritten note from Russert to Fitzwater: Dear Marlin, One more time. Our time has come. Thanks, Tim.

August 24, 1992—Handwritten note from Fitzwater to Russert: Tim: Thanks for your note. New team in place here. We'll see. Marlin.

September 28, 1992—Russert Letter to Bush: Dear Mr. President: With five weeks to go until the campaign, I would like to invite you once again to be our guest on Meet the Press. You would be our sole interview for the entire hour. The panelists would be Tom Brokaw and John Chancellor. We are not interested in playing "gotcha," but rather engage in a substantive and civil discussion of the issues confronting our nation and your plans to deal with them. I do thank you for your consideration.

September 28, 1992—Handwritten note from Russert to Fitzwater: Dear Marlin, I read I'm on the "blacklist." Someday I'd love to hear how I earned that dubious honor. Nevertheless, I hope you will consider this request. It would be a fair, substantive program. Many thanks, Tim.

October 1, 1992—Handwritten response from Fitzwater on copy of Russert's note: Tim: NO black list. That's Lesley Stall's [sic] paranoia. The President got your letter. Hope something works out. Marlin.[53]

During 1992, the general press strategy that had been in place since the start of the administration had not changed, even while Bush was in the heat of a reelection campaign. Making sure that the president appeared in dignified and presidential settings, appearing to be above the political fray of the campaign, remained a top priority. However, White House memos suggest that the president's usual public strategy had shifted a bit to not only accommodate the demands of a reelection campaign but also the challenges posed by both Bill Clinton and Ross Perot's use of newer media formats. A list of potential media activities for June and early July 1992 included the following interviews and television appearances:

6/10—Satellite, Remarks on Balanced Budget, Purpose: To present your arguments for use by television.

6/11—Depart Rio, Departure Statement, Andrews Air Force Base, Purpose: Coverage on 7 A.M. newscasts would allow a direct explanation of your procedures and goals in Rio to the American people.

6/15—*CNN International Hour*, Live from White House, Frank Sesno to discuss Yeltsin visit, Rio, etc. Purpose: To highlight your foreign policy experience in an international forum that is directly transmitted to the world.

6/18—*CBS Today*/Paula Zahn, 15 minute interview from White House: To allow an interview that is friendly and informative, and unique because you have never done a morning show interview before. This is perhaps the one CBS show we would recommend.

6/23—*20/20* Barbara Walters, 30 minute President/30 minutes Mrs. Bush, 10 minute together, Purpose: Maximum exposure to 10–15 million people with an interviewer who is dignified and respected.

6/25—*New York Times* Interview, Purpose: *The Times* has assigned reporters to produce a 6-part series on the Bush Administration's record in the first 3 ½ years. This interview would be your account of your major accomplishments and achievements.

6/30—Jim Lehrer Interview, *McNeil/Lehrer Report*—PBS, Purpose: To provide an interview with a respected newsman, on television's most-respected news show, and one which would generate coverage by other media.

7/2—*Today Show* with Bryant Gumbel from the White House, 1 hour call-in, Purpose: All 3 networks morning shows invited the Presidential candidates to an hour call-in show. Bill Clinton and Ross Perot participate this week. Moving your show to July would offer an opportunity to discuss the American scene just prior to the July 4 holiday. This is a dignified forum for you to communicate directly with the American people.

7/3—Press Conference—Room 405—Economic Summit with foreign reporters, Purpose: To discuss the Economic Summit with foreign reporters.

7/22—Larry King at the White House, 1 hour Call-ins, Purpose: To show your ability to handle questions from a large call-in audience on a variety of subjects, to answer questions from "real" people, with the White House as a back-drop.

July/August—Brinkley Interview[54]

Similarly, in July 1992, the goals of presidential media opportunities included: "Media exposure that allows the President to express his views in full. Dignified, 'Presidential' settings. A 'personality' emphasis that displays personality and character. Family exposure." The "tools" for achieving those goals included interviews with Barbara Walters on ABC's *20/20*, Jim Lehrer on PBS, Brian Lamb on C-SPAN, oval office interviews with David Brinkley on ABC's *This Week* and Charles Kuralt on CBS's *Sunday Morning*, a primetime East Room press conference, a photo essay in *Time*, satellite interviews with local broadcasters, and a handful of Saturday radio addresses with "news peg."[55] It is telling that memos found in open files to date in the Bush Presidential Library show an overwhelming emphasis on traditional news outlets such as the three networks, the *New York Times*, and *Time Magazine*, even in 1992 as the Clinton campaign began to rely on new media outlets; there is little mention of any newer media outlets or news sources as ways for President Bush to bring his message to the public. The "newer" innovations during Bush's reelection campaign, like weekly radio addresses and satellite interviews with local reporters, had already been introduced as standard communication strategies in the Reagan administration. Despite Clinton's (and to some extent Perot's) success with more innovative media outlets, like talk shows (*Larry King Live*, *Phil Donahue Show*, *The Arsenio Hall Show*, for example) or appearances on non-traditional outlets like MTV, the Bush team mostly stayed the course with a more traditional press strategy.

Like other presidents before him, most notably Gerald Ford and Jimmy Carter, Bush miscalculated in the belief that more access for reporters would provide positive coverage. During the television age, journalists representing all mediums now interpret the news, rather than just report events, and much of Bush's difficulties came from the news media's analysis of his leadership. According to Mark Rozell, this interpretation by the press left much to be desired for Bush, since "modern journalists are much more like public teachers, and much less like stenographers, than they used to be. They do not merely report the president's activities. They also evaluate his actions and even speculate about possible underlying motivations."[56] Also, the difference between entertainers and journalists had been getting "fuzzier and fuzzier to Americans in the 1980s and 1990s, and shock 'journalism' seemed to have replaced traditional issue-oriented reporting. Washington journalists were seen by the public as personalities or opportunists seeking only self-aggrandizement and sensational stories about White House embarrassments."[57] According to Fitzwater, Bush was tremendously frustrated by his negative press coverage: "[T]o the last day of his administration, [Bush] could not understand how the press could be so bad to him when he had been so good to them."[58] Bush often showed his impatience and testiness with the press; "[Bush devoured] everything printed and broadcast about him and [seemed] to take criticism personally."[59] Critical stories about members of his family, like stories about his son Neal's involvement in the savings and loan banking scandal, upset Bush more than any other coverage. According to C. Boyden Gray, White House counsel to Bush, "I think he was increasingly disenchanted with the hammering he and his family were getting. He knew that public scrutiny and public criticism came with the territory and didn't complain about it publicly, but he would complain to me privately. His bitterness about the press may have taken some of the fun out of the job for him."[60]

By all accounts, the Bush years were a period of a rapidly changing news media environment when technology began to drive presidential news more than any previous era. While the challenge of managing a presidential image and message would have been immense for any team of advisors working for any president during those years, Bush's more traditional view of the presidential-press relationship at times seemed out of step with the political environment in which he attempted to govern. Nonetheless, Fitzwater's adept handling of the White House press corps, which can be a hostile crowd to any president or press secretary who attempt to manage the news, proved to be a strong asset for the Bush team. In January 1993, during the waning days of the Bush administration, Fitzwater received the following handwritten letter from Chris Matthews, then Washington bureau chief for the *San Francisco Examiner*:

> Dear Marlin—While you remain in the chair of honor I want to put it on record that nobody has handled that job better than you. I know all the old, tired bone [*sic*] about Hagerty. But, he had Ike and didn't have the crowd in today's press world. Whenever I think if I could handle that job of yours I think of the simple powerful fact that you, Marlin, don't make mistakes. I don't know how you do it, but there's bound to be some pay dirt out there for a guy who has

> performed so professionally in a world & time that hardly matches the staid, respectful world of Jim Hagerty, Ike and those pompous establishment types who wanted nothing more than the great general's favor. Congratulations on being the best at a time that's far tougher, meaner, and less fun than any before. Best, Chris.

Matthews' letter, along with Fitzwater's handwritten response, seems to sum up the type of relationship that the latter developed with the White House press corps: "Chris: Thanks my friend for your kind comments. It's been a good ride. Even fun. Thanks for thinking of me. [signed] Marlin F."[61]

It is important to note that not only had the news media industry itself changed by the early 1990s, but so too did the White House strategy in how to craft presidential images and messages. In this regard, Bush often failed where Reagan had succeeded before him (mastering the art of image and style) and Clinton succeeded after him (using the new media outlets and technologies to promote his message). Where Bush did not act strategically in regards to the changes within the news industry, the theme of the Clinton team, once they took office in 1993, was "out with the old, in with the new" as far as press relations were concerned. According to media critic Tom Rosenstiel, Clinton's advisors declared "the end of Old Media and the beginning of the new science of a more substantive, more precise form of communication by political leaders through targeted use of the New Media, new technology, and local reporters. . . . Clinton had learned to manipulate his message in a way that was entirely 'new.' He had 'honed' the strategy of 'narrowcasting' that began with shades and sax on Arsenio Hall's talk show, using new technology and specific media to reach the public with direct, targeted messages—'accurate, immediate and politically sensitive transmission of his policies.'"[62]

That is not to say that the old-style media could be ignored either, as Bush and his successors still needed to understand the needs of the press in order to manage the message coming from the White House. But Bush seemed reluctant to develop a strategy for either the old or new media, making the task of managing his message even more complex in the face of changing technology and the increasing number of news outlets.[63] With a news industry in transition and a White House communication strategy that was moving away from stagecraft and packaging the news, Bush often ended up looking like an unrhetorical, non-strategic president. An interesting irony for Bush is that not only were his reelection chances hurt by the impact on voters of the recession of 1991–92, but the news media as an industry was also hit hard by the recession—layoffs, salary freezes, collapsing advertising bases—so that when Bush complained about how the economic recovery was not being reported, those that he wanted to report it were feeling the pain of the recession perhaps more than other industries. In addition to the many structural changes occurring within the news industry, another important trend impacting coverage of the Bush White House (and the subsequent Clinton, Bush, and Obama administrations as well) was the increase in "soft news." Defined as news having no real connection to substantive policy issues, or as the opposite of "hard news" that includes coverage of breaking events or major issues impacting the daily routines of U.S. citizens, soft news has steadily increased during the past two decades in response to competition within the marketplace. The bottom line is that the "new" news—soft, entertainment, and market-driven news—is much more profitable than the traditional "who, what, where, when, and why" of traditional political news. Journalism has also become increasingly critical in its tone toward government officials in an attempt to grab more viewers and readers, to which some scholars point as evidence of "weakening the foundation of democracy by diminishing the public's information about public affairs and its interest in politics."[64] Unfortunately for Bush and his advisors, all of this represented an inhospitable political environment in which his style of governing made it difficult to succeed.

The Public Connection: Bush and Polling

A president's approval rating is one of the best indicators of whether or not a communication strategy with the U.S. public is working. While many outside factors, including the economy, international events, and the political environment in general, all shape how the president's job performance is evaluated, above-average approval numbers can at least suggest that a president is succeeding somewhat in the area of public leadership. It is important to note, however, that being liked by many Americans does not always translate into an effective method of governing in the public arena. When looking at Bush's public approval ratings throughout his four years in office (see figure 1), a striking paradox is evident. For a majority of his time in the White House, with 1992 as the obvious exception, Bush enjoyed above-average approval ratings, yet his managerial style of governing did not afford many opportunities (with the exception of the Gulf War) to capitalize on his public support. Political scientists have known for decades the importance of public support in the equation of presidential success. By the time Bush took office in 1989, presidential popularity was just as important as ever, and perhaps even more complex, because approval ratings had become more volatile through an increasingly critical public as well as divided partisan support within Congress.[65]

Presidents can also be victims of circumstances that are beyond their control. Bush initially enjoyed the carryover success of public support for the Reagan years early during his administration. The public rallying event of the Gulf War, beginning with the military buildup in the Persian Gulf in 1990 and concluding with the victorious return of U.S. troops in 1991, provided Bush with then-record-high approval ratings. News coverage during the Gulf War in 1991 was closely monitored and tightly controlled by the government. Only Pentagon-approved pool reporters were allowed to report on action, stories were subject to military censorship, and most coverage consisted merely of official military briefings. Unlike Vietnam, when fighting on the battlefields was brought into the living rooms of Americans on a nightly basis via the network news, coverage of the Gulf War maintained the visual image of U.S. military strength until Iraq

Figure 1: Bush Approval Ratings - Gallup

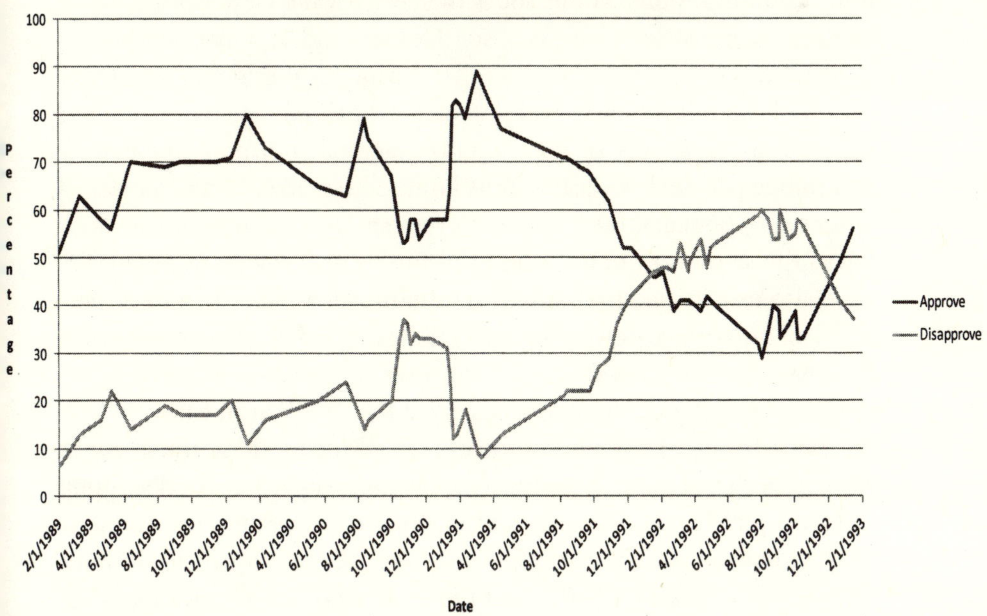

urce: The Gallup Poll, 1989–1993.

surrendered. "Persian Gulf coverage was a classic example of government and the media collaborating to manipulate popular passions and shape our nation's political discourse."[66] This helped Bush achieve high public approval ratings during the conflict, as high as 90 percent in some polls in February 1991 for approval of job performance.[67]

As the nation turned its attention to the sagging economy by late 1991 and early 1992, Bush's approval ratings plummeted just as he was readying for his reelection campaign. The recession, while not the worst or the longest that Americans had ever endured, would nonetheless hurt Bush's presidency in a variety of ways. First, the news media provided a running narrative about the recession that blamed the Bush administration and its domestic policies, or lack thereof, as a large part of the problem. Second, the tighter economic climate for the news media industry made for tougher competition, which resulted in more critical coverage of the Bush administration. Third, the news media in general, and the White House press corps in particular, were still recovering from the "PR machine" and its manipulations during the Reagan era.[68] As a result, Bush was the unfortunate recipient of negative coverage, especially during his reelection bid, and he often showed his impatience and testiness with the press.[69]

An important factor in public approval ratings for presidents is personality, which was always good news for Bush, since most people liked him. Routinely, polls would show that Americans viewed him as "an intelligent, industrious, cautious, solid leader" and as someone who was "warm, sincere, relaxed, and secure."[70] During his presidency, and especially in his public remarks and statements, Bush was "neither harsh nor contentious. He avoids the use of confrontational or disunifying rhetoric and public personality clashes, thus limiting the target and strategies of potential opponents. Bush rarely if ever espouses unpopular causes or bucks the trends of public opinion."[71] Bush's high marks in popularity were also usually tied to dramatic international events; when "domestic problems intervened or were forced on the White House, the polls returned close to the presidential average."[72] However, while Bush's approval rating soared during the U.S. military success in the Gulf War in early 1991, as the United States–led coalition forces pushed the invading Iraqis out of Kuwait, by the start of 1992—Bush's reelection year—the president's poll numbers plummeted. According to journalist Hugh Sidey, the dramatic drop in Bush's approval ratings, from a high of near 90 percent in mid-1991 to a low of around 30 percent in early 1992 was perplexing: "One might have thought that George Bush would have received credit for his success in foreign policy. After Desert Storm, he had 91 percent approval ratings in the polls, and then the rating plummeted. I do not know what caused this plummet, but George Bush told me that it happened because he could not communicate. When I asked him what he meant, he said that he tried to tell the people that the economy was improving after the small recession that the country had just come through, but he just could not get that point across."[73]

While Bush had little control over external polling about his presidency, internal polling was an important element of the overall White House communication strategy. Like several prior administrations, the Bush White House relied on polling—both within and outside of the administration—in an attempt to "lead the public" in support of the president's agenda. Presidents dating back to Richard Nixon have relied on such polls and have been criticized for developing a "permanent campaign" mentality while attempting to govern, with the inference that presidents are too often checking the pulse of the nation through a poll prior to making a policy decision. The White House polling operation since the Nixon years has become an institutionalized aspect of the presidency by influencing how and to whom presidents can choose to communicate. According to Diane J. Heith, "the poll data enabled the production of a presidency-centered constituency strategy, which linked the president's initial electoral coalition to a viable reelection coalition. Thus, polling altered the target and framework of presidential persuasion toward an increasingly segmented and adversarial conception of the president's supporters."[74]

In Bush's case, like many of his predecessors, his staff devoted "substantial time, money, and attention to a White House public opinion apparatus."[75] An "Opinion Digest" was also used to track the results of outside polling operations, such as Gallup or the various media-sponsored polls, on the public's mood on important policy issues.[76] Poll meetings were routinely held for staffers, and while Bush did not regularly attend such meetings, he exchanged a greater number of "poll memos" with his staff than Presidents Nixon, Ford, Carter, or Reagan. For example, Bush received a memo from Ed Rogers in July 1990 to present the president with "Recent Polling Data":

> To follow-up our conversation of last Tuesday, attached please find an analysis of recent polls. I assume you saw yesterday's *New York Times* poll which showed a drop of 6 points—from 69% to 63%—roughly the same result as our poll. In addition to the information printed

> in the paper, Tab A provides another set of Gallup questions. A Sindlinger poll shows a drop of 13 points—from 72.8% to 60%. This latter poll's sample is largely slanted toward economic issues (see Tab B, part 1) which they say is why it appears to be such a dramatic drop. Also, part 2 analyzes the conclusions drawn from Wirthlin's "Right Direction/Wrong Track" question which you asked about on Tuesday. The Wirthlin poll was conducted before your budget statement. A new Wirthlin poll is due for release next week. The *Houston Post* article that cited 70% approval was based on June's Gallup approval which was 69%. Finally, a *Wall Street Journal* poll, that ran today, mirrors the results of our own poll last week, and in fact, is a few points better. Even more encouraging, this poll was taken over a week later than ours. The conclusions we can draw from this information are as follows: We will not take a big hit as a direct result of your budget statement, due in large part to your personal credibility, as indicated by the *New York Times* poll in which 75% consider you "sincere" and just 18% consider you "insincere"; and reading between the lines, you will have a strong benefit-of-the-doubt factor working in your favor when we do begin to promote a budget package.[77]

While the overall goal of the Bush White House may have been to step back from the public relations emphasis during the Reagan years, it is worth noting that more than seventy Bush staffers were involved in polling within the following White House units: Office of Economic and Domestic Policy, Chief of Staff, Political Affairs, the Cabinet, Intergovernmental Affairs, as well as eight other offices and assorted pollsters independent of the White House.[78] The Bush White House relied on polling as an attempt to move public opinion in line with the president's policy preferences on minor initiatives such as the national tree-planting program, a component of the president's larger clean air initiative. Some success was achieved in shaping public opinion on this issue in 1989 and 1990, as evidenced in a memo to Bush from Roger Porter in October 1990:

> Some interesting and encouraging news suggesting that repetition and persistence pays. A recent Market Opinion Research survey reveals widespread awareness of, and support for, your tree planting initiatives. Half of the electorate is aware of your support for

> tree planting. Women are more aware of your efforts in connection with tree planting than men. Republicans and conservatives are more aware than Democrats and liberals. Awareness is also greater among higher income and well educated voters. Eighty-five percent of those surveyed believe your request for Americans to plant trees is a good idea to help the environment and that the idea will work. Voters across all demographic groupings agree that your request for Americans to plant trees is a good idea. Half of the persons polled said that they or someone else in their family has planted a tree or has been involved in a tree planting activity in the past twelve months. "He plants trees to benefit another generation." Cicero quoting Caecilius Statius (220–169 B.C.) in De Senectute, VII.[79]

By 1991, the oncoming recession limited the president's ability to shape public opinion on the larger issue of the environment (which the tree planting effort was supposed to help), as well as many other issues. In October 1990, Bush pollster Richard Wirthlin sent a message to John Sununu to report good news on Bush's poll numbers and that the president had survived the budget battle with Congress: "All in all, we have made up good ground in the last three days. Now the issue is not on the budget, but on leadership."[80] But by the end of 1991, the White House mood over poll numbers had dramatically shifted as evidenced in a memo to Bush from Fitzwater to provide talking points for photo opportunities where the press was expected to ask about Bush's falling approval rating. The talking points for Bush included:

> These polls show people are anxious and very concerned about the economy.
>
> I don't worry about polls in terms of my personal political situation, but I do worry about peoples' views of our general economy. It's clear consumer confidence is down, and the economy is in serious trouble.
>
> We are working on a series of options to turn the economy around. 1) New Highway Bill: Several hundred thousand jobs. 2) Asia Trip: A chance to push for market access and more U.S. exports. Every billion dollars in exports means 20,000 new jobs. 3) Various measures to stimulate the economy are being considered as part of our Fiscal Year 1992 budget process.[81]

* * *

By January 1992, the White House was looking for any good news in polling numbers for the president's reelection bid. Bush received a memo from Deputy Press Secretary Judy Smith with the subject line "Overnights!!" on January 23, 1992: "The latest NBC/Wall Street Journal poll showed both positive and negative results. NBC made an executive decision from New York to put a positive spin on the results because they think the poll has bottomed out to about 50 percent. In addition, NBC talked to voters in New Hampshire and the voters believe many factors contribute to the current economic situation."[82] It is important to note that the Bush White House, like others before it, did not abandon their control over the legislative agenda based on public opinion, nor did it adopt a permanent campaign strategy in place of traditional governing.[83] Like many of his predecessors, however, Bush, along with his advisors, closely monitored his approval rating and understood what a sagging approval rating could mean for both legislative initiatives and a reelection campaign.

Conclusion

Like other presidents before him, Bush endured a complex relationship with the press; while he liked many reporters on a personal level and for many in the White House press corps the feeling was mutual, that did not guarantee positive press coverage. According to Helen Thomas, throughout his four years in office Bush was friendly with reporters and often entertained them in Kennebunkport. However, Bush partially blamed the press for his defeat in 1992: "Bush remained friendly to the press until the presidential campaign in 1992, when he seemed to feel he was not getting a fair shake. He had been riding high in the aftermath of the Gulf War with popularity polls as high as 90 percent, and he appeared unbeatable." Thomas recalled how First Lady Barbara Bush also took a dim view of the press, especially after her husband's defeat in 1992: "In the White House tradition, in November 1992, Mrs. Bush invited Hillary Rodham Clinton to visit her future home. When she arrived at the White House and was welcomed by Mrs. Bush at the diplomatic entrance, the South Lawn was jammed with reporters and photographers witnessing the moment. With a smile, Mrs. Bush gestured to the media horde, looked at Hillary and said, 'Avoid this crowd like the plague. And if they quote you, make damn sure they heard you.'"[84]

In the simplest of terms, Bush was unlucky to inhabit the White House during this time of substantive and structural change within the news industry. While those who have closely studied the Bush presidency have surmised that he was a substantive president who often lacked public style, it is difficult to view him as a successful leader, particularly in regards to the public presidency, in the long shadow of the Reagan years. And in an historical context, Bush's public legacy will also be shaped by not only who he followed in the White House but who followed him, since Clinton is credited with not only better understanding the needs of the news media but being able to survive harsh media attacks as well. On the one hand, that assessment might seem a bit unfair, but on the other hand, the circumstances of the political environment were such that some aspects of the public presidency were out of Bush's control. Others, however, were not; key moments in Bush's tenure point to what turned out to be a more difficult relationship with the press than he had anticipated. According to historian John Robert Greene, "Bush perhaps met with the press more often, but the press instinctively knew that Reagan liked them more.... An angry Bush, publicly castigating purported leakers from within his own administration, began to withdraw from the press. For example, on the way to a February 1990 drug summit in Columbia, a visibly angry Bush went back to the press seats on Air Force One. He condemned stories that had been written on his tendency for secrecy and announced that from that point forward, 'we've got a whole new relationship.' That relationship continued to sour as the press felt itself—rightfully, as the evidence shows—to have been closed out of the field of battle in both the Panamanian and the Persian Gulf conflicts. By 1991 there was an open hostility between Bush and the press that had become difficult to contain."[85]

Ultimately, the Bush administration viewed the press differently than Reagan had, and this affected the relationship. While the news media was a vehicle through which Reagan excelled at communicating, Bush's advisors considered the press more of a hindrance. Bush's lack of initiative with the legislative agenda, as well as declining interest in political news, had placed White House news in a secondary role during the Bush years. The president was no longer leading the newscast, and Bush was seen on television about one-third as often as Reagan had been. While Bush had been "generous in providing quotes and more understanding of the needs of reporters than any other president had been since Kennedy . . . his accessibility certainly did not tone down press criticism, keep embarrassing questions off the agenda, or make the American public feel all warm and fuzzy about their president."[86] Because the presidential-press relationship is such an integral component of the modern public presidency, it is easy to understand Bush's frustration with the White House press corps. Given the media environment in which Bush attempted to govern, however, coupled with Bush's view about the public aspects of the presidency, perhaps his public performances were as good as could have been expected of this particular president in this particular moment in political time.

CHAPTER 4

Bush's Major Public Addresses

The Inaugural and State of the Union Addresses

The significance of symbolism and ritual to the U.S. presidency cannot be overstated. In recent decades, as technology has continued to expand the myriad opportunities for presidents to communicate with and be seen by citizens (U.S. and global alike), the image of the president as a national leader and the presidency as a powerful institution is perhaps more pervasive in the public realm than ever before. From the moment the president delivers his inaugural address until he waves goodbye to well-wishers on the day he leaves office, the president lives his life on center stage and must live up to the public expectations that come along with the job. As such, presidential communications make up a large part of the symbolism attached to the office; beyond the presidential seal on the podium, the sounds of "Hail to the Chief" when the president enters a public event, or the ever-present Secret Service agents and the White House press corps trailing the president's every move, a major public address by the president epitomizes both the symbolism and the ever-increasing public role of the office. While a major public address is one of many options that the White House will consider as a means for the president to communicate, such an event is often the centerpiece of the overall communications strategy for a particular decision or policy initiative. As presidential advisors in recent years have developed more innovative ways for a president to communicate with both the U.S. public and the news media, public expectations for effective communications during such high-profile events have also increased. The office of the presidency now demands strong communication skills, even if the president himself falls short of that expectation. While less than stellar communication skills does not disqualify someone from winning the presidency (as has happened more often than not during the television age), a president cannot escape the public aspects of the job once elected.

George H. W. Bush is such an example. The fact that Bush was not a gifted public speaker in the television-age tradition of John F. Kennedy or Ronald Reagan was not a surprise to the journalists who had covered the 1988 campaign or even the voters who helped to put together Bush's winning electoral coalition. Presidential campaigns are often a good indicator of what the public can expect from their president, particularly in regards to public leadership. If the candidate does not engage in lofty and soaring rhetoric on the campaign trail (which Bush did not), that is usually a good indication that such a style of communication will not be forthcoming once the president takes the oath of office (it was not with Bush). However, while a president's communication skill level may change White House strategy, it does not eliminate the growing public responsibilities that go along with the job. Major public addresses and other presidential public activities are essential in signaling the president's policy agenda to other relevant political actors as well as to the public. The president's performance at such events can also influence resulting news coverage of the president as well as public approval ratings. As a result, and as with every president in the television age, Bush could not escape the inevitable public expectation of him as president to embrace the public aspects of the job as "communicator-in-chief." Bush did not place a high priority on giving speeches or using the public relations apparatus within the White House to govern; he seemed to view the public aspects of the job as a necessary evil, and he did not match the public style and performance of his predecessor (Reagan) nor would he adopt a strategy of campaigning to govern like his successor (Bill Clinton). Yet his speeches and public appearances would nonetheless play a significant role in governing during his four years in office.

This chapter and the next will analyze the major public addresses, major policy addresses, and related public activities during the Bush presidency. The inaugural address and state of the union addresses will be considered here, and major policy addresses and related public events will be considered in chapter 5. Major public addresses are defined as rhetorical moments when the president addresses the nation, or when his address to a smaller group can expect a larger (and perhaps national or international) audience through mass media dissemination. While presidents during the television age have relied on various public strategies in an attempt to publicize their policy agendas and to improve their standing with the U.S. public, there are certain major public addresses that are required and expected so as to leave no doubt that the president will deliver them (even if he is not a gifted speaker). These include the inaugural address and the annual state of the union address. Other major policy addresses are also expected of the president, including televised addresses to the nation in times of crisis or national urgency (usually involving national tragedy, U.S. military action, natural disasters, or economic crises), as well as policy addresses with the expectation of national news coverage, thus having an effect on the public agenda (usually delivered before a large group such as a national convention for a particular interest group or a university graduation).

A case study approach is used in these two chapters to better understand the Bush strategy, as well as the feedback from the news media and the public, for the major public addresses, major policy addresses, and related public activities of the Bush presidency. To examine the inaugural address and the state of the union addresses, the content of the speech is analyzed to determine the policy focus, and the strategy for the event is assessed (including the political environment in which the president delivered the address). The resulting news media coverage is then assessed to determine how major news outlets viewed or rated the president's performance. The case study approach for major policy addresses and related public activities differs somewhat depending on the type of event. For example, while an inaugural address or a state of the union address receives mass coverage from all press mediums, there is no relevant question as to amount of coverage. These events dominate political news coverage when they occur, and it would take an extraordinary story to bump the president off the top of the news. However, a major policy address before a national convention of a large interest group may provide the president with an opportunity to outline specifics of an important policy goal, but news coverage on a national level is not guaranteed. Therefore, it is important to assess the White House strategy for a major policy address and related public activities to better understand not only who the intended audience was, but whether or not the president's message was heard by the targeted audience.

The Inaugural Address

On January 20, 1989, George Herbert Walker Bush took the oath of office and was sworn in as the forty-first president of the United States. Inauguration day represents an important political ritual for U.S. citizens, as it serves as a time of renewal of faith in the U.S. constitutional system of government to witness the peaceful transition of power from one leader to the next. It is the one day on the political calendar where partisanship is mostly set aside, and the events surrounding the incoming president are filled with optimism, even if the nation is facing a crisis. Presidents look to the inauguration, and in particular the inaugural address, as an opportunity to set the tone for their tenure in office with the public, other political actors, and even the news media; it is also a time to talk about broader political principles and not specific policies. This is one of the many symbolic acts in which a president engages and is the first time that he can address the U.S. public—the national constituency that he uniquely represents within the political system—as president. Each president also faces unique circumstances on the day he takes office and, therefore, may have different strategies and goals that he and his advisors are attempting to achieve. As such, the inaugural address represents an opportunity for the incoming president to unify the audience, set forth the political principles under which he will govern, and renew the constitutional bond between himself and the U.S. people by reminding them of the limitations of executive power. According to Karlyn Kohrs Campbell and Kathleen Hall Jamieson, "Inaugurals transcend the historical present by reconstituting an existing community, rehearsing the past, affirming traditional values, and articulating timely and timeless principles that will govern the administration of the incoming president."[1]

Some of the most memorable and quoted inaugural addresses have occurred during times of great national crisis, such as Abraham Lincoln's address in 1861 (often remembered for the "better nature of our angels" line at the end of the speech) or Franklin D. Roosevelt's first inaugural address in 1933 (when he told Americans "the only thing we have to fear is fear itself"). Other presidents, such as John F. Kennedy in 1961 ("ask not what your country can do for you" and "the torch has been passed to a new generation of Americans") and Ronald Reagan in 1981 ("government is not the solution to our problem; government is the problem"), were skilled public speakers and used the inaugural address to present a recurring theme for their presidencies. However, in 1989, Bush took office in a relatively peaceful and prosperous time for the nation; his election also did not signify a major shift in the balance of political power in Washington. While no one expected Bush to be Reagan in the public aspects of the job, he was nonetheless responsible for carrying on the Reagan policy agenda and was seen as a president who would represent stability and continuity, all while working with a Congress controlled by the Democratic Party.

One of the biggest challenges facing Bush on inauguration day came from the contentiousness of the 1988 campaign, which at the time was considered one of the most negative on record in the television age. Bush had enjoyed a sizable victory over his opponent, Michael Dukakis, with a popular vote margin of 53 to 47 percent and winning forty states for an electoral vote margin of 426 to 111, but he had no mandate to govern with the Congress still controlled by Democrats.[2] Bush had also struggled to define his image during the campaign—was he the competent and experienced public servant who had served as Reagan's vice president for eight years in addition to his previous positions as CIA director, U.S. representative to the United Nations, ambassador to China, head of the Republican National Committee, and member of the House of Representatives? Or, was he a wimp not tough enough for the job (as the cover of *Newsweek* had declared in October 1987) or merely Reagan's lapdog while vice president (as *Washington Post* columnist George Will labeled him in 1986)? Throughout the campaign, Bush had struggled with defining his political identity as a national leader and in developing a vision for where he wanted to take the country as president (what Bush himself dubbed "the vision thing" in a moment of irritation with his press coverage on the campaign trail in 1988), a challenge that would remain for his speech writers and communication advisors once he took office.[3]

Bush's inaugural address was written by Peggy Noonan, a speechwriter in the Reagan White House who had also written Bush's acceptance speech at the Republican National Convention in 1988. The convention address had contained what would become the politically infamous line "read my lips, no new taxes," but Noonan had also helped to craft the other well-known lines associated with Bush about the "thousand points of light" (referring to the tradition of volunteerism in the United States) and Bush's desire for a "kinder, gentler America." Bush had emphasized the latter two themes on the campaign trail, and the same general themes made their way into his inaugural address as well. Political change, particularly in regard to the weakening of communism around the globe and the forthcoming end to the Cold War, also appeared as a prominent theme in the inaugural address, which fit well with Bush's own interest and expertise in foreign policy. In the early section of the speech, Bush gave what is perhaps the most memorable line: "We live in a peaceful, prosperous time, but we can make it better. For a new breeze is blowing, and a world refreshed by freedom seems reborn." Bush then moved on to the changing global scene: "Great nations of the world are moving toward democracy through the door to freedom. . . . We know what works: Freedom works. We know what's right: Freedom is right. We know how to secure a more just and prosperous life for man on Earth: through free markets, free speech, free elections, and the exercise of free will unhampered by the state."

Bush then gave a hint as to what he considered important domestic issues by providing a call to national service: "We as a people have such a purpose today. It is to make kinder the face of the Nation and gentler the face of the world. My friends, we have work to do. There are the homeless, lost and roaming. There are the children who have nothing, no love and no normalcy. There are those who cannot free themselves of enslavement to whatever addiction—drugs, welfare, the demoralization that rules the slums. There is crime to be conquered, the rough crime of the streets. There are young women to be helped who are about to become mothers of children they can't care for and might not love. They need our care, our guidance, and our education, though we bless them for choosing life." Bush then touched on the pressing problem of the budget deficit and national debt: "The old solution, the old way, was to think that public money alone could end these problems. But we have learned that that is not so. And in any case, our funds are low. We have a deficit to bring down. We have more will than wallet, but will is what we need. . . . I have spoken of a Thousand Points of Light, of all the community organizations that are spread like stars throughout the Nation, doing good. We will work hand in hand, encouraging, sometimes leading, sometimes being led, rewarding. We will work on this in the White House, in the Cabinet agencies. I will go to the people and the programs that are the brighter points of light, and I'll ask every member of my government to become involved."

In addition, Bush offered a call for political unity in working with the Democratic majority in Congress: "We need a new engagement, too, between the Executive and the Congress. The challenges before us will be thrashed out with the House and the Senate. And we must bring the Federal budget into balance. And we must ensure that America stands before the world united, strong, at peace, and fiscally sound. . . . For Congress, too, has changed in our time. There has grown a certain divisiveness. We have seen the hard looks and heard the statements in which not each other's ideas are challenged but each other's motives. And our great parties have too often been far apart and untrusting of each other. It's been this way since Vietnam. That war cleaves us still. But, friends, that war began in earnest a quarter of a century ago, and surely the statute of limitation has been reached. This is a fact: The final lesson of Vietnam is that no great nation can long afford to be sundered by a memory. A new breeze is blowing, and the old bipartisanship must be made new again."[4]

In assessing the delivery of the speech that she had written, Noonan wrote that Bush delivered the inaugural address "in a forceful voice," but that it was "a quiet speech."[5] According to Timothy Naftali, Bush's inaugural address "was more articulate and stirring than many had expected" in that no one had anticipated a grand rhetorical moment in the tradition of Kennedy or Reagan, yet the speech was nonetheless significant in its content and delivery.[6] The speech did, however, include traditional themes common in many previous inaugural addresses—a call for political unity, asking Americans to embrace public service, and a discussion of changes to come as the president outlined general governing principles. The speech was also an attempt to "separate [Bush] from his predecessor."[7] Bush received both praise and criticism from the press for his departure from the rhetorical flourishes of the Reagan era; despite what had been a rather smooth presidential transition, some journalists complained that Bush had yet to clearly define his policy goals for the nation and that he placed "an emphasis on the virtues of volunteerism and charity."[8] Nonetheless, most coverage extended a feeling of good will toward the new president while withholding judgment to see if he could actually follow through on the tone and principles set forth in his inaugural address. An editorial in the *New York Times* described the inaugural address this way: "Yesterday George Bush spoke, in measured tones, about a new breeze and the age of the offered hand. Why so measured, so modest? . . . The question doesn't do justice to the new President's resolutely decent message. The test of an Inaugural Address is not eloquence in a vacuum; it's how well the speaker relates to the politics of his time. President Bush, taking office in a tranquil time, did that admirably. . . . How out of synch, therefore, were the laments from commentators that the new President failed to lay out stirring plans for his Hundred Days. . . . Mr. Bush thus spoke not with alarmed hyperbole but with moral conviction and a realistic agenda. . . . The President's ideas still lack tangibility and will require elaboration. But even so, on day one, George Bush's agenda for America 1989 rings with inspiration."[9]

Other editorials in major newspapers offered a similar analysis. For example, an editorial in the *Boston Globe* acknowledged that the "new president, who succeeds a president known as the Great Communicator, is no stunning orator. But his sincerity shone through as the wind whipped through his hair on 'democracy's front porch.' . . . The Bush presidency will be judged on deeds, not on words in 'a vow made on marble steps.' . . . The most refreshing notion in the Bush agenda was his commitment to the kinder, gentler and older notions."[10] According to the *Washington Post*, "George Bush authenticated something yesterday: his own political identity and that of the administration he plans to lead. . . . But you don't have to suspend all your critical faculties or otherwise go overboard to note that Mr. Bush, speaking words that were neither high-flown nor rhetorically self-important, did exactly what he should have done: he laid strong claim to the best part of the Reagan legacy and moved out and away from the part that richly deserved to be left behind. He did this tactfully, modestly—and unmistakably. It was a skillful and credible performance. . . . [h]e sounded like a man trying to call a prospering and somewhat heedless nation back to its better instincts. The test will come in the programs and policies President Bush puts forward to this end. But that he spoke these things and so evidently meant them bodes well."[11] And in the *Los Angeles Times*:

> Americans have become accustomed to rancorous and dramatic changes in presidential administrations from one political party to the other, signaling breaks with the past and sharp turns in direction. . . . In a fashion that Ronald Reagan never did, George Bush reached out to all Americans, and specifically to his Democratic opponents in Congress, to join him in moving the country ahead in bipartisan unity. . . . Bush's offer of conciliation will not alter the great differences over such issues as the budget deficit and taxes. But it certainly enhances the opportunity for the sort of accommodation that serves the national purpose rather than narrow partisan satisfaction. . . . Bush's speech was simple and direct in many ways, and at times eloquent. There were no grand designs for great new programs expressed in soaring rhetoric, no excessive expectations raised. That would not have been appropriate either to the times or to George Bush the man. . . . Not a simple task, but a worthy undertaking by a modest and natural man in an area where a concerned President can make a difference.[12]

Columnists were a bit more pointed in their analysis, yet some were nonetheless mostly complimentary of Bush given the challenge of succeeding Reagan in the White House. According to David Broder of the *Washington Post*, "the new occupant of the White House may be less like

Ronald Reagan, the retiring president to whom he and the nation bade farewell yesterday, than he is a curious mix of qualities associated with two very different Democratic presidents, Jimmy Carter and Franklin D. Roosevelt. . . . If Bush seemed almost Carter-like in the contrast he drew to the Hollywood glamour of the Reagan years, even more striking was his implicit rebuke to the 1980s' acquisitive spirit, which, he suggested, has made Americans so 'enthralled with material things [we are] less appreciative of the nobility of work and sacrifice.'"[13] David Gergen, former Reagan communications advisor, offered Bush sage advice in *U.S. News and World Report*: "With his government slow in forming, Bush will advance few, if any, grand strategies and proposals. . . . Historically, America's strongest presidents have been those who began with clear goals and wrestled events to the ground. . . . Unless he takes special care, he could wind up closer to Jimmy Carter, who had no clear vision for his presidency, than to Ronald Reagan, who did."[14] Stephen Kurkjian wrote in the *Boston Globe*, "President Bush yesterday used Norman Rockwell strokes to paint himself and his presidency as homespun and Yankee, the good neighbor ever willing to lend a hand to the less fortunate. . . . By the first measure, George Bush's 20-minute speech yesterday will not rank as one of the more memorable inaugural addresses. But he did succeed in presenting a clear picture of his character and in drawing a clean line of difference between himself and Ronald Reagan that was not evident during the past eight years or the presidential campaign. . . . [Bush is a] practical, straight-forward man who appears more comfortable with working the levers of government rather than expressing its goals."[15]

Other commentators were not quite as charitable, suggesting that Bush had not succeeded in clearly defining himself or his agenda in the inaugural address, nor that he could succeed in the tasks that lay ahead for his presidency. In the *Los Angeles Times*, Robert Shogan wrote, "Indeed, discarding traditional high-flown rhetoric along with his topcoat, Bush made clear on this bright and blustery day that his view of his new job was far from grandiose or imperious. Instead, with the sun on his face and the wind in his hair, Bush presented himself as your basic plain-spoken, good-intentioned, friendly neighborhood chief executive. One with a patrician sense of duty and bent toward good works. . . . But Bush may not care whether his words go down in history books. In his first day on the job, he seemed more concerned with trying to convince voters who last November entrusted him with the nation's destiny that they made the right choice."[16] Wrote Paul Gigot in the *Wall Street Journal*,

> Washington's long underestimation of George Bush has given way to inaugural deference, but this week's ritual good will is a phony peace. Soon enough the capital will revert to its habit of devouring presidents. . . . Though he takes office with pomp and media flourish, Mr. Bush today becomes the leader of the weakest of the three branches. The presidency, most scholars and witnesses agree, is striking mainly for what it cannot do (get its budget enacted, for example). . . . Ronald Reagan, by leaving on a surge of good will, paradoxically leaves Mr. Bush a harder act to follow. He has shown a president can succeed, but he has bequeathed Mr. Bush fewer tools to ensure his own success. . . . The vulnerability is enhanced by television. The media focus their daily attention on the White House, heightening expectations and exaggerating mistakes.[17]

Also in the *Wall Street Journal*, Robert Bartley wrote,

> In the past year George Herbert Walker Bush has evolved from a wimp into a meanie into a soothing pragmatist. An amazing chameleon act, if you choose to believe the faddish wisdom. While in fact George Bush is probably pretty much the same guy who left Connecticut to fly in World War II, it is true that he comes to the presidency today having revealed no clear public blueprint. . . . For the past eight years, it has been impossible to slip a piece of rice paper between Vice President Bush and whatever President Reagan decided. In the campaign, Candidate Bush promised not to raise taxes and to support the flag. In picking his cabinet, he emphasized experience and team play, virtues by which he himself lives. This is no doubt prudent, given the prevalence of slash-and-burn politics in Washington. But it does mean that the essential character of the Bush presidency remains to be defined.[18]

In general, Bush received a mostly positive response to his inaugural address. News coverage and commentary reflected the challenges facing Bush as Reagan's successor, not only in terms of his communication style and approach to the public aspects of the office, but as the heir-apparent to Reagan's conservative policy agenda as well. In some respects, the coverage provided a bit of a harbinger for future press treatment—the more liberal editorial voices at a newspaper like the *New York Times* were hopeful that Bush would make a break from the Reagan years with a more centrist and pragmatic approach to governing, while more conservative voices at a newspaper like the *Wall Street Journal* were already showing skepticism about not only Bush's ability to govern but his commitment to the conservative agenda. In addition, the news media had set a tough—and perhaps unreasonable—standard for Bush in terms of his public performances and policy agenda in the post-Reagan years. According to Mark Rozell, "These early criticisms of Bush's leadership reveal not only the rapid pace by which journalists begin to define a presidency but also their strong bias in favor of immediate presidential policy activism. Even though Bush had sought the presidency promising policy continuity and only incremental change, journalists held him to a very different standard—one demanding bold policy action during the first one hundred days."[19] From his first day in office, Bush was already facing the changing news media environment in which he was expected to govern. The press set the stage for Bush in a way that gave the new president an opportunity to succeed while at the same time giving him a high standard to meet, emblematic of both the increasingly competitive nature of the news industry and the higher public expectations placed on the president by the end of the 1980s.

State of the Union Addresses

In the modern era of the presidency, the president's annual state of the union address is perhaps the most anticipated and analyzed of all presidential speeches. Article 2 section 3 of the U.S. Constitution requires that the president "shall from time to time give to the Congress information on the state of the Union and recommend to their consideration such measures as he shall judge necessary and expedient," but there is no requirement that the president give this information in an address to a joint session of Congress. Although George Washington and John Adams submitted this information in person to Congress, presidents Thomas Jefferson (1801–1809) through William Howard Taft (1909–13) met this constitutional requirement by submitting a written report to the Congress on the state of the union. Pres. Woodrow Wilson (1913–21) revived the practice of delivering an address to Congress, which has continued most every year since.[20] It is important to note that the first state of the union address for George H. W. Bush in 1989, Bill Clinton in 1993, George W. Bush in 2001, and Barack Obama in 2009 are technically not state of the union addresses. Instead, they are addresses to a joint session of Congress to lay out administration goals. The attention paid to and impact of these speeches, however, is so similar to an actual state of the union address that they are considered comparable for research classification purposes.[21]

Traditionally delivered near the start of the calendar year, the state of the union address is not only a report to Congress on the actual "state" of the union but also a statement of the president's proposed policy agenda for the upcoming year. This has evolved as a unique opportunity for modern presidents, in upholding their constitutional duty, to remind both the audience in attendance (Congress) and those watching and listening at home (the U.S. public) of the president's role in shaping the national agenda. According to Campbell and Jamieson, the state of the union is a "uniquely presidential genre of discourse" that gives to the president "in the role of national historian, the opportunity to reconstruct the past in order to forge the future. . . . More eloquent presidents have seized the opportunity to reshape reality and to imprint that conception on the nation. . . . By the sheer fact of its delivery, the address reminds the country that presidents have a unique function in our system of government."[22] In recent decades, the state of the union address has involved an extensive White House communications and media strategy plan for events prior to, on the day of, and after the actual speech. The goal is to try to maximize the president's exposure to the news media and the U.S. public through an event where he looks and sounds presidential, since he is both addressing the Congress and speaking to the nation with all the attendant pomp and circumstance that the event brings with it; this is one of the most ritualistic of presidential public events.

1989

Bush delivered his "Address on Administration Goals before a Joint Session of the Congress" on February 9, 1989. Just short of three weeks past the inaugural address, Bush had an approval rating of 55 percent in early February prior to this speech. With the budget deficit looming as one of Bush's highest policy priorities, and one of the only issues he had addressed specifically in his inaugural address, White House advisors viewed the speech as "the President's first opportunity to place his mark on the budget process and the priorities for the Nation."[23] In a memo outlining White House strategy and goals for the speech, advisors determined that the communications plan "should focus on ensuring that the President's message is not just 'communicated' but, through aggressive outreach, is understood by the media, the public and constituency groups. As the first major initiative of the Bush Administration, it is also important that the efforts involved—communication, policy, political, press etc.—be perceived as first rate and professionally handled." Regarding media coverage, the memo suggested the following: "Several avenues will be employed to provide the media with information both prior to the speech and following. This includes briefings, materials distribution, interviews, and mailings. . . . Targeted mailings to specialty and selected media tentatively including: editorial page editors, financial writers, black media, environmental media, business media, women's media, education media."[24] Constituency group outreach was also a priority, including a series of short constituency group briefings to accomplish two goals:

> A. to ensure that those individuals most likely to be contacted by the media for comment will be fully briefed on the details of the President's overall proposal as well as the specific initiatives in their particular areas. B. to use the address as a means to outreach and establish a working relationship with a larger number of people in individual issue areas. An individual group or cabinet agency would be contacted for each issue area to serve as defacto "sponsors" of the briefing (including Education, Drugs, Homeless, Child Care, Balanced budget/U.S. Chamber, Conservatives, Environment, RNC political, Black colleges). A question remains on the briefing of Members of Congress in advance. Providing a pre-speech briefing in the afternoon almost guarantees portions of the speech on the network news that evening. A decision on implementing a Congressional briefing needs discussion. . . . A decision on what materials to provide the Cabinet remains as well as the action on producing them. An advocacy factsheet is being produced. . . . This factsheet and any additional talking points should be provided to departmental public affairs heads in advance of the speech either directly or through the appropriate Cabinet member. They will be asked to get the specifics of their individual programs out to their constituency or media lists.[25]

Press Secretary Marlin Fitzwater also provided a more detailed media plan for a seven-day period surrounding the February 9 speech. Two days prior to the speech, the plan included: "Open photo/writing pool coverage of the President meeting with his budget team (Sununu, Darman, Brady, Boskin). This demonstrates the President's direct involvement in the decision process. If coverage allowed of meeting, allows the President to answer a question or two on the budget." The day before the speech, there would be a "White House photo released of the President working on a draft of his speech. This, along with the briefing, demonstrates the President's direct involvement in the speech and decisions regarding the budget." Press activities for the day of the speech, and for four days following the speech, included:

Thursday, February 9 (SPEECH DAY)

2:30 P.M. Roosevelt Room Briefing for White House Staff. Attendees: Secretary Brady, Governor Sununu, Dick Darman, Michael Boskin, Dave Demarest, Jim Cicconi, Steve Studdert, Alixe Glen, B. Jay Cooper, Steve Hart, Andy Card, Ed Rogers, Tom Scully, Fred McClure, and Barbara Clay.

7:00 P.M. Darman Backgrounder for Print Reporters.

Speech texts are given out at 7:30 P.M., embargoed to delivery. No quotes are given out for use by the nightly news.

Fact sheets, prepared by OMB [Office of Management and Budget] in coordination with Demarest's shop, are distributed at same time as embargoed texts.

9:00 P.M. The President delivers his speech to a Joint Session of Congress.

Recommendations for people to appear on TV with anchors analyzing speech: Drew Lewis, Bob Dole, Alan Simpson.

Friday, February 10 (The President goes to Canada)

Morning Shows:

Friday

ABC *Good Morning America*: Jeff Greenfield and George Will; David Stockman. Tentatively Boskin.

CBS *This Morning*: Governor Sununu

NBC "Today": Dick Darman; Senator [Lloyd] Bentsen and Congressman [Dan] Rostenkowski

PBS *McNeil-Lehrer*: Dick Darman

The President, on his way to Canada, visits with the Air Force One pool to follow-up on his speech, providing reaction to the reaction that likely came from Congress and others.

Gov. Sununu holds background sessions with the weekly magazines for "tick-tock" on budget decisions.

Administration officials appear on shows (live or taped) such as

McNeil-Lehrer, Moneyline, Nightly Business Report, and *Financial News Network.*

Saturday, February 12

CNN *Evans and Novak*: Michael Boskin

CNN *Newsmakers*: To be determined

Sunday, February 12

Administration officials appear on the Sunday shows:

NBC *Meet the Press*: To be determined

CBS *Face the Nation*: Dick Darman, Senator Sasser

ABC *This Week with David Brinkley*: Secretary [James] Brady or Michael Boskin.

Monday, February 13

The President has an interview with *The Wall Street Journal* to follow up on his speech. This is already on the schedule.

Thursday, February 16

The President holds a 2 P.M. press conference in Room 450.[26]

Given the importance of the speech to address the federal budget and prioritizing Bush's economic policies, three members of the administration played a prominent role in providing information and interviews to the press: Richard Darman, director of the Office of Management and Budget; Michael J. Boskin, Council of Economic Advisors; and Nicholas Brady, secretary of the treasury. Coverage in business-oriented publications was also emphasized as part of the press strategy.

The speech itself touched on a wide variety of domestic and international issues, although the federal budget and other economic issues factored prominently. Continuing with the general theme presented in the inaugural address of how he intended to work with Congress, Bush began by stating to members of Congress that "the hand remains extended; the sleeves are rolled up; America is waiting; and now we must produce. Together, we can build a better America. . . . I feel as if I'm returning home to friends. And I intend, in the months and years to come, to give you what friends deserve: frankness, respect, and my best judgment about ways to improve America's future." Bush then turned to the federal budget deficit and outlined his plan:

> [W]e must make a very substantial cut in the Federal budget deficit. Some people find that agenda impossible, but I'm presenting to you tonight a realistic plan for tackling it. My plan has four broad

> features: attention to urgent priorities, investment in the future, an attack on the deficit, and no new taxes. This budget represents my best judgment of how we can address our priorities. . . . We cannot settle for business as usual. Government by continuing resolution, or government by crisis, will not do. And I ask the Congress tonight to approve several measures which will make budgeting more sensible. We could save time and improve efficiency by enacting 2-year budgets. Forty-three Governors have the line-item veto. Presidents should have it, too. And at the very least, when a President proposes to rescind Federal spending, the Congress should be required to vote on that proposal instead of killing it by inaction. And I ask the Congress to honor the public's wishes by passing a constitutional amendment to require a balanced budget.

The president then discussed a long list of his domestic and economic budget priorities, either announcing actions he intended to take himself or urging Congress to join him in taking action on the following initiatives: economic growth, parental choice in education, funding for the National Science Foundation, a permanent tax credit for research and development, a task force on competitiveness, funding for the National Aeronautics and Space Administration (including a manned space station and the space shuttle program), a cut in the capital gains tax rate, education initiatives to improve school performance, stopping the flow of illegal drugs, funding for AIDS treatment, environmental issues (including the Clean Air Act and clean coal initiatives), offshore oil drilling, toxic waste dumps, full funding of Medicaid, preschool funding, a cost-of-living adjustment for Social Security, the problem of homelessness, statehood for Puerto Rico, reforms to the savings industry, and the cleanup of nuclear weapons plants (in that order). On the issue of education, Bush also reminded his audience that he had made the issue a priority during the 1988 presidential campaign: "I've said I'd like to be the 'Education President.' And tonight, I'd ask you to join me by becoming the 'Education Congress.'"

Bush then turned to matters of foreign policy and national security:

> America is a stronger nation than it was in 1980. Morale in our Armed Forces has been restored; our resolve has been shown. Our readiness has been improved, and we are at peace. There can no longer be any doubt that peace has been made more secure through strength. And when America is stronger, the world is safer. . . . Secur-

> ing a more peaceful world is perhaps the most important priority I'd like to address tonight. . . . And it's a time of great change in the world, and especially in the Soviet Union. Prudence and common sense dictate that we try to understand the full meaning of the change going on there, review our policies, and then proceed with caution. . . . The fundamental facts remain that the Soviets retain a very powerful military machine in the service of objectives which are still too often in conflict with ours. So, let us take the new openness seriously, but let's also be realistic. And let's always be strong.

Bush stated his support for continuing to pursue the Strategic Defense Initiative, a ban on chemical weapons, and continued support for "self-determination and democracy in Central America, including in Nicaragua." He then announced that Secretary of State Baker would travel to Europe to meet with NATO allies and that Bush himself would be traveling to "the far reaches of the Pacific Basin, where the winds of democracy are creating new hope and the power of free markets is unleashing a new force."

Bush concluded the address with what he termed a Lincolnesque call to service for all Americans, including young people (through a new program called YES, Youth Entering Service to America), men and women in business (to avoid the "temptation of quick and easy paper profits"), members of the military ("your calling is a high one: to be the defenders of freedom and the guarantors of liberty. And I want you to know that this nation is grateful for your service"), the farmers of America ("we appreciate the bounty you provide [and] will work with you to open foreign markets to American agricultural products"), parents (to urge more involvement in children's schooling), inner-city youth ("say no to drugs"), disabled Americans ("you belong in the economic mainstream"), and "to the families of America watching tonight in your living rooms, hold fast to your dreams because ultimately America's future rests in your hands. . . . There are voices who say that America's best days have passed, that we're bound by constraints, threatened by problems, surrounded by troubles which limit our ability to hope. Well, tonight I remain full of hope. We Americans have only begun on our mission of goodness and greatness."[27]

Overall, the speech was balanced in terms of diversity of topics in the general categories of domestic, foreign, and economic policy—the basic categories that presidents are expected to cover in a state of the union address. (See table 2.)[28]

Table 2. 1989 Address on Administration Goals, Policy Categorization (by Paragraph)

Domestic Issues
Crime – 6
Defense – 5
Education – 3
Environment/Energy/Land Management – 5
Health Care – 1
Reform – 5
Science/Technology/Transportation – 3
Welfare/Entitlement Programs – 4
Economic Issues
Domestic Fiscal/Monetary Policy – 9
Unemployment/Jobs – 1
International Issues
Diplomatic/Military – 7
Trade/Economic – 0
Non Policy/Ceremonial – 9
Total Paragraphs – 58

A president's first major address is always highly anticipated, as it represents the first opportunity for the new president to clearly spell out his policy priorities in a governing, as opposed to campaign, mode. The expectations for Bush's first major address, like with any new president, were quite high. While Bush had received mostly modest praise for his inaugural address, many political observers were still waiting for Bush to more clearly define his goals as president. As David Gergen in *U.S. News and World Report* observed a few days prior to the speech, Bush needed to seize the opportunity to define himself as president: "Folks beyond the Beltway, while pleased with his spirit and tone, are still puzzled by the President. Many do not know where he is heading and wonder whether he knows himself. Bush needs to get tough again. . . . A President without a strategy is like a sailboat without a rudder—open to capsizing. In his nationwide address to Congress this Thursday, a speech that now rivals the inaugural in importance, Bush must present a credible, fair plan for wiping out the budget deficit. He can neither break his pledge on taxes nor hide behind the discredited economic forecasts of the Reagan team. . . . Equally important, Bush must seize this occasion to spell out long-term priorities. . . . His speech Thursday ought to be only the first in a continuing series to reach out and rally the country."[29]

Following the address, a general consensus seemed to emerge among the nation's leading journalists that the content of the speech, as well as Bush's performance, was adequate but not great. The content of the speech was judged as being heavy on symbolism yet light on specifics, while the style of the speech was judged to be mediocre. From members of Congress, Bush received praise from many Democrats for not sounding too much like Reagan and his antigovernment rhetoric and praise from Republicans for highlighting conservative issues like a capital gains cut and a balanced budget amendment. Even though skepticism remained about whether or not Bush could actually achieve anything on his agenda, many commentators were still feeling the optimism of a new presidential term. An editorial in the *Los Angeles Times* the morning after the speech declared, "The official launching of the Bush era Thursday night was strong on symbolism and short on dollars. But that was no surprise, given the hangover of budget deficits from the Reagan era. In setting his own budget priorities, George Bush generally was true to his campaign promises and his inaugural address. In spite of differences in personal style between Bush and Ronald Reagan, this is a transition, not a revolution. Bush is fine-tuning over time, not remaking government in the flurry of a hundred days. After all, George Bush is a Reaganite, too. . . . In discussing national security, Bush broke little new ground. . . . There is nothing wrong with symbolism, so long as the Bush Administration backs up the symbols with specifics and resources. . . . Bush did not lecture or berate. He offered to meet Congress half-way. That is a good, strong first step."[30]

In Bush's first major address since the inaugural, comparisons to Reagan in style and substance were perhaps inevitable. As observed in the *Orange County Register*, "George Bush is no Ronald Reagan. But his speech Thursday night, although lacking some Reaganesque excitement, pleased Orange County's representatives in Washington."[31] Similarly, in the *Boston Globe*: "The Reagan Revolution gave way to a simpler call to Build a Better America last night, as President Bush, employing a less inflexible theme, set a more restrained agenda for the country. . . . To be sure, Bush talked of severe budget restraints and no new taxes. He rolled out some old Reagan proposals such as the line-item veto and the balanced budget constitutional amendment. . . . The tone of the Bush speech was more conciliatory than those of Reagan's addresses, and complemented Bush's inaugural speech in which he extended a hand of cooperation to the Democrats. . . . Congress will be looking for more leadership than Bush displayed in the televised speech."[32] And from the Associated Press: "Inaugural addresses are the style, but budgets are the substance of new administrations. With his first spending plan, George Bush completed the transition from the Reagan to the Bush presidency. . . . What he set forth was a shift in direction, not a reversal or a sharp turn. While the direction remained conservative, it was a direction that was clearly his own. A dependence on growth and an opposition to taxes remained central to his plan for the economy. He stood fast on Star Wars. But in many of the priorities and most clearly in the tone, this was George Bush, not Ronald Reagan."[33]

The content of the speech, which included a broad array of policy and spending priorities, also provided opportunities for comparisons to Reagan's agenda. Having emphasized issues such as the environment and education, Bush did differentiate himself somewhat from his former boss. As noted in the *Los Angeles Times*, "The United States will not just be a kinder, gentler nation if George Bush diligently pursues the environmental initiatives that he has launched. It will be a cleaner, healthier nation. . . . The Bush Administration at least seems to understand that environmental progress is worth pursuing for its own value. . . . This is a welcome and critical change in attitude from the recent past."[34] Similarly, Maureen Dowd in the *New York Times* wrote that Bush "echoed the themes of cooperation, compassion and optimism that he struck in his Inaugural Address last month. He said America 'is headed the right way' as a result of the Presidency of Ronald Reagan and should continue to strive for fewer regulations and less bureaucracy. But he put aside the strongly conservative oratory that marked Mr. Reagan's budget addresses, and encouraged the country to 'rediscover' words like 'goodness' and 'mercy' and to help those who have been left out of the economic recovery of the 1980's. . . . Mr. Bush also used the address to strike a moderate tone in foreign policy, speaking of a need to be realistic about East-West relations but also to work for peace with the Eastern bloc."[35]

However, to some, the speech had a decidedly pragmatic and somewhat Democratic tone, as E. J. Dionne of the *Washington Post* observed:

> For eight years, President Reagan delivered speeches to Congress that were long on inspiration and relatively short on programs. President Bush's understated address tonight lacked Reaganesque flourishes, but it offered a long list of minor spending increases covering fields from education to outer space. . . . This gave the speech a distinctly Democratic flavor, despite Mr. Bush's opening pledge that his Administration would build on the Reagan legacy. . . . To be sure, many of Mr. Bush's ideas were anything but new. . . . Still, after years of President Reagan's talk against big government, the speech Mr. Bush delivered tonight was anything but an attack on the power of the state. It represented not so much a choice of direction as a promise that Government could do many good things, and the accent was on issues—drugs, homelessness and education—that the polls show are the central concerns of the voters.[36]

A stronger critique of the content of the speech, and its list of budget priorities, came from Walter Shapiro of *Time*:

> By the time the new President made his triumphal entrance into the House chamber . . . the stage was set for the programmatic speech that would boldly launch the Bush Administration. By those inflated standards, Bush fell far short—and for want of a coherent message, an important opportunity was lost. Unlike the Inaugural Address, the speech contained no inspirational phrases, no soaring metaphors, just commonplace sentiments. . . . In sharp contrast to Reagan's stiff-necked philosophic rigidity, Bush was eager to touch every point on the ideological spectrum. . . . But instead of clear priorities, the President offered a clutter of programs, almost all marginal adjustments in the status quo. By awkwardly trying to match the concerns of a liberal Democrat with the means of a parsimonious Republican, Bush ended up with an incoherent philosophy that might be dubbed Reaganomics with a human face. . . . The President's a-little-something-for-everyone approach to Government, lurching from new national parklands to a statehood referendum for Puerto Rico, at times sounded as if it had been borrowed from Lyndon Johnson. . . . Hemmed in as he is, the risk for Bush is that his Administration could drift for months without major victories—or, worse, be burdened with a mortifying setback. Already, the uplifting sermons have begun to

> sound repetitious and a trifle hollow. . . . In the interim, Bush should have more than enough time to grapple with that transcendent—but still unanswered—question: What precisely does he want to accomplish as President?[37]

Commentary on a presidential address, particularly a major speech early in a president's term such as this address to a joint session of Congress, always offers the press an opportunity to assess a new president's public leadership style. Bush himself thought the speech went well, writing in his diary that "speech went well. . . . I felt in command and in control, no nervousness—it was almost like coming home."[38] Despite the feelings of good will towards the new president from many in the national press corps, Bush could not avoid an assessment of his first substantive performance that served to point out many of his weaknesses. In *USA Today,* "In politics, more often than not the initial impression is a lasting one. Unfortunately for President Bush, his first budget address to Congress is being perceived as unimaginative, inflationary and ill-advised. . . . Just 21 days on the job and the liberals' perception of George Bush standing tough against tax increases is now at risk in light of his readiness to compromise and even reverse the Reagan-era principles and priorities."[39] In terms of pure performance, this assessment came from media critic Tom Shales of the *Washington Post*:

> For such a manifestly uninspiring speaker, George Bush gave a moderately competent speech on the budget to a joint session of Congress last night. Unfortunately, from a performance point of view, the speech was also infernally boring to watch. The speech was carried by all the major networks, and some minor ones too, disrupting what otherwise would have been a captivating evening of prime-time diversion. Ronald Reagan always tried to make his speeches entertaining for home viewers, with anecdotes and guest stars and a winning, highly polished delivery. Bush lacks the facility for nearly all of that. As a speaker on television, Bush has the prim, proper air of a stern schoolmaster—maybe a substitute teacher, the wet blanket who shows up one day when everyone is hoping the jolly, ingratiating regular teacher will be there. Alas, we'll be doomed to the substitute from now on unless Ronald Reagan is brought in as designated speechmaker.[40]

* * *

The content of Bush's first major address, along with the news media's reaction to it, is both suggestive of the political environment in early 1989 as well as the challenges Bush would continue to face throughout his four years in office. Bush often found himself in a political bind as Reagan's heir apparent—on the one hand, he was expected to continue the Reagan policy legacy, yet he was also expected to more independently define himself as president beyond Reagan's shadow. As a result, a more moderate stance on policy issues, such as education or the environment, highlighted his attempts to be a consensus builder with a Democratically controlled Congress, yet at the same time, such moves alienated the conservative base of his party for not being more like Reagan. Similarly, while many in the press opined about how important it was for Bush to move beyond the harsher rhetoric of the Reagan years, Bush was constantly criticized at the same time for not being Reaganesque enough in his presentation and public style. Not only did Reagan leave a tough act for Bush to follow, but it took only a matter of weeks before the comparisons emerged in the national dialogue in a way that set nearly an impossible standard for Bush to live up to. The commentary following this address to Congress, in effect the first if unofficial state of the union event, provides early evidence of the fact that Bush would not be allowed to escape the Reagan public legacy. However, it is important to point out that Bush did improve his public approval rating following the speech, which rose to 61 percent by the end of February 1989, suggesting that the inside-the-beltway commentary from an ever-increasingly competitive news environment did not always match up with public perceptions of the president from a broader sample of U.S. citizens.

1990

On January 31, 1990, Bush delivered his first official state of the union address before a joint session of Congress. During the first week of January, Bush enjoyed an 80 percent approval rating. Throughout 1989, as the Cold War moved closer to its end and the world witnessed the Berlin Wall coming down, Bush's expertise in foreign policy had an opportunity to emerge as a major component of his governing style as he traveled around the globe talking about emerging democracies. In addition, Bush's high approval ratings stemmed in part from the successful U.S. military invasion of Panama in December 1989 to oust Manuel Noriega from power, after which the military dictator was captured and brought to the United States to stand trial for drug trafficking. In terms of domestic policy, while 1989 had not been a year of major legislative achievements, Bush had nonetheless spent a great deal of time working on education initiatives, sending a proposed Education Excellence Act to Congress in April 1989. While the bill itself was limited in scope, Bush gave a speech in March 1989, convened a two-day education summit in September 1989, and engaged in other public events related to education, which kept one of his major campaign promises high on the public agenda.[41]

As White House advisors began preparations for the State of the Union address at the end of January 1990, reigning in the budget deficit was still a high priority for the Bush administration. Assessments of Bush after his first year in office, despite a high approval rating, tended to point out the dual nature of the Bush presidency—an experienced and effective leader when dealing with foreign policy while an ineffective and uninspired leader when dealing with domestic issues. Advisors viewed the State of the Union as an opportunity to effectively outline major policy initiatives in both domestic and foreign policy; Bush had been criticized for lacking more policy specifics and bolder action on domestic policies throughout 1989.[42] White House memos leading up to the speech suggest that a variety of topics and themes were debated among advisors for inclusion. For example, as early as November 1989, advisors were thinking ahead to how global events, particularly the fall of the Berlin Wall, could translate into a successful state of the union address in early 1990. In a memo to David Demarest, speechwriter Edward McNally suggested "a five-point plan for [Bush] to become the architect of the most popular presidency in modern history," with point five being "a State of the Union Address that (without proposing any defense reductions) focuses on visionary proposals on space, the environment and the like—proposals fitting what may be a new era."[43] Other advisors suggested focusing on the issues important to Bush voters in 1988, which would bolster voter support on issues "crucial to our candidates as they wage the President's mid-term election battles" in 1990; the issues included education, the environment, law and order, "true deficit reduction," and reminding voters of Bush's "read my lips, no new taxes" promise.[44]

In January 1990, Deputy Chief of Staff James Cicconi urged Chief of Staff John Sununu to use the speech to focus on key economic issues:

> As you know, we have endorsed or will soon put forward three significant proposals which relate to the economy: capital gains, a permanent R&D tax credit, and a plan to boost domestic savings. All three will assist growth industries in the U.S., particularly high tech businesses, and enhance competitiveness. Accordingly, I would hope we will link these as part of a 'competitiveness package' designed to boost investment in America's future. Such a link would enhance the legislative prospects for all three ideas. . . . Of the above, the R&D tax credit, which could do perhaps as much for corporate investment as any of our other ideas, should not get short shrift in our legislative and communications strategy. A permanent credit came close to passage in both the House and Senate last year, and could pass this year with sufficient Administration support. Packaging these proposals and presenting them rhetorically as such will help provide that support. It is also a way of having some 'old' ideas appear new for State of the Union. If you agree with the above, we can see that it is presented accordingly in the State of the Union and subsequent speeches.[45]

Other suggestions demonstrated the lobbying efforts that often go on among White House and executive branch officials to get a mention in the president's state of the union address for a specific policy or proposal. For example, Sununu was advised to make the state of the union the moment Bush would make his strongest push to Congress for passage of the Americans with Disabilities Act. Wrote Evan Kemp, a commissioner at the Equal Employment Opportunity Commission, "It is critically important that the President call for passage of the Americans With Disabilities Act (ADA) during his State of the Union Address. The President's statement during the campaign proved that 34 words embracing the goal of mainstreaming disabled Americans could garner him half of the 13 million votes cast by this traditionally Democratic voting bloc. A strong statement by the President in support of this legislation can be used by the Republican Party during this year's congressional campaign and in 1992 to woo disabled Democrats and hold disabled Republicans. *Moreover, should the House pass a markedly weaker version of the bill, the President can use his statements of support for the legislation to lay the blame on the Democrats, where it belongs* [emphasis in original]."[46]

The White House Counsel's office recommended that Bush claim credit in the address "for having achieved comprehensive ethics reform. It may be worth noting that the scheduled date of the address is exactly one year to the day after the President established the President's Commission on Federal Ethics Law Reform. . . . Taking credit for ethics reform could be used to lead into a call for bipartisan cooperation in achieving comprehensive campaign finance reform."[47] Similarly, the policy office suggested taking credit for progress on chemical weapons: "Here are the points you asked for. We've tried to write them in a way so that you can use the overall structure or just separate out the points which fit best into the structure you've already developed. One point we don't stress enough is chemical weapons; given the President's personal interest in a total ban and his UN proposal, we'd recommend highlighting the steps we've taken."[48] Major foreign policy players within the Bush administration were also discussing the content of the speech, as evidenced in the following note from Secretary of State Jim Baker to National Security Advisor Brent Scowcroft: "Brent, If we're going to make an effort on earmarks or an effort to give the President some flexibility regarding security assistance, we need something along these lines in the State of the Union."[49] Finally, White House advisors also solicited comments on the upcoming speech from key Republican Party leaders in numerous state party organizations who had been active during the 1988 presidential campaign.[50]

Unlike the 1989 budget address delivered to a joint session of Congress just weeks after taking office, in which the president touched on a broad array of topics, Bush's first official state of the union address focused more on international issues, the state of the U.S. economy, and specific domestic issues such as education and the environment (see table 3). Bush began his address by talking about "the changes we've seen, the challenges we face—and what that means for America. . . . The events of the year just ended, the Revolution of '89, have been a chain reaction, changes so striking that it marks the beginning of a new era in the world's affairs." Those changes included the U.S. invasion of Panama, the emerging democratic governments in Poland and Czechoslovakia, and the fall of the Berlin Wall. Bush referred to the global changes as consistent with American ideals: "As this new world takes shape, America stands at the center of a widening circle of freedom—today, tomorrow, and into the next century. Our nation is the enduring dream of every immigrant who ever set foot on these shores, and the millions still struggling to be free. This nation, this idea called America, was and always will be a new world—our new world." Bush then turned to the importance of U.S. competitiveness in the global economic arena: "In the tough competitive markets around the world, America faces the great challenges and great opportunities. And we know that we can succeed in the global economic arena of the nineties, but to meet that challenge, we must make some fundamental changes—some crucial investment in ourselves. Yes, we are going to invest in America. This administration is determined to encourage the creation of capital, capital of all kinds. . . . Let me tell you, if we ignore human capital, if we lose the spirit of American ingenuity, the spirit that is the hallmark of the American worker, that would be bad. The American worker is the most productive worker in the world."

Moving on to more domestic matters, Bush introduced his idea for a Family Savings Plan, his support for a capital gains tax cut, the continued

Table 3. 1990 State of the Union Address, Policy Categorization (by Paragraph)

Domestic Issues
Crime – 0
Defense – 0
Education – 8
Environment/Energy/Land Management – 2
Health Care – 1
Reform – 4
Science/Technology/Transportation – 0
Welfare/Entitlements Programs – 2
Economic Issues
Domestic Fiscal/Monetary Policy – 6
Unemployment/Jobs – 3
International Issues
Diplomatic/Military – 19
Trade/Economic – 1
Non Policy/Ceremonial – 14
Total Paragraphs – 61

need for research and development, a housing initiative to help first-time homebuyers, and drug-free programs for children. Bush then highlighted his education initiatives, including his fall 1989 education summit with state governors and increased funding for Head Start: "Education is the one investment that means more for our future because it means the most for our children. Real improvement in our schools is not simply a matter of spending more: It's a matter of asking more—expecting more—of our schools, our teachers, of our kids, of our parents, and ourselves. And that's why tonight I am announcing America's education goals." Those goals included having children better prepared for starting school, an increased high school graduation rate, student assessment, drug-free schools, and U.S. students being first in the world in math and science achievement by the year 2000.

Bush then reported that "we're getting our own house in order" by making progress on reigning in federal spending and moving toward a balanced budget. He spoke about the importance of protecting the environment: "And there's something more we owe the generations of the future: stewardship, the safekeeping of America's precious environmental inheritance. It's just one sign of how serious we are. We will elevate the Environmental Protection Agency to Cabinet rank—not more bureaucracy, not more redtape, but the certainty that here at home, and especially in our dealings with other nations, environmental issues have the status they deserve." Before returning to international issues, Bush reminded members of Congress that "the American people did not send us here to bicker. There is work to do, and they sent us here to get it done. . . . Let's work together to do the will of the people: clean air, child care, the Educational Excellence Act, crime, and drugs. It's time to act. The farm bill, transportation policy, product-liability reform, enterprise zones—it's time to act together." Social security and health care reform were also mentioned, as was the need for public service: "The state of the Union depends on whether we help our neighbor—claim the problems of our community as our own. We've got to step forward when there's trouble, lend a hand, be what I call a point of light to a stranger in need."

To conclude the address, Bush recognized the service of an army medic who had died during the invasion of Panama and then reminded those listening of the prediction Pres. Harry Truman made four decades earlier in an address to Congress that someday change would come to the Communist world. Bush declared,

> Today, that change is taking place. For more than 40 years, America and its allies held communism in check and ensured that democracy would continue to exist. And today, with communism crumbling, our aim must be to ensure democracy's advance, to take the lead in forging peace and freedom's best hope: a great and growing commonwealth of free nations. . . . Here in our own hemisphere, it is time for all the peoples of the Americas, North and South, to live in freedom. In the Far East and Africa, it's time for the full flowering of free governments and free markets that have served as the engine of progress. It's time to offer our hand to the emerging democracies of Eastern Europe so that continent—for too long a continent divided—can see a future whole and free. It's time to build on our new relationship with the Soviet Union, to endorse and encourage a peaceful process of internal change toward democracy and economic opportunity.

Despite a period of "great transition," Bush urged for the continuation of strategic offense modernization and the Strategic Defense Initiative, a conventional arms control agreement, and a "coherent defense program that ensures the U.S. will continue to be a catalyst for peaceful change in Europe," which included a reduction in U.S. troops in Central and Eastern Europe while sustaining NATO's defense strategy. Bush ended with the following: "Here at home and in the world, there's history in the making, history to be made. . . . The anchor in our world today is freedom, holding us steady in times of change, a symbol of hope to all the world. And freedom is at the very heart of the idea that is America."[51]

Media reactions to the speech varied from complimentary to critical. For example, Ted Koppel of ABC News called the speech "effective," while Katie Couric of NBC's *Today Show* said that the president was "long on rhetoric, short on specifics." CNN's Bill Schneider claimed that Bush seemed "more relaxed" with his personality coming through during the speech but that he did not have "a sense of agenda" despite the "politics of good intentions." The *Washington Times* called Bush's speech "upbeat" and the *Wall Street Journal* called it "relentlessly upbeat," while R. W. Apple Jr. of the *New York Times* reported that there were "no new programs of note [and] the tone of the domestic portion of the speech was largely hortatory."[52] Similarly, David Gergen of *U.S. News and World Report* pointed out that the speech was a political success yet lacked policy substance:

> With his opponents still gasping over the political success of his first year, George Bush is deftly moving to ensure that his second year is even better. There is a good chance he'll succeed. He has no apparent game plan, but as a politician, Bush has become the best open-field runner since "Crazy Legs" Hirsch, the Los Angeles Rams halfback who merrily zig-zagged through the opposition. Whenever the Democrats try to tackle him—on Panama, China, defense—Bush slips away and scores. Last week, in his state-of-the-union address, he did it again. In his calls for more troop cuts in Europe and higher standards in schools, Bush scampered past his Democratic foes just as they were preparing to pounce on him for complacency. Never mind that his new budget reduces education spending in real dollars; politically, Bush had another winner.[53]

Regarding polices, Bush received criticism for lacking a substantive domestic agenda and higher marks for foreign policy initiatives. In the *New York Times*:

> President Bush lent oratorical flourish and the weight of his office to his domestic agenda tonight but added little new substance to policies outlined earlier this week in budget proposals that Democrats have already criticized as inadequate. . . . Mr. Bush, smiling as he was announced into the House chamber, got two standing ovations before he spoke. . . . He brought most of the audience to its feet when he spoke of the Panama invasion. He drew his longest applause when he said his new budget would reduce the deficit without raising taxes. The Republicans stood. The Democrats sat, applauding quietly, and Mr. Bush laughed as Republicans waved at the Democrats to stand. At times, the speech was quintessential George Bush, filled with the litany of his campaign oratory—drug-free schools, help for the disabled and homeless and commercial enterprise zones, without the offer of substantial money to back the programs.[54]

And the *Los Angeles Times*:

> Taking advantage of events tumbling his way, George Bush has put together a striking proposal that is the foreign policy equivalent of motherhood and apple pie. In this case, as he surveyed the political

> scene, he found on this side of the Atlantic a Congress growing increasingly reluctant to foot the bill for 305,000 U.S. troops stationed in a post–Cold War Europe. On the other side, he found an Eastern Europe throwing off the communist yoke and pressuring the Kremlin to pull its troops back to behind Soviet borders. What to do? Seize the moment. And so he did. Wednesday night, the President whose foreign policy watchword has been prudence, suddenly called on the Soviet Union to join him in agreeing to make further massive cuts in the forces arrayed along the thoroughly frayed East-West divide—forces which appear each day less likely to be called to combat. And Bush managed to accomplish the announcement in what has become true Bush fashion: when it was least expected.[55]

Bush also received the usual comparisons to Reagan, although several commentators pointed out that, for better or worse, Bush had finally begun to move away from his predecessor in policy and tone. According to the *St. Louis Post-Dispatch*,

> In his first state of the Union address, President George Bush was no Ronald Reagan. It was a new president. . . . Although the heir to the Reagan mantle, Bush was a different leader with a more moderate message and a less theatrical style Wednesday night than the man who delivered all but one of the State of the Union messages in the 1980s. . . . There were no trumpet calls to remake the federal government. . . . There was no call to ban abortions, bring prayer back into the public schools, overhaul welfare or to pass a constitutional amendment to require a balanced budget. Bush spoke movingly of faith and family, but did not press the hot button of conservative social issues that dotted Reagan's State of the Union messages. And there was little of the gimmickry and theater of the Reagan messages. . . . In some ways it almost sounded like a Democratic president's State of the Union speech.[56]

Similarly, Bill Schneider in the *National Journal* wrote, "George Bush has finally made a sharp break with Ronald Reagan. . . . In his first State of the Union address . . . Bush defiantly set off on his own course. . . . At last, Bush can say he is his own man. . . . The rest of the speech was very much in the Reagan mold—a feel-good speech. Things are fine, and we're going to make them even finer.... A State of the Union speech is supposed to be a call to action in which the President lays out an agenda. Bush refuses to do that, beyond a long list of lofty goals.... That's one reason Bush, with an 80 percent job approval rating, has far less clout with Congress than his predecessor had with a 50 percent rating."[57] According to the *Boston Globe*, "President Bush demonstrated in his State of the Union address last night that he is a president for his times, a mirror of the American public that elected him and approves of him so heartily. Like them, Bush came across as alarmed by America's slippage in a fiercely competitive world but uncertain what to do about it and unpersuaded that there should be a major federal role in addressing the threat. After a year spent trying to persuade the country that he is a more alert and involved commander-in-chief than his predecessor, Bush in his remarks on domestic policy chose not to view the future through President Reagan's rose-colored glasses. Instead, he donned a pair of his own."[58]

However, Tom Shales of the *Washington Post* remained unimpressed with the president's performance, despite his high approval ratings:

> One of the most distinctive things about George Bush's first State of the Union address . . . was that it wasn't very distinctive. It was your standard basic generic presidential speech. If someone pries it out of a time capsule a hundred years from now, they won't get much of an idea about what life was like in the United States in 1990, except that we had a pretty dull president. Bush's speech and his delivery of it were competent, goodhearted, uninspired and uninspiring, although the blandness didn't discourage the assembled legislators from interrupting it with applause. They interrupted it 35 times, or roughly once per minute. It was a little like listening to sheep clap. If sheep could clap . . . In terms of his speaking style, it is much improved, and yet Bush still seems something of a bitter pill, even when trying to convey good news. He's getting those quixotic hand gestures under control, although he had a relapse when talking about lowering the federal deficit. His gestures suggested a Marcel Marceau routine called "wrapping a box." He spoke in complete sentences, not in the sing-songy phrases lampooned by Dana Carvey on "Saturday Night Live."[59]

While Bush's approval rating had dropped to 73 percent by the second week of February 1990, the president was still enjoying high public approval immediately following his state of the union address. Bush had used the address to "articulate a programmatic vision" and talked about how the nation needed to act in the areas of education, health care, the economy, the environment, and housing; however, "journalists were quick to point out that the president had submitted a budget that failed to reflect a bold domestic agenda."[60] The press also continued to criticize Bush for lacking a coherent domestic agenda, as well as continuing to remind Americans that Bush lacked the public skills of Ronald Reagan. While Bush used the state of the union to discuss a broad array of domestic issues, many observers in the press still wanted more specific policy proposals. As a result, Bush was often viewed as having much more credibility on foreign policy issues as opposed to domestic issues as reported by many in the news media, which tended to portray Bush as a bi-polar leader and only in charge of one half of the nation's agenda. The credit that Bush received for his foreign policy expertise would help to carry him through the public aspects of the presidency with high approval ratings in 1991 and the Gulf War but would prove problematic as the nation turned its attention to more domestic matters by 1992.

1991

Bush delivered the 1991 state of the union address January 29. At this time, the Gulf War dominated the news and the Bush presidency. Due to the U.S. military's ongoing success in pushing the Iraqi military out of Kuwait, Bush enjoyed an approval rating of 83 percent in the days leading up to this address. Despite his approval rating, Bush continued to fight the public perception of the dual presidency—successful in the international arena yet ineffective at setting a strong domestic policy for the nation. This idea was perhaps best exemplified by *Time* magazine's choice of Bush as its 1990 "Men of the Year: The Two George Bushes." In one of the articles that corresponded with the annual cover story, Michael Duffy reported that "many Americans concluded that in George Bush they had elected two Presidents: a highly capable captain of foreign policy and a dawdling, disengaged caretaker of domestic affairs."[61] It was this political environment in which Bush delivered the state of the union and attempted to address the criticisms in the area of domestic policy while basking in the glow of his initial success in the Gulf as commander-in-chief.

In developing the text of the state of the union address, White House advisors expressed concern over a lack of specific domestic proposals on the president's agenda. In a detailed memo from Charles Kolb to Roger Porter, both domestic policy advisors, Kolb says that the state of the union "represents the last opportunity for us to lay out a thematic domestic policy agenda before the 1992 election cycle begins." Kolb then gives a thematic breakdown by paragraph of the 1990 state of the union address and concludes that "there are relatively few broad themes which actually make it into the text. Assuming that the address is to be something more than a framework for listing what's in the budget (and it's not just a budget summary; last year the President explicitly stated at the beginning that he would not be emphasizing programs or numbers) then it behooves us to determine as soon as possible what our basic message should be."[62] The memo continues with suggestions on how to develop the necessary themes. Kolb notes that "two themes are likely to dominate the foreign policy aspects of the speech: the collapse of the Soviet empire (and possibly the Soviet Union itself) accompanied by the democratization of Eastern and Central Europe, and Iraq's invasion of Kuwait. In the former, the blossoming of individual freedom has led to reunifying Germany and the institution of Western-oriented democratic and capitalistic governments. The second theme, unfortunately, reflects the (temporary) loss of individual freedom of the Kuwaiti people, but it nonetheless shows the United States squarely on the side of democracy in calling for the unconditional withdrawal of Iraq from Kuwait." On domestic policy: "The transition from foreign to domestic policy, in my judgment, should emphasize individual freedom, decisionmaking, and choice. Our model of democratic capitalism was what inspired the revolutions in Poland, Czechoslovakia, East Germany, even the Baltics. These countries have borrowed our model—our system—and are holding it up for the world to see. This triumph affords us the opportunity to reinforce the values and principles upon which our Republic was also founded." Kolb then suggested highlighting the following initiatives:

> Empowerment: "[T]he Economic Empowerment Task Force is seeking ways to reinvigorate individual choice in American life. . . . the Task Force has recommended a series of budgetary and legislative initiatives in areas such as education, child care, housing, job training etc. that will increase the extent to which individuals—rather than bureaucracies—have a say over the governance of their lives. In his speech, the President could praise the efforts of [various individuals] who are redefining the ways in which civil rights, education and

housing services, plus anticrime efforts are being delivered. It might be too Reaganesque, but some of these empowerment 'heroes' could even be invited to sit in the gallery during the speech. The message to those on the floor below would be stunning!"

Growth: "We know from the 1980s . . . that growth incentives work; command-and-control economic models that are premised on confiscatory tax rates don't. The address should emphasize the importance of solid growth incentives as the best way to ensure a sound economy. We should lay out a clear agenda which also includes a stern warning against excessive *re*regulation. . . . A reference to cost-effective environmental regulation might comfort those who worry about the cost of implementing the Clean Air Act."

Education: "[T]he President needs to announce a series of actions that will have a dramatic and visible impact on education at the local level. If we are subject to any criticism for what we have done thus far in education, it is that we have failed to penetrate beyond the beltway and governmental elites. I still believe the President should call for school contracts in every elementary and secondary school in America in order to establish the responsibilities of parents, teachers, principals, and students when it comes to learning. Additionally, the President could agree once a month to teach a class on television."

Civil Rights: "We should take this issue on directly by announcing that we will be introducing a new anti-quota, pro-jobs civil rights bill that will have as its centerpiece the principle of personal economic opportunity and liberty. . . . In short, ours must be a populist civil rights agenda, emphasizing things like repeal of Davis-Bacon and other structural impediments to good jobs, housing, safe streets, and equal opportunity."

Crime: "As part of our civil rights discussion, we need to recognize that freedom from crime is one of the most important civil rights and a key responsibility of government. Since the Warren Court, the focus of liberals has been on the rights of criminals; the President can help turn this around by emphasizing that safe streets and drug-free schools foster an environment which is itself conducive to advancing civil rights: economic opportunity is enhanced when people are better educated; people have greater access to work when they can travel to and from a job without fearing for their lives."

> Adoption: "What better example of a kinder, gentler theme? There are tens of thousands of families that would like to adopt children, and the availability of children is certainly there, too. The President could announce that he will be offering model legislation that States could enact to streamline adoption rules and procedures."
>
> Litigation: "Imagine the headlines if the President simply acknowledged the extreme costliness of litigation to the American way of life. The available factoids on this one would be more entertaining than *Jake and the Fatman*. . . . Merely framing this issue will put the President on the side of the vast majority of Americans who dislike lawyers."
>
> Congress: "This one will hit close to home for the audience, but the President should not shrink from calling for major reforms in the way the Congress operates."
>
> Miscellaneous themes: "In addition to these suggested themes, there are a few other themes that I would recommend including: GATT and the results of the Uruguay Round, Making Government Work—a powerful theme which can be bolstered by gripping examples, Americans With Disabilities Act and Child Care bills—we should commit to timely and cost-effective implementation, Financial Institutions—news stories have suggested looming problems with banking and insurance sectors; the President should be reassuring there as well as on the overall state of the economy, and Volunteerism—we got the tree-planting initiative and the Thousand Points of Light Foundation. They should be mentioned. Energy—presumably we'll have a national energy strategy to announce that will reduce our overall vulnerability.[63]

As the strategic plans for the state of the union address continued to make their way up the chain of command within the White House, a consensus emerged for Bush to deliver a thematic, as opposed to programmatic, speech. As Porter reported to Sununu at the end of December 1990, "The programmatic approach easily cascades into a laundry list of particular programs. It may please some specific constituencies that they were mentioned, but it rarely inspires the listener or conveys a sense of direction."[64] The eight-page memo also detailed the four themes to be covered in the speech: foreign policy, economic policy, domestic policy, and values. Regarding foreign policy, Porter concluded that the changes within the previous year (including the fall of the Berlin Wall and nearing the end of the Cold War) as well as the ongoing situation in the Persian Gulf should play a "prominent" role in the speech: "This is an opportunity to convey a tone of *prudent decisiveness* [emphasis in original]. The Vietnam experience is still a vivid memory in the minds of most adult Americans. . . . This is also an occasion to place events in the Middle East into a larger context of what has happened during the past two years and of the new world order the President is seeking to establish during this decade." Regarding economic policy, Porter acknowledged that Bush faced a challenge in addressing this topic: "The National Bureau of Economic Research will have technically declared that we are in a recession by January 29. The economic data that will be released between now and the State of the Union will almost certainly not be encouraging. . . . Perhaps more than anything else, the portion of the speech dealing with the economy needs to convey *confidence* both in the short-term and the longer-term [emphasis in original]. It is important that the President convey that he is following economic developments closely, and that he remind Americans of the fundamental strength and resilience of the U.S. economy."[65]

On domestic policy, Porter pointed out that the state of the union should be viewed as an opportunity to articulate important issues on Bush's domestic agenda: "Inside the Beltway, and in much of the press, recent weeks have witnessed a steady stream of stories suggesting that the Administration has a limited (or little in the way of a) domestic agenda." According to Porter, three domestic themes should be highlighted: kinder and gentler (a phrase "favorably identified" with Bush relating to more government resources for programs such as Medicaid and Head Start); opportunity and empowerment (by championing issues such as civil rights, crime control, and self-reliance, "the President can observe that America has always been a land of opportunity where individuals have had rights and have also accepted responsibility"); and a sense of stewardship (to highlight Bush's policies in the areas of environmental protection, including the Clean Air Act, and national service). Finally, regarding the theme of values, Porter wrote: "The values that run through the speech are freedom, growth, opportunity, and responsibility. They are the elements that make for a strong nation and strong families."[66] By January 9, 1991, the speechwriters began incorporating the ideas for themes and specifics into the draft of the speech, with the directive that "Porter says that virtually all the powers that be agree we should go thematic." Other directions included the following: "We should express confidence and optimism, but we need evidence to back it up. . . . Let's put recession into historical perspective, showing hey—it's not all that bad. Suggestion of using very simple graphics to show comparison. Just a blip on the screen. . . . Latest polling data suggests that people think the best thing we can do to ease the recession is to CUT WASTEFUL GOVERNMENT SPENDING. . . . Idea of holding up the documents of specifics in administration's proposals shows: here's the beef. . . . POTUS may be signing several executive orders on SOU [state of the union] day. Shows action, command, decision. Also shows what he can do without Congress. . . . Must reduce [Roger Porter's] technocratic language to laymen's terms. Make it sing, letters, anecdotes."[67]

Other internal memos from various agencies also suggested highlighting specific domestic initiatives during the state of the union address. From the Department of Education:

> Our primary suggestion is that the President should make civil rights one of the themes of both the message and the Agenda. The recent veto of the Civil Rights Act of 1990 has raised the salience of civil rights issues, and we believe the President should confront civil rights issues head on, rather than letting the Democrats seize the initiative and put the Administration into a defensive posture. Thus, the President should state that he wholeheartedly supports the expansion of civil rights where warranted, and take a share of the credit for passage of the Americans with Disabilities Act. This reflects his campaign pledges and commitment to disabled Americans. He should also assert that he opposes unwarranted expansion of civil rights standards where they go beyond a commitment to nondiscrimination and instead encourage reverse discrimination and quotas, and that the Civil Rights Act of 1990 represented such an overextension"[68]

Similarly, the following was sent to Porter from Health and Human Services:

> [t]he President would be left open for criticism if he ignored health care in this year's state of the union, something he last year said is "one more problem we need to address." I would suggest a frank approach would be to say (1) Secretary Sullivan has found slogans aplenty but no consensus, (2) cost is the largest problem, both in terms of its economic effect and its effects on access, and (3) reaf-

> firm the commitment to bringing the staggering costs of health care under control. Controlling the effects of medical liability might be offered as one way to bring costs under control. A new equation of cost with access would give pause to the Congressional momentum behind more pernicious approaches to access. It would have the effect of shifting the debate, much as our tax credit based approach to child care blew holes in the police state approach to child care that appeared to have so much momentum before the Administration spoke.[69]

Finally, from the National Space Council: "Enclosed are some suggestions about space to be used as a potential insert in the State of the Union address. I assume that, as last year, space will be among the topics touched upon in the address. I further assume that, as last year, the speech will be broadly thematic. I would imagine that the President's discussion of space would best fit under the general heading 'Investment in the Future.' In this regard, I believe it is crucial that he focus whatever attention he can on space to the rallying point of the recently completed Augustine report (*Report of the Advisory Committee on the Future of the U.S. Space Program*). This will be our central focus and our point of departure for the coming years."[70]

The proposed media plan for coverage of the state of the union focused, as with earlier public events, on portraying the president as actively engaged on various agenda items, with key surrogates helping to make the case for the administration:

> Friday, January 25: Still photographers take photo of the President working on speech at desk in Oval Office. This will play over the weekend and in Monday editions of magazines. Sunday, January 27: Governor Sununu on *Brinkley*. Richard Darman on *Face the Nation*. Tuesday, January 29 (Speech Day): 6:00 P.M., quotes given to TV Networks for nightly news. 6:00 P.M., distribute one page talking points, prepared by Dave Demarest, to Administration spokesmen and surrogates. 7:00 P.M., background briefing by OMB Director Darman, Governor Sununu, General Skowcroft, and Roger Porter. 7:00 P.M., embargoed text released. Embargoed fact sheet, prepared by OPD [Office of Policy Development], is released with text. 9:30 P.M., people to appear on TV for after speech react: Dole, Simpson,

> [Robert] Michel, [Dick] Cheney, and Sununu. 10:00 P.M., ABC-TV *State of the Union Special.* 11:30 P.M., Richard Darman on CBS *America Tonight.* Wednesday, January 30: 7:00 A.M., Sununu and Porter on morning shows. 11:00 A.M., the President speaks at 50th Anniversary of FDR's Four Freedoms Speech. Thursday, January 31: 8:00 A.M., the President addresses National Prayer Breakfast. Friday, February 1: 11:00 A.M., Presidential Press Conference on the State of the Union and the Gulf.[71]

Just thirteen days after the start of Operation Desert Storm, Bush's state of the union address not surprisingly included a strong foreign policy component by providing the nation with a reminder of why U.S. soldiers were fighting in the Persian Gulf, stating that "we stand at a defining hour." The speech also included a long list of domestic and economic policy priorities despite the initial intent to make the speech less programmatic (see table 4). Bush began with a broader statement about "a new world order" to explain his foreign policy objectives: "What is at stake is more than one small country; it is a big idea: a new world order, where diverse nations are drawn together in common cause to achieve the universal aspirations of mankind—peace and security, freedom, and the rule of law. . . . The community of nations has resolutely gathered to condemn and repel lawless aggression. Saddam Hussein's unprovoked invasion—his ruthless, systematic rape of a peaceful neighbor—violated everything the community of nations holds dear. The world has said this aggression would not stand, and it will not stand. . . . With few exceptions, the world now stands as one. The end of the cold war has been a victory for all humanity. . . . Germany is united. Europe has become whole and free, and America's leadership was instrumental in making it possible." The president also stated that he remained "concerned by violence in the Baltics" and was committed to pursuing the "triumph of democratic ideas in Eastern Europe and Latin America."

Bush then turned to domestic matters and revisited a familiar theme of public service and personal sacrifice: "Tonight I come before this House and the American people with an appeal for renewal. This is not merely a call for new government initiatives; it is a call for new initiatives in government, in our communities, and from every American to prepare for the next American century. . . . We have within our reach the promise of a renewed America. We can find meaning and reward by serving some higher purpose than ourselves, a shining purpose, the illumination of a

Table 4. 1991 State of the Union Address, Policy Categorization (by Paragraph)

Domestic Issues
Crime – 2
Defense – 5
Education – 0
Environment/Energy/Land Management – 0
Health Care – 1
Reform – 7
Science/Technology/Transportation – 1
Welfare/Entitlements Programs – 0
Economic Issues
Domestic Fiscal/Monetary Policy – 12
Unemployment/Jobs – 2
International Issues
Diplomatic/Military – 28
Trade/Economic – 2
Non Policy/Ceremonial – 7
Total Paragraphs – 67

Thousand Points of Light. . . . Together, these last 2 years, we've put dollars for child care directly in the hands of parents instead of bureaucracies; unshackled the potential of Americans with disabilities; applied the creativity of the marketplace in the service of the environment, for clean air; and made home ownership possible for more Americans." The economy also played a prominent role in the early part of the speech: "I know that tonight, in some regions of our country, people are in genuine economic distress. And I hear them. . . . But there are reasons to be optimistic about our economy. First, we don't have to fight double-digit inflation. Second, most industries won't have to make big cuts in production because they don't have big inventories piled up. And third, our exports are running solid and strong. In fact, American businesses are exporting at a record rate. . . . since 1981, we've created almost 20 million jobs, cut inflation in half, and cut interest rates in half. And yes, the largest peacetime economic expansion in history has been temporarily interrupted. But our economy is still over twice as large as our closest competitor. We will get this recession behind us and return to growth soon."

The next portion of the speech included Bush's list of policy priorities, including "a budget that promotes investment in America's future—in children, education, infrastructure, space, and high technology." Bush began with various budget issues like developing a "pay-as-you-go plan" to control deficit spending, the creation of tax-free family savings accounts, penalty-free withdrawals from IRA's for first-time home buyers, and a reduced tax for long-term capital gains "to increase jobs and growth." Other proposals included: legislation to achieve "excellence in education" by making "America number one in math and science; a blueprint for a new national highway system, a critical investment in our transportation infrastructure; a research and development agenda that includes record levels of Federal investment, and a permanent tax credit to strengthen private R&D and to create jobs; a comprehensive national energy strategy that calls for energy conservation and efficiency, increased development, and greater use of alternative fuels; a banking reform plan to bring America's financial system into the 21st century so that our banks remain safe and secure and can continue to make job-creating loans for our factories, our businesses, and home buyers." Bush continued by urging Congress to work with him to expand U.S. exports and develop a Mexican free trade agreement; to create new incentives to create jobs in inner cities by encouraging investment through enterprise zones, including tenant control and ownership of public housing; to reduce crime and combat drug abuse; to develop health care prevention initiatives; to enact term limits; and to provide more funding for various state programs. He also urged Congress to join him in continuing the work on civil rights as "crucial to protecting equal opportunity. Every one of us has a responsibility to speak out against racism, bigotry, and hate. We will continue our vigorous enforcement of existing statutes, and I will once again press the Congress to strengthen the laws against employment discrimination without resorting to the use of unfair preferences."

The final section of the speech returned to foreign policy issues: "As Americans, we know that there are times when we must step forward and accept our responsibility to lead the world away from the dark chaos of dictators, toward the brighter promise of a better day. Almost 50 years ago we began a long struggle against aggressive totalitarianism. Now we face another defining hour for America and the world." Bush then offered a tribute to the men and women serving in the military and noted that the wife of Gen. Norman Schwarzkopf, commander of the U.S. forces in the Persian Gulf, was in attendance to represent the servicemen and women. With a brief mention on his direction to refocus the Strategic Defense Initiative to "providing protection from limited ballistic missile strikes," Bush devoted the remainder of the speech to the U.S. objectives in Iraq:

> The war in the Gulf is not a war we wanted. We worked hard to avoid war. For more than 5 months we—along with the Arab League, the European Community, the United Nations—tried every diplomatic avenue. . . . But time and again, Saddam Hussein flatly rejected the path of diplomacy and peace. . . . Tonight I am pleased to report that we are on course. Iraq's capacity to sustain war is being destroyed. Our investment, our training, our planning—all are paying off. Time will not be Saddam's salvation. Our purpose in the Persian Gulf remains constant: to drive Iraq out of Kuwait, to restore Kuwait's legitimate government, and to ensure the stability and security of this critical region. . . . But the world has to wonder what the dictator of Iraq is thinking. If he thinks that by targeting innocent civilians in Israel and Saudi Arabia, that he will gain advantage, he is dead wrong. If he thinks that he will advance his cause through tragic and despicable environmental terrorism, he is dead wrong. And if he thinks that by abusing the coalition prisoners of war he will benefit, he is dead wrong. We will succeed in the Gulf. And when we do, the world community will have sent an enduring warning to any dictator or despot, present or future, who contemplates outlaw aggression. . . . The winds of change are with us now. The forces of freedom are together, united. We move toward the next century more confident than ever that we have the will at home and abroad to do what must be done—the hard work of freedom.[72]

As with many of Bush's public performances, the media reaction to this state of the union was mixed, reflecting a dual image of a successful president handling foreign policy while a mediocre president dealt with domestic and economic policies. The morning of the state of the union, a *Washington Post*/ABC News poll was released that supported this idea, with eight out of ten Americans satisfied with Bush's handling of the

Persian Gulf War, while two out of three Americans stated that "the nation's already weak economy was worsening."[73] Alan Brinkley of the *New York Times* previewed the speech this way: "If anyone has reason to be grateful for the war in the Persian Gulf, it is the unfortunate White House speechwriter responsible for President Bush's State of the Union Address this evening. Without an international crisis, what would the President have to talk about? Perhaps no Administration in this century has completed two years in office so devoid of domestic accomplishments and so uninterested in setting a domestic agenda. And there is no suggestion that anything will change soon. John Sununu captured the essence of the Administration's emptiness recently when he answered a question about what remained on the President's domestic agenda with a curt, 'Not that much.' Were it not for Saddam Hussein, the Bush Presidency would be nearly invisible."[74]

Following the speech, Margaret Carlson's assessment in *Time* seemed to capture a common theme in the press coverage of the event:

> No speaker is more compelling than one who believes what he is saying. As the camera pulled in tight on the President's face during last Tuesday's State of the Union address, the millions of people tuning in saw a President who was finally projecting the vision that all the high-priced media handlers had been unable to supply for him. . . . But when Bush moved from the state of the world to the state of the country, he left his vision at the border. The domestic side of the speech, with its reform plans, blueprints, comprehensive strategies and dynamic program life cycles, sounded as if it had been cobbled together by a committee of tightfisted accountants. There was no hint of significant spending cuts or new taxes to finance the plans, and not even a mention of the deficit, which has risen from $150 billion to a projected $300 billion since Bush took office. Yes, there is a recession—but it is regional and temporary, and we will grow our way out of it.[75]

Described in the *St. Petersburg Times* as looking "calm and confident [while] sketching some of the domestic initiatives he will propose in the budget he sends to Congress next week," Bush was also widely criticized for a lack of detail and specifics regarding his domestic and economic agenda.[76] As argued by an editorial in the *Boston Globe*,

> After dozens of rewrites, his cheerleader's address to the nation continued to stress the rightness of the war against Iraq and the belief that the distressed US economy would soon somehow rebound. Though earlier versions purportedly were dominated by comments justifying the war and assuring a victorious outcome, the final version put more emphasis on domestic priorities, on "a new American Century." New proposals spoke to energy and banking reform, as well as more money for anticrime efforts, housing for the poor, educational-choice programs and measures to combat infant mortality. Alas, few details were offered. Nonetheless, the shift in emphasis was well taken. Hours before the speech, news services tapped into the public's state of mind about the nation's condition. Neither Bush's optimism about the economy nor his assurance about the war is widely shared. . . . Bush could not afford to get too far out of step with the public. His bow to the domestic side of the agenda was clear, but he offered no substantive guidance or assessment on the state of the nation's economy. A more factual appraisal would have served him and the American people better.[77]

Similarly, John Yang wrote in the *Washington Post*, "President Bush's State of the Union address last night offered a modest outline for domestic programs in the year ahead, a sharp contrast to the expansive role he mapped out for America in the world. Bush offered a minimalist approach on several domestic issues, and said little about difficult economic problems. He didn't mention the record size of the federal deficit. . . . On civil rights, [Bush] offered no new proposals, pledging only to 'continue our vigorous enforcement of existing statutes' and to oppose hiring quotas, an issue Republican candidates put to good use in last year's congressional elections."[78] And Richard Wolf of *USA Today* pointed out the stark contrast between the foreign and domestic policy sections of the speech: "Congress greeted President Bush's dramatic State of the Union address with one voice on the war abroad but a cacophony of division about the problems at home. The unity over the war was reflected by the longest standing ovation in most lawmakers' memory—when Bush cited the sacrifices of the troops. . . . But while Bush's defense of the war won praise, his staccato list of domestic priorities was panned by Democrats."[79]

Bush received a more positive assessment for the foreign policy elements of the speech. According to Kenneth Walsh in *U.S. News and World*

Report, "Even though Bush's State of the Union address last week was hardly heroic or inspirational, it won wide praise even from Democrats for demonstrating that Bush was firmly in charge of the war."[80] Maureen Dowd of the *New York Times* said of the speech: "intended less to offer a new domestic agenda than to explain the war with Iraq and give courage to Americans fearful of a long and bloody conflict, the President harked back to images of the years leading up to World War II. . . . The President spoke in measured, sober tones, a contrast to his first State of the Union Message, in which Mr. Bush spoke triumphantly of 'Communism crumbling' and of a new relationship between the United States and the Soviet Union. Today he spoke of challenges in the new superpower understanding in light of the Soviet crackdown in the Baltic republics and war in the gulf."[81] But this part of the speech also lacked the specific policy details some were looking for, as noted in the *Boston Globe*: "Bush, in a State of the Union address less than two weeks after embarking on a war against Iraq's occupation of Kuwait, provided a report on the conflict's goals and progress that was strong in rhetoric but modest in specifics. . . . But while millions of Americans, restive about the war, watched the speech hoping that the president would provide assurances that the war would be over quickly, Bush offered no such promises, nor any breakthroughs on the military or diplomatic fronts."[82]

Media critic Tom Shales of the *Washington Post* provided his usual harsh critique of Bush's public performance:

> Okay, so he's not a great communicator. But he's a greater communicator than Saddam Hussein! George Bush's State of the Union speech, televised live from the House of Representatives on four networks last night, was quite satisfactory, which for Bush is a step up. For a wartime president, Bush kept saber-rattling and name-calling basically to a minimum, especially considering how well it would have played in front of Congress. Saddam was rarely, if ever, mentioned by name, perhaps partly because Bush has so much trouble pronouncing it. He stuck mostly to terms like "tyrant," and "brutal dictator" and "threat to decency and humanity." . . . Bush's speaking style has improved. People used to say his voice reminded them of Jack Nicholson's but last night, some of the reediness and the dry phrasing seemed more reminiscent of Henry Fonda. Unfortunately, Bush still sometimes lapses into a sour Nixonian scowl and this does not serve his purposes well. . . . The State of the Union was not a

> speech to echo through the ages, but how many do anymore? Bush acquitted himself well, read smoothly, and spoke for only about 15 minutes too long. He looked happier when it was over than he did when it began, and so were we.[83]

Even with the tepid response from the news media about the domestic agenda Bush laid out in his state of the union address, the public continued to respond more resolutely to the president's role as commander-in-chief; Bush enjoyed a public approval rating of 82 percent right after the speech. Unfortunately, the public's attention would turn within a few months to domestic and economic matters when U.S. troops victoriously came home from the Persian Gulf and as the recession became more widespread on a national scale. Despite the need for bold global leadership when dealing with Bush's self-described "new world order," his status-quo agenda at home did not lay the groundwork for continued public support after the military achieved victory against Saddam Hussein. The oncoming recession, along with a Democratic Congress not interested in working with a Republican president looking forward to his re-election campaign, combined to consistently drive down Bush's approval ratings throughout the rest of 1991. This also seemed to play right into the media narrative that had already been presented of Bush as a strong president abroad while weak at home. According to Rozell, "Bush had failed to meet a journalistic criterion for leadership: the willingness to turn presidential popularity into national support for an activist agenda."[84] That narrative proved difficult for Bush to shake during the remainder of his time in the White House.

1992

Entering his reelection year in 1992, Bush faced major challenges on the domestic front. In terms of timing, the recession and his falling approval ratings (down to 46 percent, with a disapproval rating of 48 percent) in January of that year could not have come at a worse time (although the two were not mutually exclusive). This was the first time in Bush's tenure that his disapproval rating registered higher than his approval rating with the American public. Billed as the "defining moment" of the Bush administration, the state of the union, delivered January 28, attempted to lay out a dramatic domestic and economic proposal to get the country back on track; it was to be "brief and thematic, avoiding the standard laundry list approach."[85] However, the press corps labeled the speech as lacking in vision and without a broad theme, a "grab bag of tinker-at-the-margins initiatives that did not add up to an action agenda."[86] Understanding the significance of this state of the union address from the reelection campaign angle, Bush sought the help of Peggy Noonan and media adviser Roger Ailes, two veterans of the 1988 campaign, "to add glitz to this pivotal moment," which in turn "helped the president deliver a respectable crafted speech and a respectable performance."[87]

In addition to seeking out help from past advisors, Tony Snow had joined the Bush White House team in 1991 as Bush's head speech writer (and a media advisor by later in 1992). Snow had strong conservative credentials from his time as editorial page editor of the *Washington Times* and had been hired by Sununu to help re-craft the president's speeches to clarify Bush's domestic message while solidifying support from the Republican base with the approaching 1992 election.[88] In a memo Snow wrote to speechwriters and researchers in which he reported that "the State of the Union is taking shape, in ways that we will like," Snow presented the following strategy:

> I talked with Bob Teeter today, and he outlines what we should do in the weeks leading up to SOU, and the two weeks beyond. A summary: Phase One: Friday through next Wednesday (Jan. 10–15)—crow about the Asia trip and reiterate the link between foreign policy and jobs. The Cold War is over. We won. Now we must compete in a global economy, one in which our fate is tied to the fates of our trading partners. We want open markets, free trade. If everyone plays by the same rules, everyone rises and falls together: If they starve, so do we. If they thrive, so do we. The President has taken some important first steps to create a new world trade structure—and he will continue to do so. The better the structure, the more jobs we will create. Phase Two: Wednesday until SOU—play to whatever audience we're addressing while also outlining the criteria for a true-blue, no-BS economic growth package. Here are the parts (in Teeter's words: We should try to devise snappy labels): 1) A good growth package gets us competitive in the world economy, builds upon our growing export business, and creates jobs; 2) It understands that you don't create jobs out of thin air. Investors have to make the initial cash outlay; entrepreneurs have to take risks; people have to buy the product; workers have to work—and none of this starts without the fundamental—an investor's investment. We're going to

> make it easier for investors to invest. (We also should walk through the other stuff and demonstrate that we'll stop punishing risk; we'll reward success, and so on.). 3) It restrains budget growth. Heck, we may even cut the budget. 4) It preserves the value of people's basic assets—starting with home values. . . . 5) It assures all Americans, and especially low- and middle-income Americans, that they will be able to afford the cost of raising a family, educating children, providing for health care, and making life better for every new generation. . . . 6) It does not increase the deficit. 7) It works—and gives people the confidence they need to invest for the future. . . . Phase Three: In the 12 days following the SOU, POTUS will deliver four major think speeches (at least according to the latest unofficial plan): An economic growth speech, a defense reform address, a health care speech, and a GOP "family of America" talk that incorporates everything from crime and drug policies to welfare, to schools, to whatever else really matters to Real America.[89]

Other potential, and specific, policy proposals were also being considered by various White House advisors for inclusion in the state of the union address. One memo presented "a list of 'top ten' ideas for the State of the Union," including:

> 1. The Citizen's Charter Approach to Government
> 2. The *Next* Step in Choice in Education
> 3. The Next Step on Privatization [transportation]
> 4. GOP Governors are Blazing New Paths
> 5. Emphasize Achievements: Drugs—The War on Drugs is a corking success according to the statistics. Besides, this President can claim to have cleaned up a conduit of drugs the size of an entire nation, namely Noriega's Panama.
> 6. Economic Liberty: Anti-Credentialism/Deregulate the Poor
> 7. Responsible Populism: Term Limits
> 8. *Beck* Decision Enforcement
> 9. Economic Growth: Tax & Budget Proposals—These proposals can be presented together as a package. . . . A critical factor on the economic growth issue is the public's awareness of the *prospect* of economic growth. The President's agenda must show activism and hope.
> 10. New Principles

The memo concluded:

> Finally, the President ought to expound some principles that knit his concrete policies together. These can supplement the broad rubrics which we traditionally rely upon, namely Stewardship, Investing in the Future, Creating Opportunity, Maintaining Growth. Already implicit in the President's idea of Thousand Points of Light, they can be thought of as chapter headings underneath these broader titles:
>
> Family: The family must be encouraged.
>
> Results: Policies should be guided first by whether they produce "outcome," i.e., results, not by what the "inputs" are (e.g., money, personally, etc.).
>
> Competition: Competition among service-providers to the poor should always be encouraged.
>
> Community: Organizations and decision-making should be community-based.
>
> "Little Platoons:" Mediating structures of society (family, associations, religious institutions, etc.) will be encouraged.[90]

Other suggestions for the speech included forming "a broad-based winning business coalition around our economic growth package," as well as encouraging provisions designed to help the real estate sector and health care reform issues related to small business owners. Advisors also acknowledged that "in order to excite a broader base . . . the President needs to state that he will not raise rates or taxes."[91] Several memos during this time show the concern among White House advisors that Bush be perceived as taking action to get the economy back on track. Charles Kolb wrote to Tony Snow:

> Some final thoughts about the State of the Union speech. After this, I promise to leave you alone. First, I'd recommend that we say something solid about welfare reform. Middle class voters *do* care about this issue, and they don't like seeing their tax dollars go to support otherwise able bodied people. We'll keep our safety net intact for those who need it, but not forever, except in the case of the permanently disabled. The attached article from last Sunday's *New York Times* bears reading. The President, in my view, needs to position himself to the right of Clinton on this

> issue. Second, when the President finishes next Tuesday night, *our* supporters should think to themselves, "Damn right!" Litanies of programs and spending increases don't provoke a "Damn right!" response. Nor does caring by itself. A Republican staffer for a very loyal GOP Congressman called me last week with the following comment: "Sure, we all know the President cares. But save the Hallmark cards. What is he going to *do*?" In my view, we get a favorable response by explaining to ordinary folks just what the President's initiatives mean for them. Program and budget talk is inside-the-beltway talk. Results are what people care most about and, to boot, results are positive, forward-looking. Hope the above is helpful.[92]

The planning of press activities related to the State of the Union address remained consistent with previous years. A memo from Fitzwater included the following strategy:

> State of the Union Press Activities: Tuesday, January 28—Full schedule of morning shows with administration representatives, a potential press conference with Dick Cheney to address defense budget cuts and new strategies for the military [this did not occur]; afternoon briefings by COS Skinner and Secretary Brady on economic growth package with tv business writers, columnists and talk shows; release advance text, followed by a press room briefing by Skinner; post speech interviews by administration officials (including *Nightline*); Wednesday, January 29, morning talk shows, budget briefings by various departments throughout the day; Thursday, January 30, "11:00 A.M. Presidential Press Conference to reflect on the State of the Union"; followed by Sunday talk shows and Monday morning talk shows (the latter with Republican governors in town for the GOP Governors' Meeting).[93]

Similarly, the Office of Media Affairs provided an "aggressive media plan" for the State of the Union address to

> be sure the President's words resonate into every community in America. To that end, the Office of Media Affairs
>
> • has participated in every issue roll-out meeting, prior to the State of the Union;

- has set-up and coordinated media opportunities for surrogates and regional coverage of the President on the Environment, Education and Crime/Drugs pre-State of the union roll-outs;
- has provided technical support and coordinated set-up for the CNN pool covering the address;
- has served as White House liaison for House Radio & TV, the Clerk's office, the House Recording Studio, the Architect's office, the Doorkeeper's office, the Capitol Police, the Sergeant-at-Arms, and of course, CNN;
- has orchestrated senior Administration official media availabilities for the day of, and weeks following, the State of the Union;
- has coordinated the activities of all Public Affairs operations, including all Agencies and the RCN, throughout the State of the Union roll-out;
- will provide materials to the above for their use and dissemination. We will get the President's speech, fact sheets and talking points to the Public Affairs shops which, in turn, will disseminate to their respective press corps;
- will hand-deliver the advance text and fact sheets to the National Press Club and other news chains, providing Washington-based reporters for national and out-of-state media quick and easy access. In addition, we will provide the same materials *directly* to the Editors and/or Editorial Boards of those papers, hitting not only the Washington representatives of many national papers, but the papers themselves; and finally
- will reach virtually every radio station, TV station, magazine and newspaper across the country as well as special interest groups and trade media representatives who focus on business, health, education, etc.[94]

The speech itself had a much stronger emphasis on domestic and economic policy than Bush's previous state of the unions (see table 5). The speech also represented the opening of Bush's reelection campaign, leaving the president with the daunting task of sounding decisive in the face of an economic recession and amidst sinking approval ratings when domestic and economic matters had not been the hallmark of the Bush administration. Bush began the speech by proclaiming, "I mean to speak tonight of big things, of big changes and the promises they hold, and of some big problems and how, together, we can solve them and move our country forward as the undisputed leader of the age." Immediately reminding everyone that the United States had won the Cold War, Bush then spoke of the opportunity to now "look homeward even more and move to set right what needs to be set right." With an acknowledgement of the sacrifices made by servicemen and women since the beginning of the Cold War, Bush also spoke of the sacrifice of the U.S. taxpayer: "No one ever thinks to thank the people who pay a country's bill. . . . But for half a century now, the American people have shouldered the burden and paid taxes that were higher than they would have been to support a defense that was bigger than it would have been if imperial communism had never existed. . . . We liberated Kuwait. Soon after, the Arab world and Israel sat down to

Table 5. 1992 State of the Union Address, Policy Categorization (by Paragraph)

Domestic Issues
Crime – 1
Defense – 5
Education – 1
Environment/Energy/Land Management – 0
Health Care – 4
Reform – 5
Science/Technology/Transportation – 1
Welfare/Entitlements Programs – 4
Economic Issues
Domestic Fiscal/Monetary Policy – 17
Unemployment/Jobs – 1
International Issues
Diplomatic/Military – 10
Trade/Economic – 2
Non Policy/Ceremonial – 14
Total Paragraphs – 65

talk seriously and comprehensively about peace, an historic first. . . . Much good can come from the prudent use of power." Bush then talked about needed cuts in military spending and in nuclear weapons while urging Congress to pass the Strategic Defense Initiative: "But even in the midst of celebration, we must keep caution as a friend. For the world is still a dangerous place. . . . This is a fact: Strength in the pursuit of peace is no vice; isolationism in the pursuit of security is no virtue."

The remainder of the speech focused on domestic and economic issues, although the president used familiar rhetoric to rally the cause for dealing with the recession, harkening back to his steadfast resolve about removing Saddam Hussein from Kuwait: "And now to our troubles at home. . . . unemployment is too high, some industries are in trouble, and growth is not what it should be. Let me tell you right from the start and right from the heart, I know we're in hard times. But I know something else: This will not stand. . . . in this Chamber we can bring the same courage and sense of common purpose to the economy that we brought to Desert Storm. And we can defeat hard times together. I believe you'll help. One reason is that you're patriots, and you want the best for your country. And I believe that in your hearts you want to put partisanship aside and get the job done because it's the right thing to do."

Bush laid out both a short-term and long-term plan to encourage investment, create new jobs, and to "clear away the obstacles to growth: high taxes, high regulation, redtape, and yes, wasteful Government spending. . . . There are certain things that a President can do without Congress, and I'm going to do them." The short term plan included a ninety-day moratorium on new federal regulations that could hinder growth; approving "pro-growth" expenditures like construction and maintenance projects for roads, bridges, and railways; a change in the federal tax withholding; and pursuing monetary policies to keep interest rates and inflation down. Bush also told Congress that it must pass a change in the alternative minimum tax, help for homebuyers, a cut in the capital gains tax, and an extension of unemployment benefits. Bush also acknowledged the charged political environment in which he was speaking, relative to the start of the 1992 presidential campaign: "I pride myself that I'm a prudent man, and I believe that patience is a virtue. But I understand that politics is, for some, a game and that sometimes the game is to stop all progress and then decry the lack of improvement. But let me tell you: Far more important than my political future and far more important than yours is the well-being of our country."

Bush's long-term plan included an extensive list of broad-based policy initiatives for "long-term improvement in our economic position." The first item on the list was trade: "We will work to break down the walls that stop world trade. We will work to open markets everywhere. And in our major trade negotiations, I will continue pushing to eliminate tariffs and subsidies that damage America's farmers and workers. And we'll get more good American jobs within our own hemisphere through the North American free trade agreement and through the Enterprise for the Americas Initiative." Second, education: "We must be the world's leader in education. And we must revolutionize America's schools." The remaining items included a permanent research and development tax credit for businesses; programs to combat crime and drug use; home ownership initiatives; increased spending on Head Start; reforming health care (without moving to a nationalized system); and controlling the federal deficit. On controlling government spending, Bush stated that his plan "would freeze all domestic discretionary budget authority, which means no more next year than this year. I will not tamper with Social Security, but I would put real caps on the growth of uncontrolled spending. And I would also freeze Federal domestic Government employment. And with the help of Congress, my plan will get rid of 246 programs that don't deserve Federal funding. Some of them have noble titles, but none of them is indispensable. We can get rid of each and every one of them. You know, it's time we rediscovered a home truth the American people have never forgotten: This Government is too big and spends too much. And I call upon Congress to adopt a measure that will help put an end to the annual ritual of filling the budget with pork barrel appropriations."

Rounding out the long-term list, Bush urged Congress to "enact the bold reform proposals that are still awaiting congressional action: bank reform, civil justice reform, tort reform, and my national energy strategy." He then announced a new "Commission on America's Urban Families," asked Congress to raise the child personal tax exemption for every family and allow families to deduct student loan interest, and urged reform of the welfare system. Bush then concluded the speech:

> There's a mood among us. People are worried. There's been talk of decline. Someone even said our workers are lazy and uninspired. And I thought: Really? You go tell Neil Armstrong standing on the moon. Tell the men and women who put him there. Tell the American farmer who feeds his country and the world. Tell the men and

> women of Desert Storm. Moods come and go, but greatness endures. Ours does. And maybe for a moment it's good to remember what, in the dailiness of our lives, we forget: We are still and ever the freest nation on Earth, the kindest nation on Earth, the strongest nation on Earth. And we have always risen to the occasion. And we are going to lift this Nation out of hard times inch by inch and day by day, and those who would stop us had better step aside. Because I look at hard times, and I make this vow: This will not stand.[95]

In the advance billing of this speech the Bush White House had defined it as the most important of the president's term, even as staffers like Fitzwater tried to lower expectations the day before the speech, saying that Democrats had set the bar too high for the president.[96] Nonetheless, the response from many in the press sounded like coverage from previous state of the union addresses—strong on foreign policy, weak on domestic and economic matters. According to Michael Duffy of *Time*, "In a speech that Bush's aides had touted as the most important of his term, the President, as usual, was at his best on foreign policy. He stole a march on Democrats by announcing deep cuts in the nation's strategic nuclear arsenal. But when he turned toward home, Bush fell short of his old standards for fiscal sanity or genuine sacrifice. When it comes to priorities, Bush made clear, his most important goal is to be re-elected."[97]

Other commentators offered similar assessments. Tom Morganthau in *Newsweek*: "His handlers hyped the State of the Union Message as one of the 'defining moments' of George Bush's presidency. But the real goal was redefinition, and the speech itself was rewritten again and again. Bush now faces a political predicament: his foreign-policy triumphs seem like ancient history, and the voters are asking, 'What can you do for us?' The answer is not much: the federal government, staggering under the largest deficit in peacetime history, cannot spend the nation out of recession, and candidate Bush can only try to convince the nation that this, too, will not stand."[98] Kenneth Walsh and David Gergen in *U.S. News and World Report*: "The Bush era has been remarkably themeless, as if the president preferred dropping in and out of history rather than shaping it to his design. As last week's State of the Union address demonstrated, the Bush administration is thinking ahead no further than Election Day. His speech, which the White House ballyhooed for weeks as a defining event, gave the president a short-term political boost, but represented neither a strategy nor a vision for the long-term future. . . . Even as the president prepares to make a formal declaration of his candidacy for re-election on February 12, his team is far more preoccupied with putting a better public face on his first term than in thinking about a second."[99] And Marci McDonald in *Maclean's*: "Billed by the White House as the 'defining event' of Bush's presidency, the hour-long address in the packed House of Representatives instead left analysts defining him as a cautious pragmatist committed to staying the course, offering a scattershot mix of quick election-year fixes and historic military cutbacks—but still unable to articulate an overriding vision of a nation poised uneasily on the brink of a complex post Cold War landscape. In fact, the speech may have boomeranged on Bush, underlining his apparent inability to heal the country's economic and psychic wounds."[100]

Major newspaper editorials, such as the *New York Times*, took a rather harsh view of Bush's speech:

> "This will not stand." George Bush's steely challenge to Saddam Hussein remains one of his most memorable expressions. Tuesday night, mired in recession and fighting for his political life, Mr. Bush invoked those words again in his State of the Union address. "I look at hard times and make this vow: This will not stand." This will not fly would be more like it. When the President resurrects the metaphor of Desert Storm to demonstrate his commitment to economic recovery, he might reasonably be expected to deliver a program to match the threat. . . . What his speech and new budget offer instead is a laundry list with no main text. What they disclose is not an anti-recession warrior but a tinkerer. . . . It's neither unexpected nor wrong for a President who's been under fire for ignoring domestic needs to look for an oratorical fix. Unfortunately, the President's rhetoric also illuminates how marginal are his remedies. Time and again, Churchillian flourishes introduced blinding banalities.[101]

The *Washington Post* also criticized Bush for his domestic initiatives: "The president provided few clues as to how he thinks the United States should conduct itself, how it should exercise leadership, what its purposes should be in the new international setting he rightly hails. His view was even more limited when he turned to domestic affairs. He outlined a dressed-up, standstill program of more of the same. His proposals struck us as being not at all up to the challenges before him: an ailing economy, hurting states and decaying cities, a health care system that sucks up a tenth of the money Americans spend yet fails to cover a seventh of the population, a $400 billion deficit. . . . Mr. Bush's solution to this array of problems is not to use the government but to shrink it. He offers an election-year laundry list of minor tax cuts that won't do a lot of good and which the government cannot afford."[102]

Political correspondents, like Ann Devroy for the *Washington Post*, reported on the strategy behind the speech: "Most State of the Union addresses are not memorable, and this one, in its substance, will not be either. . . . Rarely had a speech raised so many advance expectations. Virtually all of Bush's political aides, watching in horror and gloom, acknowledge now that the strategy of the past 10 weeks of waiting until last night to offer a program to combat the recession was a mistake. . . . Not only has Bush had no plan to offer the country, but his two most widely public appearances in recent weeks were his 'mea culpa tour' of New Hampshire and his collapse in Japan from a case of the flu. Last night offered a much more flattering contrast—barring calamity, a speech in the House chamber before a joint session of Congress is the next best thing to an Oval Office address for appearing presidential."[103] According to Tom Baxter in the *Atlanta Journal and Constitution*, "George Bush promised to deliver the speech of his life Tuesday night. In a few months we'll know if he delivered. It's not hard to judge how the president's State of the Union message measured up to the expectations he and his key aides raised for it. It didn't. This speech was worked on by more than 20 people, and it showed. Great lines from past campaigns were shoe-horned in for effect, but for an address that had this kind of build-up, this one was notably flat."[104]

But all of the news coverage was not bad for Bush, as the *Boston Globe* pointed out problems the Democrats were facing in their presidential primaries: "Measured against the demands of a restive electorate and the lofty expectations he himself set, President Bush's election-year remedy for the country's ills fell well short of the bold action that even many Republicans insist is needed to wrest the domestic political agenda away from the Democrats. But measured against the tawdry drama being played out in the Democratic presidential campaign, the president came across last night as reassuring if not convincing, underscoring Democratic concerns that a discontented electorate will not turn Bush out of office unless it finds an acceptable alternative."[105] Even media critic Tom Shales found a few things on which to compliment the president, calling his speech "lengthy, combative and relatively well delivered," with Bush coming across "as a guy who was rolling up his sleeves to fight the recession and to take a poke or two at anybody who thwarted him" even if the speech "didn't contain much that sounded innovative or bold. . . . While Bush carried off his speech with slick aplomb, an accomplishment for a president who is no great communicator, the Democrats began their response to the speech with an immediate fumble. [House Speaker Tom] Foley was seen staring off to his left for nearly 15 seconds with the camera trained on him waiting to begin. Then he turned, faced it, and launched into his remarks. This may not have been Foley's fault, but the effect was to make the Democrats look blundering, while Bush had looked like a polished pro . . . His scrappiness proved somewhat infectious in the hall. . . . Gangway, world! This guy Bush sounds like he means business."[106]

Right after the speech, Bush's approval ratings remained virtually the same as before, with 47 percent of Americans approving of his job performance, while 48 percent disapproved. However, the president found himself in a difficult position at the start of his reelection campaign, as much news coverage of the speech continued to hammer Bush over his lack of a domestic vision for the country. Other public relations debacles hurt him during this time period as well, including his bout with the flu during a trip to Tokyo just prior to the state of the union during which he vomited on the Japanese prime minister at a state dinner, as well as a widely circulated story about Bush's amazement at a supermarket scanner that portrayed him as being out of touch with average Americans (the story later proved to be inaccurate and a misunderstanding of Bush's response). Nonetheless, he "became the object of increasing public scorn" at a rather unfortunate time for his presidency.[107] Bush also became the first president to have his state of the union address covered on the new cable network Comedy Central, which provided a live ninety-minute commentary filled with political satire as Bush delivered his address.[108] Unfortunately for Bush, the environment in which he delivered his last state of the union address, as well as the response from the press and the public, would be a harbinger of things to come regarding the public aspects of his presidency for the remainder of the year.

Conclusion

A president's inaugural address, along with his state of the union addresses, are some of the most anticipated, most watched, and most analyzed moments of a presidency. While the inaugural address sets the bar quite high for a president in terms of getting his administration off to a positive start, the state of the union address also sets a high bar in that it represents an important presidential ritual that shines a bright spotlight on the president as the leader of the nation. Bush's experience with the state of the union addresses is not that different from his predecessors in that many competing constituencies within the executive branch fight to have their policy or initiative included in the address, which often results in a president reading off a laundry list of policy ideas and goals without speaking in substantive terms about where the nation has been or where it should go. Similarly, much attention is paid by White House staffers in preparing for the state of the union, including the act of writing the speech as well as the before, during, and after media events. For Bush, the state of the union strategy, particularly regarding media coverage and dissemination of the president's message, seemed to intensify each year as staffers seemed determined to convince the American public that Bush was succeeding in all aspects of his presidency.

Despite the strategies employed in the crafting of the state of the union speech as well as the "roll-out" media activities, Bush often seemed to be at the mercy of the circumstances in which he spoke (the state of the economy, world events, and public approval ratings), which often drove the resulting narrative in his press coverage. For Bush, foreign policy matters often provided a better sound bite for the news media, with the president making resolute statements about the need for military success or celebrating military victories. However, Bush could never quite escape the charge of lacking a vision for domestic and economic matters, and this continued to pose a challenge for his advisors in preparing the annual state of the union address. The continued use of "laundry lists" for domestic and economic issues did not help in this regard. Even while acknowledging that a programmatic, as opposed to a thematic approach, in writing the state of the union speech was not strategically sound, advisors could not free themselves from the practice for fear of not hitting every important policy point (and thus not recognizing every important constituency within the executive branch). This also hurt Bush's performance during the speech; while Bush was not a bad public speaker, he was not a performer on the level of Ronald Reagan, who excelled in venues such as the state of the union. As a result, by 1992, "Bush's speaking style, his unwillingness to practice and habit of ad-libbing continued to dog him."[109] Even when things were going relatively well for the Bush White House, many in the news media could never break away from the initial image of Bush that emerged during the 1988 campaign, which was also the initial strategy evoked by the Bush team—that Bush was no Ronald Reagan. That theme emerged time and again, particularly during the major public addresses analyzed in this chapter. While the White House strategy seemed to consistently focus on the substance of the message, the strategy lacked a means of conveying the message in a way that would consistently project Bush as a strong leader. While Bush often received high marks for his public actions in the role of commander in chief, the inability to articulate a strong and coherent vision for domestic policies would continue to challenge the Bush White House throughout the entire four-year term.

CHAPTER 5

Bush's Public Activities

Major Policy Addresses

Presidents now rely heavily on public events as an essential component of governing in a media-saturated political environment. A steady increase has occurred in the number of public events, particularly the use of major policy addresses, since the start of the 1980s. This can be attributed to the influence and expansion of television coverage, changes in the political environment that have encouraged presidents to go public more often, and each president's public leadership style. As the 24-hour news cycle emerged with the expansion of cable throughout the 1980s, and as the Internet emerged as a dominant medium in the 1990s, presidents found more opportunities for media coverage. This also increased the need for an effective White House communication strategy; not only did the expectation increase for presidents to be more visible on center stage, but more opportunities also existed for "photo ops" at more routine events and for advisors to craft a strategy in an attempt to keep the upper hand in how the president and his message were portrayed. It is not surprising that while expanding technologies allowed an increase in the amount and type of White House coverage, the president's schedule of public events also increased.

From the start of his administration, George H. W. Bush acknowledged that he would not be viewed as a great communicator in the vein of Ronald Reagan: "On that day back in 1989, the most important thing I told the speechwriters was, 'Listen, I'm no Ronald Reagan.' I was not the Great Communicator. Many times we had to rein in the rhetoric; often words meant to evoke emotion in the audience evoked even more emotion in me. I told them that if they wrote a speech that was a 'ten,' they'd better cut it back to an 'eight' for me. But I'd like to think that, given the historic times and the unprecedented events that unfolded on my watch, I did all right. I tried my best under extraordinary circumstances. We all did. We tried to set a tone that brought people out of themselves, out of their circumstances, to come together to serve others and build a better life for all—whether in the United States or around the world."[1] Early on, the public strategy that emerged consistently reflected a desire to not let public events dictate too much of Bush's day-to-day job of governing. A February 1989 White House memo describes pursuing the public aspects of the presidency as a way to "[keep] after it as a part of political leadership. Increasingly, this involves not only mobilizing support for policy goals and initiatives, but establishing outreach efforts to generate good will for the Administration and the President. . . . [A]11 such efforts should: *Reflect the President's personal style of leadership and communication* and at all times *respect the integrity of the office of President* of the United States; *Foster trust for the institution of government, the Administration and the President* and be *accurate and consistent* in all dealings with the public; *Facilitate policy making*—the goal is to make the policymakers,' the Administration's, and the President's job easier (not create another process with an end in itself) [emphasis in original]."[2]

The public aspects of the presidency and the process necessary for developing and implementing the public strategy did, however, require tremendous attention from White House staff. An irony of the Bush years is found in the number of public addresses in which he participated—a total of 1,972 public activities (which includes major and routine addresses) between 1989 and 1993, which represents an increase of 476 public activities from Ronald Reagan's first term (1981 to 1985). While Bush had hoped to move away from the public stagecraft and the emphasis on presidential performance during the Reagan years, the political and media environments in which he governed demanded that he nonetheless adopt a detailed communication strategy implemented through an increased number of public events in a wide variety of venues.[3] This chapter analyzes a sampling of Bush's major policy addresses and their attendant public events as part of the overall communications strategy. While a major policy address by itself demands much attention from White House staffers in various offices (including speechwriting, press, and media affairs), the ancillary events that go along with a major policy address (press conferences, presidential and surrogate interviews, photo ops, speech distribution and other advance work, and other activities) also play a large role in the communications strategy for a specific presidential speech. The major policy addresses selected for analysis include a variety of policy topics, both foreign and domestic, and also include various venues for the speech itself. The selected examples demonstrate the public strategies employed by the Bush White House in an attempt to mobilize support for administration policies.

Major Policy Addresses

Outside of inaugural and state of the union addresses, presidents rely on various settings to make a major policy announcement, including an address from the White House (including the Oval Office, the East Room, or other rooms such as the library), at the United Nations or while traveling abroad (including addresses to a nation's legislative body), at various gatherings of major interest groups or other organizations, and university commencements. These types of public activities contribute to the president's perpetual campaign style of governing, can allow the president to tailor his comments to the specific group, and can occur with frequency as "targeted appeals" to announce specific policy positions.[4] The assumption behind the strategy of such events is that the intended audience reaches far beyond those in attendance at the event. Reaching that broader audience, then, falls to the news media to convey the president's policy message. As such, the White House strategy in both the development of the speech itself and the logistics of the event, as well as accompanying interviews or briefings (with the president or surrogates) for the press, can play an important role in whether or not the news media pays attention to the event. While an "address to the nation" usually merits live television coverage, and while some other policy addresses will now be shown live on cable news networks, substantial coverage of a president's remarks is not always guaranteed. Like presidents before him and since, Bush used these types of speeches as a way to announce a variety of policy proposals throughout his four years in office.

Remarks at the Solidarity Workers Monument in Gdansk, July 11, 1989

Foreign policy expertise is one of the strongest components of Bush's presidential legacy, as international matters played an influential role in his administration right from the start. Bush found himself governing in a time when rapid changes were occurring around the globe, most notably the end of the Cold War and the United States government's changing relationship with the Soviet Union. Bush made a total of 182 foreign public appearances during his presidency, which is a significant increase from previous administrations.[5] During the first few months of his administration, Bush found himself dealing with democratic reform movements in Poland and Hungary and the Tiananmen Square protests and massacre in China. The speech scheduled for Gdansk, Poland, was part of Bush's second trip to Europe, with additional stops in Poland, Hungary, France (for an economic summit), and the Netherlands. According to Bush, on his departure for the European trip, he was visiting Poland and Hungary as "nations on the threshold of a new era, nations where the spirit of freedom is strong. In both countries, we're witnessing remarkable changes, welcome developments no one would have thought possible even a year ago. New voices are shaping the course of national affairs, and both countries are on the path towards economic rebirth and political pluralism. My visit underscores the growing importance our nation sees in the changing face of central Europe."[6]

This trip had a strong public relations element for Bush to show his support for the democratic movements in both countries. The speech itself was one of thirteen public or press events while in Poland, with the remarks at the Workers Monument in Gdansk as the premier public event.[7] The Poland trip also provided many good photo opportunities for Bush, as "the drama was provided by the setting and the crowd. . . . The crowd waved American flags and hand-painted placards and flashed the 'V' sign." The speech in Gdansk was interrupted by chants of "Lech Walesa" and "President Bush!"[8] Both Bush and Walesa were overwhelmed by the response: "Crowds turned out in the streets, and [Bush] was again deeply affected by the passion in the air and the energy and resolve of the reformers he met."[9] Bush's diary entry later that night showed his emotional response to the crowds: "There's no way to properly describe the excitement at Gdansk. There were thousands of people lining the street going into town, and then estimates of up to 250,000 people in the square in front of the shipyard. It was an emotional moment with grown men and women crying. There were all kinds of signs of affection for the United States all along the way, and there were flags; handwritten signs welcoming me; and friendship between the United States and Poland."[10] However, while Bush would routinely receive more positive coverage from the press for his foreign policy leadership, a more positive view of Bush as a foreign policy leader did not fully emerge until the end of 1989, after his meeting with Soviet leader Mikhail Gorbachev at the Malta Summit. According to Mark Rozell, "The press perceptions of Bush's foreign policy leadership in 1989 largely reflected the view that the president acted too cautiously in the face of unprecedented international upheavals."[11]

The strategy behind the Gdansk speech, which was one of many on this European trip, was specific—a good speech with a dramatic and memorable setting. In a memo to speechwriter Ed McNally, researcher Bob Simon described the public relations potential of the speech in Gdansk:

> I think the benchmark we should be shooting for is Kennedy's "Ich bin ein Berliner" speech (attached). By that I *don't* mean using some snappy Polish phrase (although there's nothing wrong with that.) What I mean is that the President is speaking at a place and at a time that could be one of the turning points in world history, assuming the Polish move toward democracy flourishes. By giving a good speech, I think we can make that moment even more dramatic. My greatest hope is that the press and the public will look back on this speech in 2 or 3 years and say George Bush helped inspire the people of Poland to fulfill their destiny to join the free people of Europe without provoking a Soviet backlash—something that just a few months ago most people thought was impossible. In terms of the structure and content, I think this speech should be short and clean, with about 5 big applause lines sprinkled throughout. Four to 4 ½ pages should be plenty. If you notice JFK's speech is quite short, and is mostly rhetoric, with few facts, policy or quotes. We are lucky in that most of the policy will be in the Sejm speech, so we are freed from the burden of having to trudge through the details. The "news of the day" may be in the Sejm speech, but I think some sound bites and color from our Gdansk event are more likely to make good TV. I think it would be helpful to quote both the Pope and Lech Walesa. . . . There is also an interesting conjunction of events on June 12, 1987. The Pope was speaking at the same site in Gdansk that we will use, and on the same day, President Reagan was at the Berlin Wall, saying, 'Mr. Gorbachev, tear down this wall!' . . . As far as appealing to the Poles' great love of history, I think we should avoid weighing this speech down with a lot of historical facts and dates. My review of Polish history does not reveal much that meets our present needs. . . . The President had some great language in his Inaugural Address that is worth echoing in Gdansk. . . . I think we could both flatter the Poles and make a powerful point by comparing the Gdansk Solidarity Monument to the Statue of Liberty as one of the greatest monuments to human freedom in the world.[12]

After reading an early draft of McNally's speech, Bush responded with the following comments: "Some minor changes: 1. Good length 2. Good material 3. Let's try to think of *one* sentence that the speech will be remembered for."[13] McNally responded with what he believed was his "best effort to deliver what the President asked for—one memorable line by which the speech will be remembered." That line appeared in the first paragraph: "Of all the people on earth, we are perhaps closer in spirit than the people of any two countries."[14] That one line did not make the final draft, but the overall speech closely mirrored Simon's original memo to McNally on the contents of the speech. Bush gave few policy specifics in the address but provided much of the rhetorical imagery that his advisors were seeking. The speech began with praise for Poland and what the nation had endured throughout the Cold War:

> [T]he spirit of the Poles has been conveyed across the centuries and across the oceans, a dream that would not die. That dream was severely tested here in Gdansk. . . . In World War II, Poland lost everything—except her honor, except her dreams. . . . But for you, the war's end did not end the darkness. The cold war brought a long and chilly night of sorrow and hardship—and the dream was again denied. And yet there were glimmers of the long-awaited dawn. In the summer of 1980, you occupied the shipyards where we stand. And a patriotic electrician clambered over these iron gates and emerged as one of the heroes of our times—Lech Walesa. And above your streets a graceful monument rose, in the tradition of our own Statue of Liberty, to become a symbol recognized around the world as a beacon of hope. . . . Today, to those who think that hopes can be forever suppressed, I say: Let them look at Poland! To those who think that freedom can be forever denied, I say: Let them look at Poland! And to those who think that dreams can be forever repressed, I say: Look at Poland! For here in Poland, the dream is alive.[15]

Bush then shifted to the U.S. commitment to the democratic movement throughout central and eastern Europe: "Poles and Americans share a commitment to overcome the division of Europe and to redeem the promise that is the birthright of men and women throughout the world. Poles and Americans want Europe to be whole and free. A more democratic Poland can be a more prosperous Poland. . . . I outlined steps that

America is prepared to take to assist Poland as you move forward on the path of reform. It will not be easy. Sacrifice and economic hardship have already been the lot of the Polish people. And hard times are not yet at an end. Economic reform requires hard work and restraint before the benefits are realized. And it requires patience and determination. But the Polish people are no strangers to hard work and have taught the world about determination." Finally, Bush ended the address by repeating some of the themes and phrases from his inaugural address six months earlier: "The magic of America is not found in the majesty of her land. And, yes, our country has been blessed. But Poland, too, is a land of natural beauty—ample timber and ore and water and coal, abundant agriculture potential—and a talented, creative people that is determined to succeed. No, the magic of America is in an idea. I described it in my first moments as President of the United States: 'We know what works: Freedom works. We know what's right: Freedom is right. We know how to secure a more just and prosperous land for man on Earth.' And today you can rediscover a new land—a land of your dreams, a land of your own making, a Poland strong and proud. Poland is where World War II began. And Poland is where, and why, the cold war got started. And it is here, in Poland, where we can work to end the division of Europe."[16]

The speech in Gdansk became the top news story from the president's busy European schedule on the network newscasts that evening and in several major newspapers the next day. The lead story on the ABC, CBS, and NBC nightly news programs began with coverage of the Gdansk speech. Coverage of the speech found prominent placement on the front pages of leading newspapers, including, for example, the *New York Times*, *Washington Post*, *Los Angeles Times*, *Boston Globe*, *Christian Science Monitor*, and a mention in the "What's News" briefs on page one in the *Wall Street Journal*. Many of the stories captured the emotion of the crowd during Bush's speech. The *Los Angeles Times* reported: "With his back to a stark monument to workers slain in anti-government strikes, and his eyes gazing across a sea of hopeful faces and fluttering American and Polish flags, President Bush on Tuesday delivered an emotional plea for freedom and democracy on the site where the Solidarity trade union was born."[17] Similarly, in the *Boston Globe*: "At an emotional appearance yesterday with Lech Walesa before thousands of cheering supporters of the Solidarity trade union, President Bush urged Polish opposition leaders to avoid a bitter political struggle and encouraged Poles to remain patient with the hardships of economic realignment."[18] In the *New York Times*,

Maureen Dowd wrote about the setting of the speech but also focused on procedure in how an interpreter was used over Bush's voice while delivering the speech to the Polish citizens gathered for the event:

> In a vigorous appeal to thousands of workers at a shipyard in Gdansk, Poland, President Bush today urged the Solidarity movement to shed 'the legacy of distrust and shattered dreams' and to pull together with the Communist Party to create a brighter Poland. . . . In a speech that the President said he considered the emotional peak of his trip, he stood before the dramatic shipyard workers' monument outside the Gdansk factory gate where Solidarity was born. . . . But a deep, melodious voice, which could be heard as Mr. Bush began to gesture and talk about 'Solidarnosc' and 'Polska,' startled the Americans in the audience. In an unusual arrangement, the President's interpreter, Wiktor Litwinski, was standing behind the stage, giving simultaneous translation in Polish. The President, meanwhile, was talking into the system that went to American television viewers. The maneuver gave the effect of a badly dubbed foreign movie. Mr. Bush's voice was barely discernable to those in the shipyard, and it appeared that he was lip-synching the Polish translation. White House aides said afterward that they had arranged the translation so that Mr. Bush, who is known for his fast-paced style, could get through his 25-minute speech more quickly.[19]

While most news coverage seemed to provide a positive spin and focus on the public relations aspects that the White House had planned for, editorials and commentaries focused more intently on the challenges looming ahead for Bush in his dealings with the changing political climate in Eastern Europe, giving the president mixed reviews. An editorial in the *New York Times* suggested that while Bush's prudent language hit the mark, his specific plans for aid to Poland had room for improvement:

> As he set off on his current trip to Eastern Europe, President Bush recalled Woody Allen's line that 90 percent of life is just showing up. The point was movingly made yesterday by the crowds waiting in the rain to greet him in Hungary, and by Mr. Bush's appearance on a Gdansk stage before the workers of Solidarity in Poland. Whatever the content of his words, just the presence of an American President in the heart of Eastern Europe radiates democratic change. But the

> other 10 percent counts too, and so far, Mr. Bush has got it almost right. His words have been sensibly modest, but the modesty of his economic aid proposals for Poland, so clearly disappointing to Poles, diminishes the effect of his visit. What improbable scenes: George Bush on the rostrum of the Polish Parliament, and on a stage near the Solidarity monument in Gdansk. What appropriate words: sympathy for the Poles' need to overcome hardship by hard work—the way Polish immigrants have done in the United States. . . . The President gave no hint in his speech or demeanor that the United States was trying to exploit the crisis in the Eastern bloc. Nothing would do more to bolster the East's opponents of reform than ham-handedness. There are things the United States can do to promote change in the East; bloviating is not one of them. But economic assistance is, and that's where the Bush performance falls short.[20]

A *Washington Post* editorial provided a similar assessment: "Poland urgently needs help from the West. But there seems to be some disappointment in Warsaw and Gdansk that President Bush spoke in terms of millions rather than billions of dollars. Even if the Western governments were prepared to finance a Marshall Plan for Eastern Europe—and there's no sign of it—a simple infusion of money would have only a temporary effect. Mr. Bush pointed Poland in a productive as well as realistic direction when he talked about trade and investment. . . . None of these measures is dramatic, and none will transform Poland's prospects. . . . The president's pledges are reliable and will endure beyond the present surge of emotion. They invite Poland into the economic system that has made the West rich. As the Poles approach this great transition, Mr. Bush has demonstrated that they have friends who are ready to make themselves useful."[21]

In assessing the speech, R. W. Apple Jr. of the *New York Times* suggested that Bush's performance did not live up to the dramatic events unfolding in Europe:

> Before the trip, both Solidarity and General Jaruzelski had told aides to Mr. Bush that he would do them no favors by disdaining or criticizing Mr. Gorbachev while here, according to senior Administration sources. They wanted no wisecracks like a White House spokesman's description of Mr. Gorbachev as a "drugstore cowboy," a Polish lawyer said, because "nobody baits a bear when it's

> in a good mood—good moods aren't that common." Inevitably, the President's basic strategic decision to accede to that advice robbed his visit and especially his speeches of some of their drama. He was further undermined by a nightmarish series of logistical errors—his parked motorcade blocking the view of those who came to see him in Warsaw, a bad translation and amplification system at the shipyard that gave his voice a surreal, disembodied quality, conflicts between the needs of the elephantine White House press corps and those of the security men, and so on. In addition, Mr. Bush had trouble summoning the kind of inspirational eloquence that he can on occasion muster, as he did, for example, at the Republican National Convention last summer. Here he seemed more at home with the Little Leaguers he bantered with, or the youngsters who joined him, wide-eyed, for a run through a forest, than he did before the legislature or the crowd at the Solidarity rally.[22]

Hugh Sidey in *Time* offered a similar critique of Bush's performance:

> He was Uncle George on a historic dash through Eastern Europe, trying to reach out and touch everyone, striving to bring down to personal terms his doctrine of homegrown political and economic freedoms and what they could mean for the burdened people of the Soviet bloc. . . . What propelled Bush was his belief that history is calling him and the leaders of Poland and Hungary to forge some kind of new partnership quickly. Some untutored White House aide had predicted a roaring reception in Poland, much like the one John Kennedy evoked in Berlin in 1963. A little Kennedy-like rhetoric was even inserted into Bush's Gdansk speech ("To those who think that freedom can be forever denied, I say let them look at Poland"). That totally missed the meaning of these dramatic days. Gorbachev is more of an ally than a threat. On this trip there was no adversary for Bush to shake his fist at while summoning hoarse defiance in the streets.[23]

Newsweek pointed out, despite how Bush did not have much to offer Poland in terms of monetary aid, his "goofy exuberance" during the trip nonetheless struck the right tone: "Bush's European tour was no superpower swagger, but a diplomatic high-wire walk. His tools of persuasion had dwindled from the grandiose handouts of decades past to a few token dribbles of economic aid. . . . The president also managed to encourage two of Moscow's onetime satellites, Poland and Hungary, to press on along the path to democracy and free markets. The Bush style in Eastern Europe had all of its sometimes goofy exuberance: he jogged, gripped and grinned, plunged into crowds, kissed babies and jollied his hosts with gee-whiz enthusiasm. But the offbeat charm struck sparks. The sight of a U.S. president in Warsaw and Gdansk brought tears to Polish eyes, and the crowds cheered and chanted Bush's name. A few waved faded American flags, clearly saved for years for just such an opportunity."[24] And in *U.S. News and World Report*, Bush was credited with taking the offensive regarding the U.S. relationship with the Soviet Union, even if his actions were constrained by other factors: "With his unprecedented trip into Eastern Europe this week, President Bush finally turns the East-West highway into a two-way street. After seven forays by Soviet President Mikhail Gorbachev into Western Europe, Bush is now taking the offensive in the Kremlin's back yard at a time when the Soviet leader himself concedes that democratic urges are transforming the region. But America's ability to seize this unique opportunity is constrained by tight purse strings in Washington and by the danger that Western missteps could derail the region's fragile evolution toward political pluralism and economic freedom."[25]

Overall, the White House strategy succeeded in having the more symbolic event in Gdansk highlighted in news coverage (as opposed to the earlier events that day in Poland or the later events that evening in Hungary) thanks to the photo opportunities of Bush with Lech Walesa and the large cheering and emotional crowd of Polish citizens. Even the critiques of Bush's policy of aid to Poland and Hungary reflected budgetary constraints mostly out of his control, as well as the need for moderation in the president's language and actions on the dramatic changes occurring throughout Europe in the early days of the demise of communism. While critiqued for his style, Bush received more favorable coverage for the substance of his visit, which seemed to reflect a bit of deference to the president and his expertise in foreign policy.

Address to the Nation on the National Drug Control Strategy, September 5, 1989

Bush had highlighted the need to solve the nation's drug problem during the 1988 presidential campaign, yet he surprised many political observers by continuing to pursue the issue once in office. Not only did he appoint

William Bennett to the newly created position of "drug czar," but he devoted his first nationally televised address to the nation to the subject. Since by the fall of 1989 Bush had not yet given an Oval Office address, there was "concern among his senior aides that he had not achieved presidential stature in the public mind, which a prime-time address from the White House could remedy."[26] Advisors believed that the topic of illegal drugs would provide Bush an opportunity to give a sober yet presidential message to Americans on not only the scope of the problem but the solution as well. As Bush later recalled, "The first Oval Office address for a president is a big deal. . . . The speech was to announce our Drug Control Strategy, as the drug problem in the country was at an intolerable level. . . . The speechwriters had come up with an idea to dramatize the drug issue through the use of a very powerful image: a bag of crack cocaine that I would show to the nation during the course of the speech. . . . I went on TV, showed the nation the bag of crack ('this stuff is poison'), and indeed, it was a dramatic moment. Problem was, afterward someone mentioned to the media that it was not only from a drug bust in Lafayette Park instead of a couple of blocks away, but that it was deliberately arranged there by the DEA to help dramatize the speech. This was news to all of us, but it gave the press a juicy angle to cover, and diverted people's attention from the real issue."[27]

The image of Bush showing a national television audience a bag of crack cocaine certainly provided a memorable visual, which was the original goal of the speechwriters while planning the address. The strategy was outlined in a memo from Ed McNally to Chriss Winston, both members of the speechwriting team:

> It's full of terrific stuff—sober, Presidential, compelling. The "visuals" are pure inspiration, and sure to be remembered. Another way to keep this speech memorable is to incorporate a recurring theme, a sound bite that sums up the President's proposals in a single, neat phrase. . . . The surveys show that Americans are sick and tired of this scourge—casual use is plummeting—7 out of 10 black Americans say drugs represent America's #1 problem. ***America is ready for action. And America is ready for change.*** The President should declare that enough is enough—no more business as usual ("All deals are off?"). The President should announce that—starting today—***"We're changing the rules."*** For about a month the papers have been posing the question of the hour, the question that will be on everyone's

> mind as they sit down in their living rooms Tuesday night. It is simple and direct: ***"What is the President going to do about drugs?"*** The President's speech will be rated by how effectively this nine-word question is answered. But coming up with a simple answer to this question isn't easy. The truth is, the Administration's anti-drug proposals are complicated and diverse. However, each of the President's comprehensive proposals—on education, treatment, enforcement, and interdiction—can be summed up in a single, four-word phrase. The answer to the question of what we're going to do about drugs is: "***We're changing the rules*** [emphasis in original]."[28]

Regarding media coverage, the drug speech communications strategy included extensive advance work to promote the president's policy announcement. In early August, "satellite media tours" were planned for the day after the speech for key administration officials (including Drug Czar Bill Bennett, Attorney General Richard Thornburgh, Secretary of Housing and Urban Development Jack Kemp, Secretary of Health and Human Services Louis Sullivan, Secretary of Education Lauro Cavazos, Secretary of Transportation Sam Skinner, and Secretary of the Treasury Nicholas Brady) in "an effort to 'hit' local media markets that have high drug usage or trafficking problems." Many other events were planned throughout August and September to promote the drug speech and policy announcement before, the day of, and after the speech, including meetings for Bush with the Domestic Policy Council and the National Security Council (regarding international interdiction); listening sessions with constituency groups, press interviews, and press conferences and briefings with various White House officials; appearances by White House officials on news program (such as CNN's *Crossfire*) or other network specials (such as an NBC special by Tom Brokaw on drugs and crime in Los Angeles); columnist backgrounders and other distributions of information to members of the press; radio actualities; op-eds by cabinet members in seventeen major daily newspapers (to run the week of the speech and to include "a brief overview of the drug strategy and attention to the Cabinet agency's angle"); appearances by White House officials on morning news shows; and a regional media briefing.[29]

In addition, Bush wrote on op-ed that appeared in college newspapers across the country, and a magazine strategy was developed to place articles on the drug plan "by Cabinet agencies over a period of several months for reinforcement value."[30] Finally, several other public events were planned for Bush on the day of and in the days following the drug speech, including remarks to reporters a few hours prior to the speech; an exchange with reporters, remarks at a meeting with foreign ambassadors and state and local leaders, and a press conference, all on the National Drug Control Strategy the day after the drug speech; a speech to the American Legion annual convention in Baltimore two days after the drug speech; and speeches to the U.S. Hispanic Chamber of Commerce and the National Baptist Convention, both in New Orleans, three days after the drug speech.

In delivering his first address to the nation, Bush began the drug speech by outlining the significance of the drug problem in the United States and also provided the crack cocaine visual early on in the address:

> This is the first time since taking the oath of office that I felt an issue was so important, so threatening, that it warranted talking directly with you, the American people. . . . Our courts, our prisons, our legal system, are stretched to the breaking point. The social costs of drugs are mounting. In short, drugs are sapping our strength as a nation. . . . Our most serious problem today is cocaine, and in particular, crack. Who's responsible? Let me tell you straight out—everyone who uses drugs, everyone who sells drugs, and everyone who looks the other way. . . . This is crack cocaine seized a few days ago by Drug Enforcement agents in a park just across the street from the White House. It could easily have been heroin or PCP. It's as innocent-looking as candy, but it's turning our cities into battle zones, and it's murdering our children. Let there be no mistake: This stuff is poison.

Bush then moved to the specifics of his plan to fight illegal drugs: "No single policy will cut it, no matter how glamorous or magical it may sound. To win the war against addictive drugs like crack will take more than just a Federal strategy: It will take a national strategy, one that reaches into every school, every workplace, involving every family. . . . Tonight, I'm announcing a strategy that reflects the coordinated, cooperative commitment of all our Federal agencies. In short, this plan is as comprehensive as the problem." The plan included four major elements: doubling the federal assistance to state and local law enforcement and enlarge the criminal justice system; working with governments in Latin America to combat the power of the drug cartels (to which Bush declared "the rules have changed"); increasing federal funding for drug treatment; and developing preventative measures, including anti-drug education programs in schools. Bush concluded with an acknowledgment of forthcoming criticism of the plan: "Now, I know some will still say that we're not spending enough money, but those who judge our strategy only by its pricetag simply don't understand the problem. Let's face it, we've all seen in the past that money alone won't solve our toughest problems. To be strong and efficient, our strategy needs these funds. But there is no match for a united America, a determined America, an angry America. Our outrage against drugs unites us, brings us together behind this one plan of action—an assault on every front. This is the toughest domestic challenge we've faced in decades. And it's a challenge we must face not as Democrats or Republicans, liberals or conservatives, but as Americans."[31]

On the three news networks, a preview of the speech received top billing on all three broadcasts the evening of September 5, with live coverage following later in the evening. Bush's drug plan also remained the top news story the following evening on all three networks, which included political reaction to the plan, and drug-related stories stemming in part from the Bush speech and plan also led the newscasts on ABC and CBS on September 7, and as the second story in the NBC broadcast stemming from the president's public events that followed the address to the nation. Major newspapers also previewed the speech on September 5. For example, the *Los Angeles Times* focused on how the drug plan would be funded even prior to the speech being delivered: "Practically from the beginning, the White House has viewed today's presidential speech on drugs as one of the highlights of George Bush's first year in office. . . . Given the nation's intense interest in the drug problem, the speech is likely to set off partisan bickering over whether Bush is presenting truly new ideas or is packaging proposals that have already been offered by Democrats or are already being implemented. And, more than that, the big question is likely to be over how to pay the bill for the drug war. Over the long term, the President risks letting the drug issue turn into a major liability. After all, in his inaugural address, he pledged that 'this scourge will stop,' and it is far from certain that he, or any President, has the power to fulfill that promise. Presidents have been waging war on drugs for decades, and, so far, drugs have won."[32]

Much of the coverage in major newspapers the morning after Bush's speech focused on the criticism from Democrats and others about the lack of funding for the plan. According to the *New York Times*: "From Capitol Hill to state capitals and city halls across the country, Democrats criticized President Bush's $7.9 billion drug control strategy as being short on toughness, imagination and, most of all, money. . . . Many Democratic state and local officials applauded the overall thrust of the President's message, which called for shifting the focus from stopping drugs at the border to targeting traffickers on the street. But they faulted Mr. Bush on the specifics, saying his proposals did not go far enough to help cash-short state and local governments do their part."[33] Similarly, the *Boston Globe* reported: "President Bush last night undertook a risky but essential political gamble in launching his attack on illegal drugs, entering a war that offers slim prospects for a big win and must be paid for by taking money from entrenched federal programs. While appealing to Americans to recognize the human and national devastation of drug abuse, Bush's strategy stopped short of asking them to pay more taxes to attack the root causes of the problem: poverty and economic despair."[34] And in the *Washington Post*: "In what he described as a 'heart-to-heart talk with the American people,' President Bush last night outlined a federal anti-drug strategy that shies away from major funding increases or radical new programs in favor of 'coordinated, cooperative commitment' to address the problem by all government agencies."[35]

An op-ed by Randolph Ryan in the *Boston Globe* credited Bush with taking on a difficult domestic issue: "President Bush's advisers saw the speech he delivered last night as a test in leadership. They spent months debating substance, then weeks trying to find just the right voice. . . . Since they took the speech so seriously, so should the president's audience. Judges of style can argue whether he sprang gracefully from the diving board, or walked the plank, but what really matters is whether he is honest in acknowledging the roots of the drug problem, and framing the drug war in a credible way."[36] Not all pundits were as charitable, like John Podhoretz in the *Washington Times*: "George Bush performed competently, but only competently, in his first televised address to the nation from the Oval Office. It was a painstakingly choreographed and stage-managed 23 minutes, marred by a bit of overproduction and the president's inability to decide what to do with his hands. The speech itself was unexceptional, featuring not a single memorable phrase. Its lack of eloquence, and the president's manner of delivery, offered the public little in the way of a rallying cry. . . . His performance was so understated, in fact, that the president failed to communicate the outrage he said he felt at the extent of the drug problem."[37]

Other journalists focused more on the political ramifications of Bush's speech, as in *Newsweek's* coverage: "His rhetoric was merely earnest and his delivery was sometimes stilted—but last week, in the first nationally televised speech of his presidency, George Bush took personal command of the war against drugs. . . . The speech, which got broadly favorable notices except among congressional Democrats, was mostly remarkable for the fact that Bush had made it at all—for many of his advisers believe the drug war is a political loser. But Bush and Bennett face two other political problems as well. The first is that, despite the presidential speech and numerous background briefings by Bennett and his aides, their strategy is still poorly understood by many voters and policymakers. The second is that, for budgetary reasons, they are trying to fight the war against drugs on the cheap."[38] *U.S. News and World Report* offered a similar assessment:

> For George Bush, it was a rude return. Before he even unpacked his vacation bags last week, Democrats unleashed their most partisan attacks of the year, claiming he was too timid and parsimonious in his new drug plan. What was astonishing about the moment was its rarity, for the President has hardly ever been the butt of Democrats' attacks. White House officials began to wonder if the season of partisan battles was finally upon them. . . . As the Bush team looks ahead, the aides are asking themselves how long the White House can hold the high ground. . . . Now, entering the final third of the year, the White House plans to renew its domestic emphasis. There will be no splashy events, just more incrementalism that, barring unforeseen disasters, should keep Bush in unusually good shape through the remainder of his first year. The strategy behind Bush's fall drives is to neutralize Democrats on issues they usually consider their own—drugs, the environment and education.[39]

And, even days after the speech, other commentators were still providing their analysis of the president's speech and drug plan in the Sunday editions of newspapers, as in this column by Anthony Lewis of the *New York Times*:

> A President who was serious in declaring a new war on drugs would do at least these things: Make a commitment to provide treatment for addicts who want to give up the habit—millions of whom cannot now get into treatment programs. Propose plans, and money, to reduce demand by getting at the causes of Americans' lust for drugs. Recognize candidly that expensive efforts to stop the flow of drugs

> into this country have been worthless, and that interdiction can never be very successful. Make no promises without committing the funds to pay for them. . . . President Bush met none of those tests last week. The "strategy" he announced for the war on drugs was virtually empty of new money, realism or candor. What it was long on was politics. . . . The trouble is that the military rhetoric does not actually solve the American drug problem. The words in the White House have just about nothing to do with the reality on the ground.[40]

While a large majority of the calls to the White House after the speech were positive (280 of 339), journalists nonetheless criticized the program for Bush's attempt to fight the war on drugs "on the cheap."[41] Congress would later add $900 million in federal spending to Bush's proposal, but, according to Rozell, commentators "nonetheless did not credit the Bush program as visionary or even far-reaching. Bush's efforts on this issue reinforced, rather than called into question, the press image of him as a president lacking leadership vision."[42] In addition, the press coverage from this speech and related surrounding events showed the difficulty the Bush White House experienced in trying to engineer positive press coverage for Bush's efforts regarding domestic policy issues. During his four years in office, Bush received little credit in the press for domestic issues despite the extensive strategy developed by his communication advisors to promote Bush as an innovative and inspiring leader who was capable of tackling important issues both at home and abroad.

Remarks at the University of South Carolina Commencement Ceremony, May 12, 1990

Presidents often rely on university commencement addresses to propose major initiatives in domestic or foreign policy, often speaking in broader terms about a key issue while leaving the specifics of the policy to a later date or forum. Two notable examples of this include John F. Kennedy's American University speech in 1963 during which he discussed world peace and disarmament, and Lyndon Johnson's University of Michigan speech in 1964 during which he laid out his plans for a "Great Society." Bush delivered a total of twenty university commencement addresses during his four years in office (five each in 1989 and 1990; six in 1991; and four in 1992). Most often, he used these occasions to discuss various aspects of foreign policy. In 1989, three of the five speeches attempted to lay out Bush's world view. As Fitzwater explained to Sununu and Scowcroft prior to the first commencement speech at Texas A&M University:

> The month of May promises to be a high visibility time for foreign policy. Expectations for the foreign policy review are extraordinarily high. We must be able to publicly demonstrate that a coherent "world view" has emerged from this process. We propose three Presidential addresses as follows: 1) May 12—Commencement Address at Texas A&M. The President would deliver a "world view" address outlining the broad results of his policy review process. The speech could center on such concepts as the rise of democracy, the failures of Communism, and the growing rise of free enterprise in national economies. This speech should wrap up the entire "review." 2) May 21—Boston University Commencement Address. The President's address would focus on US-Soviet relations including such points as an assessment of those relations, where he expects that relationship to go and how he expects to guide that relationship. 3) May 24—Coast Guard Commencement Address. This event is scheduled two days prior to departure for the NATO Summit. As a result, the President would focus on NATO, our strong European ties, and the mutual US-European commitment to defense and international affairs.[43]

The remaining two speeches in 1989, at Alcorn State University and Mississippi State University, focused on family values (along with education and volunteerism).

In 1990 all five commencement addresses were centered on the theme of democracy and its influence around the world (including Oklahoma State University, Texas A&I University, University of South Carolina, Liberty University, and University of Texas). In 1991, Bush's commencement addresses included the topics of freedom (University of Michigan), education (Hampton University), China (Yale University), defense policy (U.S. Air Force Academy), the "American character" (U.S. Military Academy), and domestic policies (California Institute of Technology). By 1992, the four commencement addresses covered four prominent campaign issues: foreign policy (Florida International University), the economy and job creation (Southern Methodist University), family values (University of Notre Dame), and war and peace (U.S. Naval Academy). As many presidents do, Bush spoke at the military service academies commencements as well as several university commencements in his home state of Texas.

In the spring of 1990, Bush's commencement addresses all followed the general theme of democracy. As he told the audience at the University of Texas on May 19, "In four commencement addresses this spring, I have examined what makes democracy such a special way of life: how democracies refuse to perish by uniting in a strong defensive alliance; how they are strengthened by the rule of law; how freedom empowers people to solve the toughest problems; and how democracy leads to progress and adventure. Tonight, in this, for me, my final commencement address of the year, I want to discuss the personal side of democracy: what it offers us and what we can make of it."[44] One week prior at the University of South Carolina, the commencement address was intended to discuss "the emerging democracies in Eastern Europe, emphasizing that—along with greater freedom and economic reform—there is also a need to develop the **rule of law**."[45] Four specific initiatives were announced in the University of South Carolina speech: extending a new line of credit to Eastern Europe from the Export/Import Bank; sending a delegation of election observers to Romania and Bulgaria; working to broaden the mandate of the Conference on Security and Cooperation in Europe; and creating a Democracy Corps to send to Eastern Europe.[46] In addition, White House advisors viewed this occasion as "a significant speech because its theme takes the public discussion about Eastern Europe one step farther. That discussion has been about the introduction there of democracy, or at least, of free elections, and the introduction of capitalism—to these is now added the rule of law and implicitly, constitutionalism."[47]

During the speech, Bush focused on the changes occurring throughout Eastern Europe, what he termed as "some serious foreign policy observations." Bush stated at the start of the speech: "we are living in exciting times. In the past year, one nation after another has pulled itself out from under communism, onto the threshold of democracy. Each has endured great suffering, tremendous economic damage. . . . But what we can't see so easily, what's beneath the surface but no less real, is the moral damage, the deep scars on the spirit left by four decades of Communist rule. . . . That's the legacy, the landscape of moral destruction. The tragic consequence of four decades of Communist rule: a breakdown of trust." Bush then turned to more specific policy goals to help bring democracy to the former Eastern Bloc nations:

> Today I want to focus on how America can help these nations secure their freedoms, become a part of a Europe whole and free. . . . Poland,

> Czechoslovakia, and Hungary stand now, in the spring of 1990, as America stood in the summer of 1787. Who will be their Franklins, their Washingtons, their Hamiltons, their Madisons, their men and women of towering genius, the nation builders who will set in place the firm foundations of self-government? . . . And today I'm pleased to announce four new initiatives, four steps that the United States will take to support democratic development in Eastern Europe. First, America will continue to act to advance economic freedom. . . . And second, the United States will work to help ensure free and fair elections in Eastern Europe. . . . Third, America will work to broaden the mandate of the CSCE, the Conference on Security and Cooperation in Europe. . . . Fourth and finally, we will work to strengthen the foundations of free society in Eastern Europe. And I am pleased to announce today the creation of a Citizens Democracy Corps.

Bush concluded by reminding the audience of the work that still needed to be done to secure democracy around the globe:

> America has much to contribute, much it can do to help these nations move forward on the path to democracy. . . . There is still work to be done. In the Baltic States, where people struggle for the right to determine their own future, we Americans, so free to chart our own course, identify with their hopes and aspirations. For, you see, we're committed to self-determination for Lithuania and Latvia and Estonia. And ultimately, the Soviet Union itself, now committed to openness and reform, will benefit from a Europe that's whole and free. Democracy and freedom threaten absolutely no one. . . . And now it falls upon you, the graduating class of this great university, to uphold our American ideals not in times of war, thank God, but in a time of tremendous excitement, helping these nations secure the freedom that your fathers and grandfathers fought for, the freedom millions only dreamed of until today.[48]

Bush delivered both the University of South Carolina and Liberty University commencement addresses on the same day (with the latter speech delivered later in the day), but it was the Liberty University address that received more attention on the network newscasts that evening. The South Carolina speech was mentioned on both ABC and NBC as part of each network's top news story about Bush and volunteerism (the topic of the Liberty University speech), as well as in the CBS story of the Liberty University commencement address as Bush's attempt to appease the right wing of the Republican Party (the fifth story in the broadcast). Each story only mentioned that Bush had given the speech, however, and did not focus on the content of the first of the two commencement speeches that day. In major newspapers, the speech did not automatically make it onto front pages across the country, and coverage in general was not extensive. In the *Washington Post*, one of the only papers to give the speech placement on page one, Bush's plan to create a "citizens democracy corps" was highlighted:

> President Bush today summoned the nation to help complete the "unfinished business" of securing democracy across Eastern Europe by exporting not only American money but also the American experience with two centuries of democracy. In a commencement address he called "a reflection on democratic change," the president announced the launching of a private-sector "citizens democracy corps" to carry American expertise to Eastern Europe. He also announced a liberalized line of credit to help Poland finance the purchase of U.S. machinery, technology and services as it tries to restructure its economy.... Addressing about 1,600 graduates of the University of South Carolina, Bush spoke of the nations of Eastern Europe on the "threshold of democracy" and the responsibility of the United States to secure those democracies by rooting them in democratic institutions. The United States, he said, must help the new democracies build "political systems based on respect for individual freedom, for the right to speak our mind, to live as we wish, to worship as our conscience tells us we must."[49]

In the *New York Times*, Maureen Dowd reported on page ten:

> President Bush said today that he would create a volunteer corps to try to strengthen the emerging democracies in Central and Eastern Europe. In one of several foreign-policy speeches before the summit meeting this month with President Mikhail S. Gorbachev, Mr. Bush said he would try to export his "thousand points of light" theme through a new Citizens Democracy Corps that would serve as an information clearinghouse for United States volunteer programs

> for Europe. Giving a commencement address at the University of South Carolina in Columbia, Mr. Bush said the volunteer corps could help the new democracies in Europe build political and legal systems to shore up their freedom. . . . Mr. Bush has been sharply criticized in Congress as missing an opportunity to help fledgling democracies overseas and in Eastern Europe in particular. Democrats have said that he and Secretary of State James A. Baker 3d have been stingy with foreign aid to fragile democracies. . . . Mr. Bush has also been accused by several conservative Republican senators of sacrificing the aspirations of the Baltic republics to the needs of Mr. Gorbachev.[50]

And in the *Boston Globe*:

> President Bush, in one of his sharpest attacks on the Soviet Union's past control of Eastern Europe, accused communist regimes there yesterday of perverting public institutions as well as the human spirit. In a commencement address less than three weeks before he meets with President Mikhail S. Gorbachev to discuss the new order of nations in Europe, Bush criticized the effect of the communist domination of Eastern Europe with some of the harshest language of his presidency. Bush has been accused frequently of not responding strongly enough to the collapse of Communism in Eastern Europe last year and, more recently, to the Soviet economic crackdown on the independence drive in Lithuania. . . . Yesterday, Bush aides expressed satisfaction with his speech, saying it showed the depth of his feelings toward the Soviet Union for its past abuses as well as his commitment toward improving the standard of living in the emerging democracies. . . . Despite Bush's intense rhetoric about the changes in Eastern Europe, however, the four steps that he announced in his speech to further the reforms were modest in scope and extent.[51]

A competing story about Bush's visit to South Carolina, however, received prominent play in many news organizations, which shows the difficulty the White House can have in maintaining press attention on the planned event. The "extra" story stemmed from an interesting exchange Bush had with the traveling White House press corps about their exercise habits (or lack thereof). The basic story line followed closely with the report provided by the *Washington Post*:

> Irked that reporters traveling with him declined to join him on an early morning run, President Bush today issued a stern lecture to the "slovenly" press for failing to share his enthusiasm for physical fitness. White House reporters got a 7 A.M. wake-up call from Bush aides reporting that the president was going running in 15 minutes and that they should report for duty. Bush invited the press, which usually watches from the sidelines, to join him. . . . When he finished, Bush approached the group watching and delivered his lecture, said to have been at least half in jest. "The rest of you lazy guys, get out there and run," he said, "A fit America is a fine America. A fit America is a strong America. A fit America should include photo dogs [his term for photographers] as well as print reporters who slovenly sit back in the grandstands while some of us are out running." Then he turned to another pet peeve, the "boom men" who hold microphones on long poles to pick up the president's words more clearly. One of them dropped his mike on a table in the Oval Office recently and Bush complained of ruined antiques there. Bush said that if they worked out, they would have more "strength in the forearms to keep these microphones up in the air." The lecture did not sit well with reporters who arose at 4 A.M. Friday to cover events until 8 P.M.[52]

Address to the Nation Announcing Allied Military Action in the Persian Gulf

U.S. military action in the Persian Gulf in early 1991 to remove Iraqi troops from Kuwait, named Operation Desert Storm, represented a high point of Bush's presidency regarding foreign policy success as well as popularity and support with the American people. Bush announced the beginning of military action in the gulf on the evening of January 16, 1991, with an address to the nation. Combat lasted until February 28; the military operation was both brief and successful. Bush had wide support through a broad international coalition of troops from many other nations and, through his public actions, had "used his rhetorical situation to authoritatively define, defend, and shape the conflict through its many states and to publicly manage issues of international authority and sovereignty."[53] Bush's popularity with the American public soared between January 16 with the start of the air attacks on Iraq until the February 28 cease-fire. Bush enjoyed strong support in the press as well, including praise from several prominent journalists who were often critical of the president. Despite media praise for his actions as commander-in-chief, and a record approval rating that hit 91 percent immediately after the cease-fire, positive press coverage of Bush would not last once the nation's attention returned to more domestic matters, with press coverage that "turned from bouquets to brickbats."[54]

Throughout the fall of 1990, with the buildup of U.S. troops in the Persian Gulf in preparation for an invasion (termed Operation Desert Shield), the Bush White House developed specific public strategies in terms of Bush's public statements and media coverage. For example, in a November 1990 memo to the president, Demarest outlined the public strategy to gain public support for an eventual invasion:

> Here is an outline of some possible communications activities which you and key senior Administration officials could perform over the next three weeks to strengthen public support for Operation Desert Shield. This communications plan would reassure the American people as to the objectives and purpose of our deployment, and would revolve around your Thanksgiving trip to Saudi Arabia. Specifically, the plan would include three stages: before, during and after the trip. *PRE-TRIP*: Op-ed pieces with leading foreign policy experts in support of Desert Shield. We are working with Secretary Cheney (for the *Wall Street Journal*), General Scowcroft (*Washington Post*), former President Nixon (*New York Times*), and possibly General Powell, Henry Kissinger, Zbigniew Brzezinski, Cy Vance, and Howard Baker. Op-eds would then be collected and distributed to our key constituent leaders. A Q&A with General Scowcroft for *U.S. News and World Report*. An op-ed for *Time* magazine. A bylined article for *Newsweek* by you. A half-hour interview by CNN, which would focus on your personal views of the crisis. A satellite media tour with the Vice President, Secretary Cheney, Governor Sununu, General Powell, General Scowcroft, and Secretary Baker. *DURING TRIP*: All speeches (Europe and Middle East) are clearly cross-linked with the theme of the new world order. Press conference in Paris, and press availability in Egypt, Germany, and Czechoslovakia. You deliver USO-sponsored T-shirt and scroll containing the names of 14,000 supportive citizens in Los Angeles to Armed Forces. Op-eds are recirculated among the largest newspapers and news wires. *POST-TRIP*: A live, 10-minute

> address to the nation which would be a personal reflection of the Gulf situation, and would talk about the troops, and their dedication and sense of purpose. This would take place immediately upon your return on Friday, November 23rd, at 9:00 P.M. A regional reporters briefing, which would include Secretary Cheney, General Powell, General Scowcroft, Bob Gates or other senior Administration officials. A "White House on the road" concept, which would involve senior Administration officials working Desert Shield speeches into existing beyond-the-beltway travel plans. Possible venues would include local American Legion and VFW halls, civic and business organizations, and conferences and conventions. Several Roosevelt Room briefings for key constituent leaders to brief them on your trip, and to allow them the opportunity to express reservations and concerns to you directly. Various groupings would include religious, business, labor, and ethnic leaders.[55]

By December 1990, as the use of military force to remove Saddam Hussein's troops from Kuwait seemed more inevitable, advisors strategized how to maintain public support with the presence of 24-hour news coverage on CNN. As Demarest wrote to Sununu, Scowcroft, and Fitzwater: "CNN's new daily feature 'Countdown to January 15th' is just a preview of the intense media interest we'll experience the first two weeks in January. No doubt every other Member of Congress will come back on January third prepared to introduce resolutions and make floor speeches and it is likely they will stay in session for the whole month. Given this, it is critical that the messages from our Administration are coherent, consistent, and well focused. Attached is a draft thematic outline that should guide all of our communication and outreach activity during January. Over the Holidays the Gulf working group will develop a plan to articulate these themes. For the last three weeks this group has generated events and activities designed to help establish a steady, drum-beat of support for our deployment in the Gulf."[56] The "Gulf Strategy January Themes and Messages" memo for January 1991 included:

> 1. The President's goals, and *the goals of the international community, are clear*: The immediate, complete and unconditional withdrawal of Iraq from Kuwait; The restoration of Kuwait's legitimate government; and A commitment to the security and stability of the Persian

> Gulf. 2. The President has *emphasized repeatedly that we want to achieve these goals peacefully*, but the U.N. Resolutions now provide for achieving these goals by the use of all necessary means, including force, after January 15, 1991. . . . 3. *As a nation, the United States is united* on the necessity of standing up to Iraq's aggression. . . . 4. We have been patient for five months waiting for the sanctions to take hold and force Saddam to withdraw his forces from Kuwait. *We cannot afford to be patient any longer*. . . . 5. *We are still prepared to "go the extra mile"* as evidence by the President's proposal for a meeting between Secretary of State James Baker and Iraqi Foreign Minister Tariq Aziz which will take place January 9, 1991, in Switzerland.[57]

The so-called "Gulf working group" was charged with coordinating the public relations aspect of military actions in the Persian Gulf, and sought national unity through congressional and public support.[58] The public statements made by Bush to the press regarding military action in the Gulf "were primarily directed toward the American people, whose support was crucial to winning over Congress."[59] During the first two weeks of January, Bush actively engaged with reporters on the situation unfolding in the Persian Gulf; he held a question-and-answer session with reporters on January 4, gave a radio address on the situation in the Gulf on January 5, had an exchange with reporters and a news conference on January 9, and held another news conference on January 12.[60] When Bush addressed the nation on the night of January 16, some of the same themes that Americans had been hearing for months were repeated about why Bush had committed U.S. troops to free Kuwait: "Just 2 hours ago, allied air forces began an attack on military targets in Iraq and Kuwait. These attacks continue as I speak. Ground forces are not engaged. This conflict started August 2nd when the dictator of Iraq invaded a small and helpless neighbor. Kuwait—a member of the Arab League and a member of the United Nations—was crushed; its people, brutalized. Five months ago, Saddam Hussein started this cruel war against Kuwait. Tonight, the battle has been joined. This military action, taken in accord with United Nations resolutions and with the consent of the United States Congress, follows months of constant and virtually endless diplomatic activity on the part of the United Nations, the United States, and many, many other countries."

During the short speech, Bush highlighted his diplomatic efforts along with the alliance he had forged with other nations:

> Now the 28 countries with forces in the Gulf area have exhausted all reasonable efforts to reach a peaceful resolution—have no choice but to drive Saddam from Kuwait by force. We will not fail. . . . Our objectives are clear: Saddam Hussein's forces will leave Kuwait. . . . Some may ask: Why act now? Why not wait? The answer is clear: The world could wait no longer. Sanctions, though having some effect, showed no signs of accomplishing their objective. . . . While the world waited, Saddam Hussein systematically raped, pillaged, and plundered a tiny nation, no threat to his own. . . . While the world waited, Saddam sought to add to the chemical weapons arsenal he now possesses, an infinitely more dangerous weapon of mass destruction—a nuclear weapon. And while the world waited, while the world talked peace and withdrawal, Saddam Hussein dug in and moved massive forces into Kuwait. . . . While the world waited, while Saddam stalled, more damage was being done to the fragile economies of the Third World, emerging democracies of Eastern Europe, to the entire world, including to our own economy. . . . While the world waited, Saddam Hussein met every overture of peace with open contempt. . . . Tonight, 28 nations—countries from 5 continents, Europe and Asia, Africa, and the Arab League—have forces in the Gulf area standing shoulder to shoulder against Saddam Hussein.

To conclude, Bush returned to his familiar foreign policy theme about achieving a new world order:

> This is an historic moment. We have in this past year made great progress in ending the long era of conflict and cold war. We have before us the opportunity to forge for ourselves and for future generations a new world order—a world where the rule of law, not the law of the jungle, governs the conduct of nations. . . . We have no argument with the people of Iraq. Indeed, for the innocents caught in this conflict, I pray for their safety. Our goal is not the conquest of Iraq. It is the liberation of Kuwait. . . . No President can easily commit our sons and daughters to war. They are the Nation's finest. Ours is an all-volunteer force, magnificently trained, highly motivated. . . . And let me say to everyone listening or watching tonight: When the troops we've sent in finish their work, I am determined to bring them home as soon as possible. Tonight, as our forces fight, they and

> their families are in our prayers. May God bless each and every one of them, and the coalition forces at our side in the Gulf, and may He continue to bless our nation, the United States of America.[61]

On the day of the address to the nation, Bush wrote the following in his diary: "I have never felt a day like this in my life. I am very tired. I didn't sleep well and this troubles me because I must go to the nation at 9 o'clock. . . . Well, it is now 10:45 at night. I am about to go to bed. I did my speech to the nation at 9 o'clock. I didn't feel nervous about it at all. I wrote it myself. I knew what I wanted to say, and I said it. And I hope it resonates."[62] After the speech, Bush learned that he had addressed the largest U.S. television audience on record, with 79 percent of television sets tuned in to hear the president announce that U.S. troops had invaded Kuwait to expel Iraqi forces.[63] Bush's speech had been covered live on all major news networks, with extensive coverage following the speech that lasted for days, with much regular television programming pre-empted as Americans tuned in to the first war broadcast live in the cable television age.[64]

During the Gulf War, Bush enjoyed some of the most favorable press coverage of his presidency. He continued to speak with reporters and take their questions in the days following the initial invasion on January 16; he had two exchanges with reporters on January 17, a news conference on January 18, and had exchanges with reporters on January 21 and January 24.[65] However, some media experts observed that the rally-round-the-flag press coverage that helped Bush's approval ratings did not meet the usual standard of the press as government watchdog. According to Marvin Kalb, during the Gulf War, "the American people were short-changed, in part because the press engaged in that most dangerous of professional practices, namely, patriotic journalism. . . . At no time was this saccharin journalism more on display, from early morning until late at night, than during the Gulf War. . . . Anchors and reporters struck up a we-vs.-they form of dialogue, which had the effect of suffocating press skepticism."[66]

Press coverage of the speech itself was mostly positive, portraying Bush as a calm and confident commander-in-chief ready to lead the U.S. military into combat. In the *Los Angeles Times*: "President Bush, asserting that the United States and its allies had 'no choice' other than war, said Wednesday night the massive bombing raids on Iraq were intended to knock out Saddam Hussein's nuclear weapons potential and to destroy his chemical weapons arsenal. . . . [Bush showed] little emotion and none of the fidgeting he has displayed in recent public appearances as the Persian Gulf crisis grew ever tenser. . . . Bush's speech had been prepared over several weeks, in anticipation of the moment that arrived Wednesday night. With much of the nation riveted by the initial, live broadcast reports of the aerial attack, the address allowed him to present to a tremendous audience a terse, point-by-point explanation for the military action and a brief listing of its objectives."[67] Similar coverage appeared in the *Boston Globe*: "Bush appeared to be calm during the 11-minute address, by far the most riveting moment of his presidency and perhaps the most dramatic White House address since President Nixon announced his resignation in 1974. . . . In his speech, Bush provided the first assessment of the operation, saying he had been assured by Gen. H. Norman Schwarzkopf, the US military commander in Saudi Arabia, that the air operations were succeeding. . . . He also bitterly denounced Saddam Hussein for allowing his troops to carry out 'unspeakable atrocities' on Kuwait and its people."[68]

Front page coverage in the *New York Times* focused, in part, on reactions to the start of the war: "Other rhythms of daily life skipped a beat as soon as the allied fighter planes began crisscrossing the Iraqi sky. The President's speech interrupted music videos on the MTV cable-television network, which played peace songs from the 1960's afterwards. In Times Square, even the strippers at the all-nude Paris Theater clustered inside the red-curtained lobby, watching television news. And some Americans worried how close to home the conflict might come."[69] For the Associated Press, Walter Mears highlighted the potential political stakes of the Gulf War for Bush:

> In the end, it came to George Bush alone to make the judgment unleashing the Desert Storm of war against Iraq, a decision that stakes his presidency on clear and relatively swift victory. . . . And all else had failed, he said in a somber television report to the nation Wednesday night as American, British, Saudi and Kuwaiti warplanes struck at Iraqi military targets. . . . Bush stressed that the strikes were by an international force, part of a 28-nation alliance against Iraq. That force, though, is overwhelmingly American. And it was Bush's administration that put the coalition together, lobbied through the U.N. authorization of force, and got the Jan. 15 deadline set as a compromise. When each of those steps failed to get Saddam out of Iraq, Bush ordered the attack, saying the Iraqi leader had "tried to make this a dispute between Iraq and the United States of America." But at times it has seemed much more personal than that: Each

> president has called the other names. Campaigning for Republicans last fall, Bush made Saddam the villain of almost every stump speech, likened him to Adolf Hitler, promised to bring him to heel. . . . With swift victory, Bush could regain the political standing he held before his budget and tax increase troubles of 1990. A long struggle, with a heavy casualty toll, could cripple him politically.[70]

Adam Nagourney offered a similar assessment in *USA Today*, along with the seemingly requisite comparison between Bush's rhetorical skills and those of Reagan:

> President Bush convincingly outlined his reasons for attacking Iraq Wednesday and—at least temporarily—rallied the public to his side, political analysts said. For a president who has never excelled on television, Bush—in one of the most important speeches of his political career—appeared calm, decisive and thoroughly convinced about the need for a mission that may cost American lives. . . . Bush spoke for 12 minutes at a desk bedecked with American flags. With a white handkerchief tucked into a deep-blue suit, he kept his hands folded and stared into the camera. He appeared sober, rather than angry or emotional. Bush has never been able to master television the way Ronald Reagan did, as was clear last night. He may have seemed strained when he attempted to employ the Reaganesque technique of quoting letters from soldiers. But analysts said that given the gravity of the speech—and the inclination of Americans to rally around a president in times of crisis—those shortcomings were insignificant.[71]

Assessments of Bush's speech in the two Washington papers offered two distinct perspectives. John Podhoretz of the *Washington Times* praised Bush's performance: "George Bush's 12-minute address to the nation from the Oval Office was direct and plain, with the simplicity that makes for sound bites and headlines. As such, it was easily the most successful speech of his presidency. Mr. Bush even borrowed from the Reagan speech scrapbook—which he has been loath to do as president—by quoting from five persons in uniform whose letters made the moral and tactical case for war. . . . The president even went in for a rare display of high-flown rhetoric."[72] However, Tom Shales of the *Washington Post* had little, if any, praise: "George Bush spoke to the nation from the Oval Office for 12 minutes, just after 9 P.M. 'Operations are proceeding according to plan,' Bush said. He referred again to 'unspeakable atrocities' and to 'terrible crimes and tortures' committed by the Iraqis occupying Kuwait, but Bush offered no evidence or examples. Still, he seemed encouragingly assured. . . . It was not a stirring speech. But Bush's never are."[73]

Evan Thomas in *Newsweek* provided an assessment of Bush's character and personality as president and the political ramifications of his actions in the Gulf:

> Every president, in wartime, has an image he wants to project. . . . George Bush wants to show self-control. According to his advisers, his model of how not to behave is Alexander Haig, the former secretary of state who announced to the nation, "I am in control" when Ronald Reagan was shot in 1981. . . . Bush wants to appear unruffled and unflappable in times of stress. To openly grieve or gloat, he has been taught since school days, is a poor show. The problem is that Bush is, by nature, an emotional man. He is an enthusiast with a kind of rambunctious, goofy charm. He can also be sentimental, weepy or blue. His private moods have swung in very human ways over the months of the crisis—from fear to resolution to impatience to calm and back to edginess again, say his aides. To choke up in public, at a time of crisis, would be unforgivable to Bush. But he has a poor poker face. As he often does in televised addresses, the president fixed an anxious half grin on his face last week as he spoke to the nation of subjects that are grave—and obviously emotional to him. His pursed lips curled up in a kind of grotesque good cheer as he recounted how Saddam had "maimed and murdered innocent children." The speech, largely written by Bush himself and seen by the largest American television audience in history, was straightforward. But it was oddly flat for so momentous an occasion. Bush's reticence must seem puzzling to a public that reads about his occasional outbursts, like his vow to legislators that Saddam would get his "ass kicked." . . . Bush knows that he is a poor public speaker, at least when he's staring into a camera. He does better when he can talk face to face. That explains why he has given 91 press conferences and only five televised addresses in the past two years.[74]

Other commentators not only focused on Bush's rhetorical skills when announcing the allied invasion but also assessed Bush's overall war strategy and policy in the Gulf. In the *Economist*: "A prophet is not without honor, save in his own house. Washington has not yet made up its collective mind about George Bush. Some of his achievements are cheered by all, or nearly all: the way in which he stitched together an international coalition against Saddam Hussein; the way he managed to use the United Nations to prosecute American policy; his courage. But he has not convinced his hometown audience that the larger goal of the Gulf war—the crafting of a new world order—amounts to more than a string of words. . . . His speech to the country on January 16th on the outbreak of war proved yet that the president is no orator. For people already inclined to be critical of Mr. Bush, it is easy to leap from saying that he cannot articulate a policy to saying that he does not have one, or that such policy as he has is flawed."[75] Strobe Talbott wrote in *Time* that while Bush may have been correct to take the action to invade Kuwait, he remained skeptical of how that action would achieve a new world order: "I am stronger than you; therefore you will do what I say. Obey, or I will use force. That was what George Bush said to Saddam Hussein. For more than five months he had been saying it with warnings, then an ultimatum. Wednesday evening he switched to the vocabulary of bombs. . . . For his part, Bush justified the violence he unleashed on Iraq as an unavoidable step toward the forging of 'a new world order, a world where the rule of law, not the law of the jungle, governs the conduct of nations.' It was the right rhetoric on behalf of the right policy. But no one should be under any illusion that the much vaunted new world order is in place or even at hand. Quite the contrary, last week's events in the Persian Gulf and on the Baltic Sea, while different in so many respects, had the combined effect of making the new world order seem all the more remote."[76]

After the allied invasion of Kuwait in mid-January, the communication efforts in the White House to shape and control the message on Operation Desert Storm remained consistent. Demarest provided the following proposal to Bush in early February:

> Three weeks into the fighting in the Gulf, the goal of our communications group is to generate activities designed to sustain public support for the effort. Among the highlights, a multi-agency surrogate speakers program is up and running. For example, in the last several weeks top ranking civilian and military officials at the Department of Defense have made nearly eighty speeches across

the country about the Gulf. Similar efforts are underway at the other appropriate agencies. Additionally, speech inserts and talking points are being developed for use by all senior administration officials. Tactically, the working group has developed a number of ideas for Presidential events over the course of the next five weeks for your review. Among the ideas for events:

- Additional visits to military bases.
- Drop by local volunteer organizations that have been recognized as a Daily Point of Light for their work in supporting our troops. This can be done in conjunction with a base visit.
- Host a White House salute to the various volunteer groups across the country who are doing things to support the troops.
- Do more to recognize the *reserves and their families* since their sacrifices may be felt more acutely than active duty personnel.
- Host a "town meeting" or other format in a small community where the reserve call-up has had a particularly hard impact. Interestingly, Harry Truman was a reservist, DOD is checking to see if his old unit has been called up yet.
- Tape a Public Service Announcement concerning employer support for the guard and reserve. Mention this issue in all speeches to business groups.
- Please note, as a result of the recent Governors meeting, Secretary Cheney will soon be sending a letter to all the Governors to review ways they can help reservists from their states.
- Record a radio address to the troops via Armed Forces Radio.
- Attend the 50th Anniversary of the U.S.O. in Los Angeles, CA on April 10, 1991. This event will be held at Universal Studios and be attended primarily by entertainers, and political and business leaders.
- Host a White House event for the *State Commanders of America's veterans groups* and/or visit their conventions in their home states.
- Produce a video, written message, or make a personal appearance for the "Salute to VA Hospitals" event hosted by the Department of Veterans Affairs next week.
- Visit the Patriot missile battery at Fort Bliss or elsewhere, working in a Strategic Defense Initiative research and development theme as well.

- Highlight "pride in American quality and workmanship" in future remarks, citing the extraordinary success of our high-tech weaponry.
- Host a White House event for the ambassadors of all the coalition partners to demonstrate the continuing resolve of all the countries involved in the Gulf.
- Hold a *press conference exclusively for foreign journalists.* Most of the participants would represent news organizations that are from international coalition countries.
- Revisit the various constituent groups including business, religious, and veterans leaders, who have been instrumental in generating public support for our efforts in the Gulf.

While we will be proposing these events through the regular scheduling process, I wanted to give you a flavor for the sorts of projects the Gulf group is working on. Please check any activities you have a particular interest in pursuing.[77]

Bush's communications team managed for the most part to successfully execute the public strategy for the Gulf War, helping Bush to earn what were then record-high approval ratings. However, that level of public support would not be seen again during Bush's remaining time in office, and in particular regarding the domestic policy agenda Bush would pursue throughout the rest of 1991 and 1992.

Address to the Nation on the National Education Strategy, April 18, 1991

During the 1988 presidential campaign, Bush had promised to be the "education president" by reforming and improving public education in the United States. At the start of Bush's presidency, the public believed that Bush would be able to achieve education reform (74 percent in a CBS News/*New York Times* poll), yet political pundits and other politicians remained skeptical. One of the problems Bush faced in attempting to do anything related to education was the fact that he wanted reform without a dramatic increase in federal spending. As a result, Bush often talked about education without substantial changes to federal policy. "[T]here [was] substantial evidence to support [Bush's] sincerity" in wanting to achieve educational reform, but the president never supported the type of sweeping reform (and increased spending) that many had hoped for.[78] In June 1989, Roger Porter sent a memo to Sununu urging the creation of an Education Policy Advisory Committee:

> One of our principal domestic policy objectives is to establish both the reality and the perception of George Bush as the Education President. The President expressed this interest and desire throughout the campaign and has repeated it on numerous occasions since taking office. . . . Thus far, in my view, too much of the education debate has revolved around dollars and whether the spending total for our initiatives, $441 million, is sufficient and constitutes a real commitment to education. . . . Moreover, we have argued that many of these changes must be brought about by state and local governments, and by the involvement of parents, teachers, business organizations, and other community groups. . . . Reinforcing these themes remains a persistent challenge for us. Using the bully pulpit is one means. There is a constant need to show presidential interest and attention to demonstrate that he and his administration are engaged in dealing with this problem.[79]

Bush's education policy sought increased ties to the business community along with a new emphasis on education outcomes and accountability based on standardized tests. In September 1989, the White House held an education summit with state governors, the first such presidential event since the Great Depression. Benchmarks were developed in several areas, with 2000 as the target date for completion, yet few strategies were developed to compliment the benchmarks. In his 1990 state of the union address, Bush also highlighted his education proposals, outlining goals such as school readiness for young children, increasing the high school graduation rate, and competency tests for fourth-, eighth-, and twelfth-grade students. Then, in July 1990, Bush created the National Education Goals Panel by executive order, which would monitor the goals and provide public reports about progress. Also that month, advisors developed an extensive communications and marketing plan (including several presidential appearances at public schools, a public service announcement, a presidential "listening" session, and other press events) for Bush's education initiatives, with the goal to "demonstrate presidential leadership" on education as well as to "communicate the Administration's education principles" and to create "a better understanding of the problems in education and why the President's initiatives will help correct these problems."[80] As the situation in the Persian Gulf continued to escalate during the summer and fall months of 1990, however, much of the education communications plan did not materialize. By October 1990, advisors were still trying to pursue domestic issues, particularly education: "It seems that another casualty of Saddam Hussein's 'naked aggression' was the Education Communications Plan of July, 1990. In an attempt to maintain a focus on the education issue, regardless of world events and the President's schedule, I would like to suggest a new strategy to promote the Administration's education agenda." This newer strategy included many of the same types of public events, yet would again not be fully realized until after military action in the Persian Gulf had ended.[81]

By April 1991, Bush finally unveiled his second education initiative, called America 2000. Under this plan, federal grants would help develop more than five hundred New American Schools, which would serve as models for other schools to follow. In addition, support would be provided for local organizing to achieve the national goals, report cards would be required on the progress of schools and districts, and federal support would be provided for private school vouchers.[82] Accordingly, in the spring of 1991, the White House sought to aggressively promote Bush's domestic agenda, as described in a memo from Demarest to Bush and Sununu:

> We are making plans for events and activities designed to aggressively promote the President's agenda within the context of themes articulated in the State of the Union speech: new world order, encouraging economic growth, investing in the future and giving power and opportunity to the individual. Factoring in potential overseas travel this spring, and given our priorities, we've made the following assumptions to guide our plans. Our assumptions are: We will attempt to keep the moral high ground through a consistent appeal for unity in purpose and action (a la Persian Gulf) and tap the rekindled optimism that has swept the nation in the wake of the war. The opposition will try to take the high-ground this spring by attacking our domestic agenda. If we are positioned as conciliatory, positive, and forward looking, they will appear petty and carping. Our primary domestic focus will be on our five priority issues—crime and drugs, education, transportation and energy. This will be reflected in speeches, his schedule, and surrogate activities. . . . Between now and the August recess we are planning seven or eight

> events to highlight education, and are planning a kick-off event to send up our legislation.

Bush commented on the memo with the following: "John/Dave, Let's not forget volunteerism, Points of Light etc. . . . As we do 'crime, drugs, education' lots of opportunity for 'points of light' approach. Citizen helping citizen literacy—one helping another etc."[83]

Bush announced the America 2000 education initiative in April 1991 in the East Room at the White House with administration officials and congressional leaders present. Earlier that day, Bush had an exchange with reporters on his education initiative prior to a meeting with the nation's governors and also delivered remarks at the White House at a National Education Strategy Meeting. The goal of the main event—the address to the nation—was for Bush to make "the first concerted effort to refute the argument promoted by Democrats and education lobbyists and adopted by much of the nation—that the solution to America's education problems lay in more federal funding."[84] In the speech, Bush described the importance of education in America: "Nothing better defines what we are and what we will become than the education of our children. . . . Education has always meant opportunity. Today, education determines not just which students will succeed but also which nations will thrive in a world united in pursuit of freedom in enterprise. . . . Nations that nurture ideas will move forward in years to come. Nations that stick to stale old notions and ideologies will falter and fail. . . . If we want America to remain a leader, a force for good in the world, we must lead the way in educational innovation. . . . Think about every problem, every challenge we face. The solution to each starts with education."

Bush then outlined the goals of his new initiative:

> As a first step in this strategy, we must challenge not only the methods and the means that we've used in the past but also the yardsticks that we've used to measure our progress. Let's stop trying to measure progress in terms of money spent. . . . Dollar bills don't educate students. Education depends on committed communities, determined to be places where learning will flourish; committed teachers, free from the noneducational burdens; committed parents, determined to support excellence; committed students, excited about school and learning. . . . We've made a good beginning by setting the Nation's sights on six ambitious national education goals—and setting for

> our target the year 2000. . . . By 2000, we've got to, first, ensure that every child starts school ready to learn; second one, raise the high school graduation rate to 90 percent; the third one, ensure that each American student leaving the 4th, 8th, and 12th grades can demonstrate competence in core subjects; four, make our students first in the world in math and science achievements; fifth, ensure that every American adult is literate and has the skills necessary to compete in a global economy and exercise the rights and responsibilities of citizenship; and sixth, liberate every American school from drugs and violence so that schools encourage learning. . . . For today's students, we must make existing schools better and more accountable. For tomorrow's students, the next generation, we must create a new generation of American schools. For all of us, for the adults who think our school days are over, we've got to become a nation of students—recognize learning is a lifelong process.

Bush concluded the speech by emphasizing the importance of community involvement in achieving education reform while highlighting his recurring theme of volunteerism:

> Finally, outside our schools we must cultivate communities where learning can happen. That's our strategy. People who want Washington to solve our educational problems are missing the point. We can lend appropriate help through such programs as Head Start. But what happens here in Washington won't matter half as much as what happens in each school, each local community, and yes, in each home. Still, the Federal Government will serve as a catalyst for change in several important ways. . . . But the centerpiece of our national education strategy is not a program, it's not a test. It's a new challenge: To reinvent American education—to design new American schools for the year 2000 and beyond. . . . The workplace isn't the only place we must improve opportunities for education. Across this nation, we must cultivate communities where children can learn—communities where the school is more than a refuge, more than a solitary island of calm amid chaos. Where the school is the living center of a community where people care—people care for each other and their futures—not just in the school but in the neighborhood, not just in the classroom but in the home. Our challenge amounts to nothing less than a revolution in American education—a battle for

> our future. And now, I ask all Americans to be Points of Light in the crusade that counts the most: the crusade to prepare our children and ourselves for the exciting future that looms ahead.[85]

Just days prior to Bush's education speech, *Newsweek* had previewed the event within the context of the political importance of the issue for the White House: "George Bush's vow to be the education president has so far consisted of more talk than action. School reformers say his midterm grade is, at best, a solid C. This week Bush will get a chance to pull up that grade when he releases what is being billed as a far-reaching—and perhaps even revolutionary—education plan. With the public increasingly angry and anxious about schools, the president is under pressure to deliver. There's a political subtext as well. Bush's advisers hope a well-received education program will insulate the president from persistent charges that he has virtually no domestic policy. . . . Given that there has been little educational leadership from Washington for more than a decade, any comprehensive plan from the White House would be revolutionary. But Bush is only playing catch-up with the rest of the country."[86]

After the speech, Bush's new education initiative was the top story that evening on ABC News, as well as the top story on NBC as part of a two-story package on education and crime. On CBS, the president's speech was mentioned in the fifth story on the bankrupt school district in Richmond, California. Coverage in major newspapers focused on Bush's emphasis on the federal government's proposed partnership with state and local governments, the lack of federal funding, and skepticism among Bush's critics that the plan would succeed. The *Los Angeles Times* reported: "President Bush on Thursday proposed a sweeping package of educational reforms that would add little to federal spending but calls on state and local governments, business and communities to join in an effort to 'reinvent American education.' . . . Bush stressed that the nation's governors would be partners in leading the program and alluded to his 1988 campaign call for volunteerism."[87] In the *Washington Post*: "Calling for 'a true renaissance in American education,' President Bush yesterday unveiled a strategy for improving U.S. public schools that would leave most of the details to states and local communities."[88] Coverage in *USA Today* pointed out the politics of the issue: "President Bush dove deep into domestic policy Thursday and came up with a broad plan to improve the quality of the nation's schools. But aside from promoting educational excellence, some strategists said Bush had political motives as well."[89] The

Boston Globe also highlighted the political fight that Bush would face on his education initiative: "President Bush yesterday launched what backers called a crusade for educational reform while skeptical Democrats in Congress expressed doubts about several aspects of his goals for the year 2000. . . . For the most part, educators responded positively to the president's plan and voiced the hope that Bush's expressed interest in education will translate into action in various layers of the government and communities."[90] And in the *San Francisco Chronicle*, a mixed reaction to the president's plan: "President Bush's plan to revolutionize American schools was received in California yesterday with a combination of mild applause by the state superintendent of schools and skepticism from many front-line educators."[91]

The *New York Times* provided a mostly positive editorial endorsing Bush's education plan while acknowledging the limited role that the federal government can play in such a policy:

> George Bush has finally made a down payment on his pledge to be the education President. . . . The plan has many sensible elements—including a bold proposal to create demonstration schools across the country to explore new methods of teaching and learning. . . . Many of Mr. Bush's responses will raise little controversy. He encourages both illiterate and literate adults to go back to school, urges greater community involvement, and proposes more flexibility in Federal programs that provide social services to children. In perhaps his most innovative proposal, the President also calls for the creation of research and development teams, financed partly by the private sector, to create at least 535 new schools by 1996. These schools would offer new ways to enrich the learning environment. . . . Education, of course, is principally a state and local responsibility. But many localities have given little more than lip service to reform. That's why it's important that Mr. Bush has finally spoken. Though the Federal role in education is small and Washington cannot infuse the system with many new dollars, its leadership can be enormously helpful, particularly in insuring equal education opportunity.[92]

A similar assessment was provided by *Business Week*: "George Bush is finally proving that he is determined to make good on his campaign pledge to be the 'education President.' . . . But the blunt fact is that Bush's education plan can have only so much impact on the nation's deteriorating public school system. The reason is simple: The federal government has little power or influence over educational policy, short of withholding federal funds. . . . Bush's main weapon to influence change is to use the Presidency as a bully pulpit. . . . Whether the country's public school systems pass or fail is up to the states and cities. But given the constraints on his options, Bush surely deserves an 'A' for effort."[93] And in *Time*: "George Bush may be the savior of Kuwait, but in 1992 the voters will want to know what he is doing to save America. One early promise was to be 'the education President,' but his marks for that endeavor have been decidedly mixed. The President has apparently been doing his homework. Last week, striving to fulfill his promise to launch a major domestic initiative, he presented an ambitious national plan. . . . The goal is lofty enough, but the President hopes to perform a miracle: he is offering relatively little federal money to back up his plan. Even so, there was a sense of relief that he was planning something. . . . Though revolution is too strong a term for the plan, it does call for firm steps to shake up the muscle-bound education establishment. It also aims to encourage creativity and competition among schools and make them more accountable to parents and taxpayers."[94]

The mixed reaction to Bush's education plan served as an important harbinger on the fate of the initiative. While Bush tried to portray the issue as a bipartisan policy effort, others "viewed it as a desperate move to prevent being charged in the 1992 campaign with having broken his earlier promise to become the education president."[95] Promoting Bush's education plan remained a communications priority in early 1992 at the start of the presidential primary campaign. In a memo from Education Secretary Lamar Alexander, long-term objectives were identified as including: "1. Establish AMERICA 2000 as one of long-term solutions to 'jobs, jobs, jobs: Better Schools mean better—and more—jobs.' 2. Establish AMERICA 2000 as example of President's leadership at home: 'We know exactly where America should be going and how to get there.' 3. Use AMERICA 2000 as example of President keeping his word: 'I will be an education President.'"[96] However, amid the optimism of some that true education reform would occur with so much attention from the president, and the critics who did not believe that the federal government should be the vehicle for such reform, Bush's America 2000 education initiative died in Congress in late 1992. Despite his commitment to the issue of education, Bush's public campaign and use of the bully pulpit was not enough to see the proposal through the legislative process, particularly during a contentious presidential campaign with Congress controlled by the Democrats.

Remarks to the Greater Cleveland Growth Association, February 6, 1992

In the heat of the presidential primary season in early 1992, Bush unveiled his plan to reform health care. The issue, along with the economy, had become a top talking point for the Democratic candidates for president, particularly Bill Clinton and Paul Tsongas. Democrats in Congress had also begun to promote a major overhaul of healthcare, what Republicans often referred to as "nationalizing" or "socialized" health care. Bush's health care initiative sought to preserve a private health care system with individual choice, as described in a strategy memo from Charles Kolb to Roger Porter:

> I wanted to offer some suggestions about the President's health care speech next week in Cleveland. First, the speech should make it crystal clear that the country is at a *crossroads* in health policy. At issue is whether we will preserve the private health care system with government and individual choice playing a role to increase that system's efficiency, or whether we will adopt the Foley/Kennedy version of a government-managed, national health care system. In my view, the President should define the differences between the two approaches and do so through stark contrasts. Second, one way to make the contrast is to characterize the Foley/Kennedy approach as one doomed to failure—just as the government-run, command-and-control economies of the former Soviet Union and Eastern Europe collapsed. Why would Americans ever favor—or even flirt with—the Democrats' approach, particularly when the rest of the world (*i.e.,* all those newly emerging democracies) is headed in a free-market direction? Third, highlight the fact that our approach to health care reform is consistent with the way we handled childcare (and other choice-driven policy models such as education, homeownership, entrepreneurial capitalism etc.). We should invite Congress to work with us to build on past mutual triumphs such as childcare. Fourth, keep it simple when it comes to the details. If people on *Jeopardy* can't name the Treasury Secretary, I'll bet they won't recognize (and can't remember) "play or pay." People who pay attention to the speech will think in terms of the bottomline: what will the President's proposals mean for me and my family. Rather than speak about the details (which should be covered in the White Paper and Fact Sheet), the

> President should describe approaches/principles and outcomes. Those are what people will remember."[97]

A second strategy memo also outlined the president's talking points on health care:

> Convey the message that the President has a plan for *comprehensive* health care reform. There are choices to be made. They are tough choices, and the President has not shied away from making them. First, *what kind of radical reform should we have*? Philly Chamber of Commerce Speech (1/30/92): "we can either go the way of greater government mandates, resulting in a system of nationalized care. Or we can reform our private system, preserving the greatest possible patient choice and maintaining the quality of care." The President is opting for the latter approach. Second, *how should we pay for greater access*? Again two choices: raise taxes or make our health care system more efficient. Again, the Congressional Democrats want the former and we want the latter. The President's approach means taking on special interests: trial lawyers (malpractice), doctors, hospitals, and insurance companies.[98]

Fitzwater had also developed a full-scale press plan for the speech in Cleveland announcing Bush's health care plan and subsequent public events:

> The President will announce his national health care plan before the Cleveland Chamber of Commerce on Thursday, February 6, 1992 at approximately 12 noon. The President will continue to San Diego, California for the night. On Friday, February 7, he will visit an immunization clinic which dramatizes the health care plan. He also will address the San Diego Rotary Club concerning the health care proposal. In addition, on February 7, the President will tape a radio actuality on health care for release in Washington on Saturday, February 8. Other media activities related to this announcement include: 1. HHS Secretary Louis Sullivan would hold a press conference in Washington, D.C. at 1:00 P.M., February 6, 1992 to detail and discuss the health care plan. 2. ABC "Nightline" is holding a town meeting the night of February 6, which would include Lynn Martin, Secretary of Labor, and Gail Wilensky, HHS Health

> Finance Administrator. The show will originate from Chicago. 3. The afternoon of February 6, the Office of Public Liaison will schedule meetings as appropriate in the White House for special briefings by HHS Secretary Sullivan or OMB Director Richard Darman. 4. Television talk shows for Friday, February 7, would be booked as appropriate with Administration health officials. 5. The Department of Health and Human Services would be asked to prepare a Sunday outlook article by Secretary Sullivan which gives examples and illustrations of how our health plan would work. 6. Other special materials would be developed by HHS, including: (A) fact sheet on the President's plan, and examples of its implementation; (B) one-page speech inserts would be distributed to all Republican members of Congress, sub-cabinet members, and campaign officials who wish to comment on this subject. The deadline for fact sheets and speech inserts is Tuesday, February 4. The Office of Cabinet Affairs will be responsible for seeing that they are produced by HHS. 7. This plan assumes that the Assistant to the President for Legislative Affairs will design appropriate notifications to Congress.[99]

In his speech, Bush highlighted the need to keep the federal government out of the business of health care:

> I've chosen to come to Cleveland this morning to address the health care crisis in our country and lay out my four-point program for comprehensive health care reform. Reform is urgent for more reasons than one. Right now, far too many Americans are uninsured, and those who are insured pay too much for health care. And we're going to do something about that. . . . American health care is first-rate. It is the best in the entire world. And right now, the vast majority of Americans have access to that health care system. But the cost has skyrocketed. . . . And in these hard times, we simply cannot accept the fact that one in every seven Americans is uninsured. . . . There's a better way. And my plan puts the emphasis on expanding access while preserving the choice people now have over the type of health care coverage and health care they receive. My plan will give Americans a greater sense of security, help ease the fears that so many Americans have that changing jobs will cost them their health coverage. And the key here is portability, changing the system to ensure people that they will always have access to health insurance

no matter where they work.

Bush also sought to emphasize the differences between his plan and those competing plans put forth by Democrats, either in Congress or on the presidential campaign trail:

> We stand at a crossroads. We can move forward dramatically to reform our market-based system, or we can force ourselves to swallow a cure worse than the disease. Some people have scribbled out a prescription for disaster. They want to nationalize our health system, put the Government in control of the system: Well, you let Government control the prices, let Government ration the kind of health care people get, let Government tell people looking for care how much they'll get, what kind, and when. . . . But there are other proposals out there that sound simple but are every bit as harmful. One's called 'play or pay.' Each employer must play, provide insurance for employees, or pay a payroll tax to finance Government health coverage. . . . Step away from the rhetoric, strip it out of there, and 'play or pay' just creates a back-door route to nationalized health care. . . . Our system should be built on choice, not central control. It should keep costs down and open up access. But above all, it should allow all Americans to rest secure when it comes to health care, to ease their worry that if they change jobs, if they or their kids develop serious health problems, they'll still be able to count on the coverage they need.

Bush concluded the speech with the specifics about his plan:

> Now, my comprehensive four-point plan meets every one of these commonsense tests. And here's how it works. Point one, we will make health care more accessible by making health insurance more affordable. . . . Point two, we will cut the runaway costs of health care by making the system more efficient. . . . Point three, we will wring out waste and excess in the present system. . . . Fourth and finally, we will get the growth in Government health programs under control. . . . These four points will create the kind of market-based reform plan that will give Americans the kind of health care they want and deserve and put an end to the worry that keeps them awake at night. Remember what people want. People want quality care, care they can afford, and care they can count on, care they can rely on. . . .

> We don't need to create another wasteful Federal bureaucracy. As President I simply will not let that happen. We need commonsense, comprehensive health care reform, and we need it now. And my plan I really believe is the right plan, a plan that meets our obligation to all Americans by putting hope and health within their reach.[100]

News coverage about Bush's health care speech focused on both the debate over how to reform health care and the politics involved, particularly within the context of the presidential campaign. The speech was the top news story on ABC and NBC news that evening and the number two story on CBS behind the top story about a National Guard plane crash. In addition, Ted Koppel hosted a town meeting of more than one thousand people on health care in America that evening on ABC's *Nightline.* A sampling of how the story was framed on the evening newscasts shows that the politics of health care permeated the coverage stemming from Bush's speech. On CNN, anchor Bernard Shaw reported, "Bush's medicine wagon stopped in Cleveland today. [His] health care message: Don't buy what those Democrats are prescribing as a solution to the affordable health care problem. . . . His election year cure-all features a mix of tax credits and government vouchers to help low and middle income people pay their medical bills." Brit Hume reported on ABC that the plan "may not give Americans all the medical coverage they need, but it might just give this president the political coverage he needs. Until this day on this issue, he was the man with no plan." NBC's John Cochran stated, "George Bush always said he wanted to be the education president and the environmental president, now he wants to be the health president." And on CBS, Dan Rather reported, "Out campaigning for re-election, President Bush made it official today, he rejects national health insurance. He rejects the idea of requiring employers to help employees pay for more health insurance."[101]

Most major newspapers gave the story front-page coverage, although the broader emphasis tended to focus on the contrast between Bush's plan and Democratic plans as well as the politics of the issue. As Ann Devroy reported in the *Washington Post*, "President Bush today unveiled an election-year health care proposal that he said would 'preserve what works and reform what doesn't' rather than fundamentally change the nation's health delivery system. Bush's proposal—built on government subsidies to help the poor and middle class purchase health insurance and cutting health care costs through a series of reforms—immediately came under attack by Democrats and some health care advocates. Some congressional Republicans active on the issue welcomed the president's proposals but characterized them as only a first step."[102] And in the *Los Angeles Times*, Bush's criticism of Democratic plans was highlighted: "President Bush on Thursday unveiled a much-touted plan that he said would cut health costs and guarantee access to care, but he offered no clear explanation of how his Administration would pay the $100-billion price tag. 'We'll figure that out,' Bush said as he began a cross-country trip to drum up support for the election-year initiative. . . . In contrast to various Democratic proposals that promise health care for all, sometimes under government auspices, the Bush plan promises only universal access to health care through tax credits and tax deductions designed to make health insurance affordable. . . . For his part, Bush used his appearance here less to discuss the details of his plan than to attack the so-called 'play or pay' approach and other Democratic-backed alternatives."[103]

Similar coverage appeared in the *St. Louis Post-Dispatch*:

> Raising the specter of government control over personal health care choices, President George Bush stumped in Cleveland on Thursday for his $100 billion plan aimed at helping the poor and middle class get health insurance through tax credits and vouchers. Democrats and other critics harshly criticized the plan as inadequate and misguided while Republicans and other supporters praised it as a step in the right direction toward solving the nation's health care problems. The tenor and reception for the official unveiling of Bush's long-awaited plan underscored the political freight carried by health care issues in this election year. In Cleveland, Bush maintained that his plan would be a comprehensive way of expanding health care to the 90 million Americans without adequate insurance. And hoping to shift the debate on overhauling the system, he accused Democrats of trying to open 'a backdoor route to nationalized health care' that would deprive Americans of personal choices.[104]

And in the *Boston Globe*: "Four years after promising a national health care policy, President Bush yesterday unveiled a complicated plan that offers tax breaks to low- and middle-income Americans for purchasing health insurance. Bush did not say how he would pay for his plan, which administration officials said would cost $35 billion a year when fully implemented in 1997. Bush's proposal was praised by many Republicans and business groups. . . . But Democrats called the program an election-year effort to shield Bush from opposition charges that he has no plan to control soaring health costs or to help the nation's 37 million citizens who lack health insurance."[105]

An editorial in the *Washington Post* did not show support for the president's plan: "The defects of the health care plan that President Bush presented yesterday are easier to toll than its virtues. The all-too-familiar, contradictory problems with the current system are that it costs too much—more than $1 of every $9 that Americans now spend—yet still leaves out a seventh of the population. The president tries to solve these problems while keeping the federal government at too great a distance. That leaves his cost-control proposals unconvincing. The benefit he offers the uninsured may meanwhile not be large enough, yet for fear of offending voters in an election year he forbears from saying how he would finance even that. The clearest suggestion he makes is to finance part of the increased care for the poor by cutting the main existing form of care for the poor: He proposes sharp restraints on future federal Medicaid payments."[106] Also in the *Post*, David Broder highlighted the political rhetoric on the campaign trail over health care: "The Democratic presidential candidates happily let President Bush set the agenda today, competing with each other to see who could find the most scathing description of the health care plan Bush formally introduced into the 1992 campaign."[107]

Coverage in the weekly news magazines also focused on criticisms of Bush's proposals and the difficulty in introducing such a plan in the heat of the presidential primaries. As reported in *Time*,

> The idea that every American should have access to affordable health care has been gathering political force since Democrat Harris Wofford used it to trounce former Attorney General Dick Thornburgh in the Pennsylvania Senate race last fall. Here, Democrats believed, was a domestic issue they could use to help drive George Bush from the White House—and Republicans feared they were right. And so last week the President, unnerved by declining approval ratings and a tepid response to the hodgepodge of tax cuts he proposed in his State of the Union address, unveiled his own prescription for reforming the health-care system. . . . The President was praised for addressing one of the major flaws in the existing insurance system: denial of company-sponsored coverage to new employees if they suffer from 'pre-existing' ailments. With Bush's plan, companies

> could no longer legally turn down applicants no matter what their health status, but the cost of private coverage would still be prohibitive. But Bush's reform plan has huge drawbacks. . . . The feverish partisan atmosphere of an election year almost guarantees that neither Bush's prescription nor any other competing scheme will be enacted before November.[108]

Coverage in *U.S. News and World Report* suggested that the White House should be focusing on the economy and not health care reform: "Fear has become the dominant force in the lives of American voters. This winter, families are drowning in discontent over the health of their finances, the vitality of their communities, the effectiveness of their leaders, the future of their children. . . . As if Democratic diversions weren't bad enough, George Bush spent the end of the week barnstorming for his new $100 billion health-care reform plan and drew attacks from many sides for his failure to attack key problems and for the plan's blatant giveaways to upper-class voters."[109] And in *Newsweek*, a grim forecast met Bush's proposal, as well as a comment about the now-infamous checkout scanner incident:

> This was not the campaign Bush expected to run. As recently as last summer, the president's aides were predicting a 1992 cakewalk pegged to Kuwait, crime and quotas—the "KKK strategy." But that scenario depended on an economic recovery by the end of 1991. Now Bush must sell himself to voters in the new role of credible domestic leader. The early results are not encouraging. The economic program he outlined in his State of the Union Message barely nudged his national approval ratings. His new health-care plan—offering tax credits and deductions to help low-income Americans buy medical insurance—is already a political DOA in Congress. Attempts to reanimate the average-Joe image he evoked in 1988 with pork rinds and country music are falling flat. At a grocers convention in Orlando, Fla., last week, Bush was "amazed" by the brave new world of electronic checkout scanners—a part of American shoppers' lives for more than a decade.[110]

Bush's health care plan proved to go nowhere politically, as did the Democratic plans proposed in 1992, which is not surprising during a presidential election year. But even Bill Clinton and a Democratically controlled Congress could not make progress on the issue in 1993 and

1994. And as Americans witnessed in 2009 during Barack Obama's first year in office, health care reform remains one of the most confounding domestic policy issues for Washington politicians nearly two decades after Bush's proposal in 1992.

Conclusion

The sampling of major policy addresses in this chapter shows that the Bush White House was attentive to the public relations needs of selling the president's agenda. While Bush may not have been as scripted as Ronald Reagan, and while Bush had a different public style than his predecessor, the public strategies were similar in how to package a presidential event (and other related public events as part of the entire communications strategy). The goal of the speechwriters and other communication strategists was to provide a coherent and consistent message prior, during, and after Bush would give a speech in the hopes of receiving positive press coverage and political support for initiatives. While none of this is surprising, it does show that the Bush White House built upon some of the successes of the Reagan years in terms of public relations, as well as the broader public strategies that have been institutionalized within the White House during the television age.

While it would be unrealistic to expect positive coverage for every presidential event and policy initiative, the policy addresses analyzed in this chapter suggest that Bush was given more latitude in the press on foreign policy initiatives than on domestic issues, which is also in line with the fact that presidents have more latitude to be active in the foreign policy arena as opposed to the domestic arena where Congress is often more engaged. Bush also enjoyed above-average approval ratings before the Gulf War in 1991, with record-high approval ratings during the war, but that would disappear, along with much of the optimism for Bush to enact domestic issues such as education reform, once both the recession and the presidential election took hold in 1992. Until Bush's last year in office, the public strategies employed by his White House were successful for the most part, but even the best political strategists could not rescue the president from the events in 1992 that would lead to his failed reelection bid.

CHAPTER 6

Conclusion

The Public Legacy of George H. W. Bush

On December 15, 1992, just thirty-six days before he would leave office, George Bush delivered an address on the foreign policy accomplishments of his administration. In the speech, what could be considered the closest thing to a farewell address that he would deliver after losing his reelection bid in November 1992, Bush talked about his vision for a new world order and emerging democracies around the globe following the end of the Cold War:

> The end of the cold war, you see, has placed in our hands a unique opportunity to see the principles for which America has stood for two centuries, democracy, free enterprise, and the rule of law, spread more widely than ever before in human history. For the first time, turning this global vision into a new and better world is, indeed, a realistic possibility. It is a hope that embodies our country's tradition of idealism, which has made us unique among nations and uniquely successful. And our vision is not mere utopianism. The advance of democratic ideals reflects a hard-nosed sense of our own, of American self-interest. For certain truths have, indeed, now become evident: Governments responsive to the will of the people are not likely to commit aggression. They are not likely to sponsor terrorism or to threaten humanity with weapons of mass destruction. Likewise, the global spread of free markets, by encouraging trade, investment, and growth, will sustain the expansion of American prosperity. In short, by helping others, we help ourselves. Some will dismiss this vision as no more than a dream. I ask them to consider the last 4 years when a dozen dreams were made real: The Berlin Wall demolished and Germany united; the captive nations set free; Russia democratic; whole classes of nuclear weapons eliminated, the rest vastly reduced; many nations united in our historic U.N.

> coalition to turn back a tyrant in the Persian Gulf; Israel and its Arab neighbors for the first time talking peace, face to face, in a region that has known so much war. Each of these once seemed a dream. Today they're concrete realities, brought about by a common cause: the patient and judicious application of American leadership, American power, and perhaps most of all, American moral force.[1]

The irony of the speech, in which Bush clearly lays out a vision for America's involvement in and leadership of the expansion of global democracy, is that it provides the type of vision that Bush was accused of not having, or at least not being able to clearly and consistently articulate during his four years in office. The consensus that has emerged since then is that Bush had many different visions for the country but did not develop one particular vision that defined him or resonated with a majority of Americans. According to Catherine Langford, "Bush's difficulty in developing, articulating, and promoting a rhetorical vision meant the public did not know who George Bush was or for what he stood. His rhetorical ineptitude and trouble with the 'vision thing' caused him to fall short of the demands of the modern rhetorical presidency."[2] In addition, Bush supposedly "failed to develop a simple, easily repeated narrative," and "more often than not, the president lacked any consistent rhetorical strategy."[3] A further consensus has emerged since Bush left office regarding his relationship with the press. According to historian John Robert Greene, "By the administration's end, by all accounts, the relationship had gone past thrust and parry; George Bush truly seemed to hate the press, and, in many journalism quarters, the feeling was mutual."[4] In addition, Greene argues that "[Bush's] public presidency was the weakest part of his tenure. He is the least introspective of men, never comfortable with articulating any abstract idea, much less with talking to the nation about what he stood for. As president, Bush consistently scorned the press' attempt to pin him down on what he derisively called 'the vision thing.' He never considered it a priority to place his actions as president in context for the American people, either during or after his tenure."[5] And, in terms of the overall public presidency, according to Martin Medhurst, "Unfortunately, George Bush was one of the worst [rhetorical presidents]. Even more unfortunate is the recognition that it need not have been so. Bush had the tools to be a perfectly acceptable, perhaps even good, public communicator. He simply refused to use those tools, or to allow others to develop them on his behalf."[6]

It is important to note, however, that for a president who supposedly lacked a vision or a consistent public or rhetorical strategy, Bush's approval ratings for most of his time in office seem to belie that fact. As discussed in chapter 3, Bush's approval ratings remained over 60 percent for most of his first three years in office, while never dropping below 50 percent during that time period. It is only when the economic recession of 1991–92 began to take hold in late 1991 that his approval rating begins to drop, which is consistent with what other presidents have experienced in terms of their approval ratings when faced with governing during an economic downturn. How, then, can a president who lacked rhetorical skill, along with a vision for the country, have maintained such high approval ratings for the better part of three years in office? While it has long been established that many factors can contribute to a president's approval ratings, with many of those things out of his control (such as the economy or international events), we do know that how a president is viewed by Americans (as in whether or not he is liked, respected, or trusted, for example) also plays a significant role. Similarly, a president's rhetorical skill or public strategy is not the single contributor to whether or not a president can govern successfully or in how he is judged by the people. As such, the assumptions that Bush was not a good public speaker, or that he lacked a consistent rhetorical strategy, or that he hated the press and they hated him in return, fails to incorporate all of the complexities of the political environment in which any president, and in particular this president, governed.

In the end, one must ask, did Bush's public strategy fail? And if so, what effect did this have on his presidency? In the simplest of terms, given the fact that Bush did not win reelection, one could easily surmise that yes, his public strategy did fail. Despite his above-average public approval ratings through his first three years in office, by 1992 U.S. voters (at least according to public opinion polls and the electoral outcome in November) had lost their faith in President Bush. Yet, while his public strategy throughout his four years in office certainly played a role in how Americans viewed Bush by 1992, and their belief that he was somehow not in touch with the needs of average Americans, many other factors played a more significant role in creating the political environment in 1992 and in the outcome of the election (like the economy, the divide between moderates and conservatives within the Republican Party, and Ross Perot's candidacy, just to name a few). However, can a president's public strategy succeed even if he does not win reelection or, as in Bush's case, if he does not have an aggressive public policy agenda seeking major changes?

Looking at this question is somewhat of a false dichotomy as it leaves out many of the nuances, complexities, and day-to-day successes that the Bush White House enjoyed during their four years in office. The public strategy developed for Bush by his advisors did succeed in that it seemed to fit the style and preferences of the president, particularly in his own goal to focus more on substance as opposed to style in his public appearances, and in the fact that he was not pursuing grandiose policy changes. However, despite the public strategy (which was extensive for certain events), the White House was often not strategic enough in developing a public style for Bush or in matching his public events to the ensuing media coverage. Advisors were certainly aware of the needs of the news media but would ignore some of those needs (such as the types of photo ops that the Reagan White House provided) to be more substantive and "presidential." Also, what the strategy did not adequately take into account was the public expectation for performance that had been left behind by Reagan. One could also surmise that perhaps Bush and his advisors put too much faith in the American public, and the news media, to appreciate a more substantive presidency with less public relations flair. It is hard to imagine that Bush could have experienced more success in terms of his public presidency had he followed Reagan's exact strategy, since being elected president does not automatically generate grand rhetorical skill in any person. Conversely, perhaps Reagan would have still succeeded as a communicator following Bush's strategy, as his stage presence and persona may have outshone any specific public relations objective. The point here is that there is only so much that any strategy can accomplish, just as there are only certain skills that any president can possess. So, within the context of what Bush was actually capable of achieving in terms of his public presidency, the answer may be very different if placed in the context of someone else's achievement (such as Reagan).

Given that, who then is to blame for the perceived failures of the Bush public presidency? Is it Bush himself for simply not having the same rhetorical skill set as someone like Reagan or perhaps his advisors for not crafting a better strategy? Usually, the blame is placed on the president himself for failings as a communicator, and since leaving office, Bush has accepted that blame for not being articulate enough.[7] But even Bush's own assessment falls short in that it does not recognize the role of many other factors, including the changing media environment, the partisan environment in Washington, and the unrealistic expectation of public leadership left behind by Reagan. The irony of this particular issue can be found in the fact that while many scholars and pundits alike argue against the power of the rhetorical presidency (that is, an imbalance of constitutional power among the branches due to the rise of the rhetorical presidency throughout the twentieth century), the public performance of presidents during the television age nonetheless offers a prominent benchmark and means of assessment for a presidency. Again, a false dichotomy can be found in some of the press coverage of the Bush years, in that Bush was often criticized for not being more Reaganesque, yet the press never developed a more adequate and accurate means of assessment for a different style of leadership following the Reagan years (even though so many complained about Reagan's news management strategy).

As a result, assuming that Bush was a poor communicator, or lacked a vision, or lacked a consistent and effective strategy is mostly an unfair, or at best an incomplete, assessment. Part of a president's context for governing, along with the environment in which he governs, comes from his predecessors and the expectations they left, but that aspect of the context often leads qualified and capable presidents to be judged unfairly or inaccurately. This is the case for the Bush presidency. For example, Bush often sought a more positive message in his public addresses, like when he talked about the end of the Cold War and future possibilities resulting from it, or his focus on "points of light" and volunteerism, or a renewed American spirit. But, he was often chided for that from critics on both the left (Democrats who controlled Congress and wanted to win back the White House) and on the right (the growing voice of conservatives within the Republican Party who believed Bush could not continue the Reagan legacy), and even in the press (who had grown accustomed to the Reagan public strategy and were facing increasing competition within their own industry). This, along with the fact that Bush was not a good storyteller or that he did not clearly define something (like communism) to fight against, contributed to the narrative that Bush lacked a vision.[8] Bush's public strategy was for the most part a substantive one, and he did succeed in stepping back from the stagecraft of the Reagan years. But the narrative that developed from the early days of the Bush administration—that he was not Reagan—often seemed to work as a self-fulfilling prophecy for how Bush would be viewed and evaluated throughout his four years in office.

Upstaging the Bush Presidency

Clearly, assessing the public aspects of any presidency is a complex process, as the importance of the public elements of the office continues to change and even dominate many of the day-to-day strategies and tasks in which a president must participate while governing. In returning to the overall theme of the book, when looking at the Bush years, what exactly upstaged the Bush public presidency? First and foremost, Bush was upstaged by Reagan and the public expectation that he left. Throughout his time in office, and even during his leadership of the Gulf War (for which he received uniformly high marks), commentators in the press continued to compare Bush's rhetorical skills, or lack thereof, to Reagan. And the comparisons were not only made to the public aspects of the two presidencies but the policy agendas as well. According to Jeffrey Cohen, "[N]o matter how hard George Bush tried to scale back these public expectations, he seemed unable to convince the public to accept a smaller presidency. This gap between what he offered to the public in terms of policy leadership and public expectations is arguably one element of his electoral defeat in 1992. Bill Clinton offered the public the traditional policy leadership to which it had grown accustomed and preferred. A political culture highly expectant of presidential policy leadership developed, and it was an expectation highly resistant to modification."[9] As such, Bush's "stay the course" policy agenda did not give him the same types of leadership opportunities that Reagan had enjoyed; even if Bush's approach was the correct one for that particular moment in time, the very fact that he seemed less active than Reagan in pursuing a grand policy agenda (like reducing taxes and the size of government or fighting to end the Cold War) left Bush at a distinct disadvantage in how he was perceived and judged in the public realm.

Second, Bush's public presidency and the communications strategy pursued were also upstaged by the changing technology and news media environment during the late 1980s and early 1990s. In what has become a steadily increasing media-dominated political environment since the days of the Kennedy administration, presidential action equals media reaction. And while a president's dominance of the political news cycle was not a new phenomenon when Bush took office in 1989, as discussed in chapter 3, Bush's time in office paralleled major changes in the news media profession. Expanding news outlets on the one hand, coupled with a tightening of budgets and other downsizing within the industry on the other, left Bush and his style of communicating at a disadvantage among the increasing competition and tabloidization of news coverage; the press wanted more personality at a time that Bush wanted to provide more substance. Bush's communication style and strategy might have been more successful at the start of the decade when CNN was first getting off the ground and the 24-hour news cycle had not yet been developed. A president who appreciated substance over style, who wanted to give access to the press to provide relevant background information on important policies, and who did not enjoy the expectation of public performance was ill-suited for the media environment that had emerged by the end of the 1980s.

Unfortunately for Bush, his governing style did not fit well with the new media environment. Bush's style was often one of nuance and diplomacy, as he was skilled at bringing everyone to the table to work out a deal. While these are usually considered positive attributes in a president, they did not translate well into sound bites or strong images of outer leadership for the public and the press to observe. Since Bush's skill at brokering behind-the-scenes deals was not on center stage (such as his success at building a strong international coalition prior to the Gulf War), he did not get the public credit that he deserved.[10] (This is similar to Lyndon Johnson's effective behind-the-scenes communication skills, known as the "Johnson treatment," which was in stark contrast to how Johnson's public performances were judged). In addition, the Bush public strategy of moving away from the "line-of-the-day" approach used by Reagan did not serve Bush well due in part to the media environment. According to Martha Joynt Kumar, "The result of this 'communications salad' approach was that the public failed to associate President Bush with any particular policies. . . . The Bush laissez-faire approach toward communications will stand as a striking example to future administrations of an approach to avoid." Kumar also points out the irony that while White House reporters had complained about Reagan's strategy of packaging the news, they also did not like how the Bush team was not telling them what to report through a one-story emphasis PR strategy.[11] While the argument can certainly be made that the press is complicit in the perceived failures of the Bush public presidency, the consequences were obviously far greater for the president.

Finally, any presidency, particularly a one-term presidency, can be upstaged by a future presidency as part of the normal cycle of assessing a president's time in office with the benefit of hindsight. For Bush, not only did he have to face the high expectation left by Reagan, but his successor also upstaged Bush in terms of public performance. For all of his political problems while in office, Bill Clinton was a gifted politician with strong communication skills; he represented a new generation of leadership that often stood in stark contrast to the Bush years. He also embraced the use of new media technologies, which seemed to fit his communication style well; as the first baby-boomer president raised in the television age, Clinton was at ease under the media glare and embraced the public responsibilities of the office. As a result, the environment in which Bush's legacy first began to develop placed the assessment of Bush as a communicator at a great disadvantage. However, later presidents can also help to place a previous president's legacy in a more positive perspective, which is the case with the George W. Bush administration. Initially, it looked as if the son's presidency might upstage that of the father, as George W. Bush achieved record-high approval ratings, along with an opportunity for strong leadership, after 9/11. Despite his own mediocre communication skills, George W. Bush's reelection in 2004 also placed him in the elite group of two-term presidents, something that his father had failed to achieve. But as more light continues to be cast on the George W. Bush administration, his father's presidency is placed in a different light, as looking at Bush through the lens of his son's presidency has tended to improve his own legacy, particularly in regards to foreign policy.

The Bush Legacy

In the end, what are we to make of the Bush legacy? The emergence of a clear picture in that regard may still be decades away; more than six decades after his death, scholars are still reassessing and reanalyzing the presidency of Franklin Roosevelt, which proves that there is no definite end date for when a final presidential legacy should emerge. Even though Bush served only four years in office, his governing and political legacies are just as complex as any other president's. In early 2009, C-SPAN released its "Historians Presidential Leadership Survey" in which Bush ranked eighteenth in the overall ranking, an improvement of his twentieth place ranking in 2000. In subcategories, Bush improved from twelfth to ninth in "International Relations," seventeenth to fourteenth in "Pursued Equal Justice for All," and twentieth to nineteenth in "Performance within Context of Times." But his rankings dropped from twentieth to thirtieth in "Public Persuasion," and twenty-eighth to thirty-fourth in "Vision/Setting an Agenda." This survey is only one small snapshot of how the

Bush legacy continues to evolve, but we can get a sense that his foreign policy leadership looks better in hindsight, while the memory of his public leadership has not improved with time. And the narrative of Bush falling short when compared to Reagan in terms of the public presidency seems to persist.[12]

At a March 2000 symposium on presidential leadership sponsored by the Center for the Study of the Presidency, journalist Steve Roberts observed that Reagan excelled at public leadership because he understood that governing was ultimately a public act—speaking, communicating, and driving public opinion. Reagan also understood that "the presidency is two very distinct jobs. It's the head of state and it's the head of government."[13] The point is especially salient in understanding Bush's public leadership—Reagan was a good head of state, while Bush was a good head of government. The public act of governing and the imagery associated with the office of the presidency matters in how the administration is viewed. Political observers, whether the news media, academics, or the public in general, tend to like good communicators. Presidents may fail at certain policies or initiatives, but skilled communicators somehow are able to soften the blow. No matter how many policy failures or personal scandals a president endures (Clinton certainly comes to mind), strong communication skills leave at least one positive aspect of the president or his administration for political discussion. And as Mark Rozell argues, "The Reagan White House understood well the relationship between positive coverage and moving forward a policy agenda. President Bush did not follow in these footsteps. Bush failed to strategically link a press relations plan with a policy agenda. Consequently, the image of the White House was one of inertia. By the end of his term, voters had no reason to return Bush to the White House other than their fear of the alternatives. That fear did not override the public judgment that the president had lost touch with his people and had no plan to deal with the domestic economy."[14]

In addition, the changes that began within the news industry during the late 1980s and early 1990s have continued to evolve and shape the political environment in which presidents must govern. It has become increasingly difficult to capture and hold the attention of American news consumers, which poses unique concerns for presidents wanting to shape the national political dialogue. According to the Pew Research Center, a growing number of Americans are beginning to lose the traditional news habit. While viewers have declined for network evening news shows, television viewing for news has not declined, with viewers looking to other time slots and different shows (including more entertainment-friendly shows found on cable outlets). The Internet has also adversely affected traditional news outlets, as it has become a prime source of news for an increasingly large segment of the population.[15] Individual control of access to news is a strong selling point for consumers, particularly younger generations of Americans whose lifestyles are driven by technological capabilities. These changes first began to emerge with the expansion of cable television outlets during the Bush years. According to Cass Sunstein, "Technology has greatly increased people's ability to 'filter' what they want to read, see, and hear. General interest newspapers and magazines are largely a thing of the past. The same is true of broadcasters. The idea of choosing 'channel 4' or instead 'channel 7' seems positively quaint. With the aid of a television or computer screen, and the Internet, you are able to design your own newspapers and magazines. Having dispensed with broadcasters, you can choose your own video programming, with movies, game shows, sports, shopping, and news of your choice. You mix and match."[16] These types of changes to the news environment raise the question, particularly for communication strategists within the White House, as to whether citizens are now opting out of hearing what the president has to say and how this might change the president's public strategy.

In spite of the many changes to the news industry in recent years, the press still remains the predominant source of information for Americans about what their government is doing. While recent and future presidents may take some comfort in knowing that journalists themselves are unhappy about the current state of their profession, believing that "journalism is going in the wrong direction" and that the "increased bottom line pressure is seriously hurting the quality of news coverage," a president is now forced to contend with the ever-watchful and ratings-driven eye of constantly changing media technologies.[17] The press has been transformed in many ways since the founding era, but the significance of its role in democratic governance has not declined. If anything, its potency as information provider, public-sphere agenda setter, and interpreter of the political scene has grown. This is why the debate has never stopped about how it can best serve as a source of essential public political enlightenment.[18] It has also been argued that many recent changes in the news industry have resulted from not only broader economic and technological changes but demographic and social changes in the country as well: "Most newspapers, television networks and local television and radio stations now belong to giant, publicly owned corporations far removed from the communities they serve. . . . Many in the news business became convinced that in an era of unparalleled prosperity and security, Americans would rather be entertained than informed. The consequences of this attitude are obvious on every television show, and in too many newspapers. The temptation to push serious news aside in favor of glitz and melodrama has too often been irresistible. A national infatuation with celebrities, both encouraged and exploited by news media, has had a profound influence on journalism."[19]

In the final analysis, a better appreciation of the political environment in which Bush attempted to govern, including the changing dynamic of the presidential-press relationship during that time, will provide a more accurate assessment of the Bush public presidency. It is not as simple as stating that Bush was not a good communicator; the analysis is and should be as nuanced as the man himself. Bush's emerging legacy is also one of many ironies, particularly when looking at the public aspects of his presidency. Bush's overall public message was based on many positive themes, which matched the times (the end of the Cold War) and his own personal values (volunteerism and public service). But the lack of a more dominant narrative throughout his four years in office, like fighting against communism, left Bush without the public opportunity for strong leadership. Perhaps it is the disconnect between the public expectations of the presidency and what really does make for a successful and effective president, since the public aspects of the office are only part of the equation, that defines the Bush public presidency most of all. Bush was better at the public aspects of the office than he was given credit for at the time, yet his public legacy is still overshadowed by that of Reagan. In the end, this may say more about the expectations of the American public, and more importantly, the U.S. news media, than it does about George Bush as a communicator, or even a president.

Notes

Chapter 1. Introduction

1. Northouse, *Leadership*, 3.

2. Duerst-Lahti and Kelly, "On Governance, Leadership, and Gender," 13.

3. Neustadt, *Presidential Power*.

4. See Skowronek, *Politics Presidents Make*, and Richard Rose, *Postmodern President*.

5. For examples of changes in the political environment, see Kessel, *Presidents, the Presidency*, and Cronin and Genovese, *Paradoxes of the American Presidency*.

For examples of the institutionalization of and leadership within the executive branch, see Burke, *Institutional Presidency*, Weko, *Politicizing Presidency*, and Warshaw, *Keys to Power*.

For examples of policy making and the president's relationship with Congress, see Jones, *Separate but Equal Branches*, Cohen, *Presidential Responsiveness and Public Policy-making*, and Lammers and Genovese, *Presidency and Domestic Policy*.

For examples of the public presidency and changes in White House communication strategies, see Kernell, *Going Public*, Tulis, *Rhetorical Presidency*, Hart, *Sound of Leadership*, Stuckey, *President as Interpreter-in-Chief*, Maltese, *Spin Control*, and Han, *Governing from Center Stage*.

6. Rockman, "Leadership Style of George Bush," 2.

7. See Han, "Public Leadership in the Political Arena."

8. Greenstein, *Presidential Difference*, 5.

9. Edwards, *Public Presidency*, 2.

10. Kernell, *Going Public*, ix.

11. Han, *Governing from Center Stage*, 2.

12. Rossiter, "The Presidency—Focus of Leadership," 14.

13. Edwards, *On Deaf Ears*, 241–46. Edwards's research suggests that rarely are presidents capable of changing public opinion on an issue, and their attempts to lead the public fall on "deaf ears." They persist in pursuing public strategies due to the routines of politics, the need to preach to the converted, and influencing elites.

14. Eshbaugh-Soha, *President's Speeches*, 157–64.

15. See Heith, *Polling to Govern*, and Jacobs and Shapiro, *Politicians Don't Pander*.

16. Canes-Wrone, *Who Leads Whom?* 192.

17. Shogan, *Moral Rhetoric of American Presidents*, 175.

18. See Han, "President over the Public," 119–37.

19. Cronin and Genovese, *Paradoxes of the American Presidency*, 152.

20. Brody, *Assessing the President*, 17.

21. Brace and Hinckley, *Follow the Leader*, 6–9, 22–24.

22. Skowronek, *Politics Presidents Make*, 415.

23. Neustadt, "Looking Back," 321–22.

24. Sunstein, *Democracy and the Problem of Free Speech*, 18–19.

25. See Tulis, *Rhetorical Presidency*, and Hart, *Sound of Leadership.*

26. Greenstein, *Presidential Difference*, 160.

27. Rockman, "Leadership Style of George Bush," 32.

28. Tiefer, *Semi-Sovereign Presidency*, x–xi.

29. Duffy and Goodgame, *Marching in Place*, and Mervin, *George Bush and the Guardianship Presidency.*

30. Mervin, *George Bush and the Guardianship Presidency*, 6–9.

31. Genovese, *Power of the American Presidency*, 180.

32. Skowronek, *Politics Presidents Make*, 430.

33. Naftali, *George H. W. Bush*, 65.

34. Greene, *Presidency of George Bush*, 1–2.

35. Skowronek, *Politics Presidents Make*, 433–34.

36. Greene, *Presidency of George Bush*, 4.

37. Neustadt, *Looking Back*, 321.

38. Tom Rosenstiel and James Gerstenzang, "Low-Key Bush Abandons Slick Image Strategy," *Los Angeles Times*, Apr. 30, 1989, A1.

39. Rozell, *The Press and the Bush Presidency*, 2.

40. Hill and Williams, "Conclusion," in *Bush Presidency*, 214.

41. Ibid., 226.

42. Ibid., 219.

Chapter 2. Internal Factors

1. Edwards, "George Bush and the Public Presidency," 148–49.

2. Maltese, "Spin Control in the White House," 112–13.

3. Skowronek, *Politics Presidents Make*, 415.

4. Nelson, *Who Speaks for the President?* 237.

5. Barilleaux, "George Bush and the Changing Context," 17.

6. Emery and Emery, *Press and America*, 474.

7. Michael Oreskes, "President Bush; He's a New Man Now, Thanks to the Press," *New York Times*, Jan. 22, 1989, sec. 4, p. 1.

8. Emery and Emery, *Press and America*, 474–76.

9. Edwards, "George Bush and the Public Presidency," 145.

10. For a discussion of Bush's many images, see Waterman, Wright, and St. Clair, *Image-Is-Everything Presidency*, 57–62.

11. Hill and Williams, "Introduction" in *The Bush Presidency*, 7.

12. Reston, *Deadline*, 447.

13. Barilleaux and Rozell, *Power and Prudence*, 50–51.

14. Rozell, *The Press and the Bush Presidency*, 148.

15. Memo from Marlin Fitzwater to George Bush, Dec. 20, 1988, John Sununu Files, Office of the Chief of Staff to the President, Formerly Withheld, NLGB Control Number 11317, George Bush Presidential Library (hereafter cited as GBPL).

16. Ibid.

17. Bush only held two press conferences in the East Room. According to David Demarest, "When President Bush finally held an East Room press conference, there were no mistakes to correct. He was always well read, well versed, and usually well briefed." Top staffers were pulled together for an Oval Office meeting to prepare Bush for his first formal press conference in June 1989, including John Sununu, Richard Darman, Marlin Fitzwater, Dan Quayle, Brent Scowcroft, Roger Porter, and Demarest. Demarest recalled, "That type of briefing was never held again because it was embarrassing. President Bush knew more than we did concerning what should be said to the press. It was clear from that moment that press conferences were going to be one of his strengths." See Demarest, "Bush Presidency and Communications," 87.

18. Bernard Weinraub, "Washington Talk: The Presidency; Bush Begins Perhaps His Toughest Job: Taming Press Corps," *New York Times*, Jan. 25, 1989, p. B6; "And Now a Question for the Press," *New York Times*, Jan. 27, 1989, sec. 1, p. 6.

19. "A Presidential News Conference," *Washington Post*, Jan. 30, 1989, p. A8.

20. James Gerstenzang and David Lauter, "Vignettes from Bush's First Week: Win One, Lose One," *Los Angeles Times*, Jan. 28, 1989, p. 19.

21. "Bush: A Matter of Style," *Los Angeles Times*, Jan. 28, 1989, p. 8.

22. Richard Cohen, "Why Have a Press Conference?" *Washington Post*, Jan. 31, 1989, p. A7.

23. Bush, however, noted in his post-presidential book *All the Best*, "Several ugly, gossipy articles appeared during the first few months of my presidency saying there was a rift between President Reagan and me. Nothing could be further from the truth." Bush, *All the Best*, 425.

24. Memo from Marlin Fitzwater to George Bush, Apr. 18, 1989, Marlin Fitzwater Files, Press Office/Alpha Files, Box 25, GBPL.

25. Mervin, *George Bush and the Guardianship Presidency*, 50–51.

26. Edwards and Wayne, *Presidential Leadership*, 152.

27. Greenstein, *Presidential Difference*, 169.

28. Jay Sharbutt, "Another Administration, Another Show; Press Corps Expects Greater Media Accessibility to Bush," *Los Angeles Times*, Jan. 20, 1989, p. 1.

29. Lang and Lang, *Politics and Television*, 186.

30. Griscom, "Great Communicator," 66.

31. Duffy and Goodgame, *Marching in Place*, 44–45.

32. Kernell, *Going Public*, 93.

33. Mervin, *George Bush and the Guardianship Presidency*, 52.

34. Fitzwater, *Call the Briefing!* 81.

35. Clayton Yeutter, "Accomplishments and Setbacks," 50–51.

36. Demarest, "Bush Presidency and Communications," 84–87.

37. Kumar, *Managing the President's Message*, 286–87.

38. See Rozell, *The Press and the Bush Presidency*, 150–52.

39. Kumar, *Managing the President's Message*, 131.

40. Ibid., 135.

41. Maltese, *Spin Control*, and Han, *Governing from Center Stage*, 216.

42. Rozell, *The Press and the Bush Presidency*, 151.

43. Memo from Marlin Fitzwater to George Bush, Feb. 2, 1989, John Sununu Files, Office

of the Chief of Staff to the President, Formerly Withheld, NLGB Control Number 11315, GBPL.

44. Memo from Marlin Fitzwater to John Sununu, Jan. 13, 1989, John Sununu Files, Office of the Chief of Staff to the President, Formerly Withheld, NLGB Control Number 13331) GBPL.

45. Twelve of the radio addresses focused on domestic or economic policy, while only one dealt with foreign policy ("Address to the Nation on the Persian Gulf Crisis," Jan. 5, 1991). The remaining five addressed topics such as national holidays, the Points of Light volunteer program, and the results of the 1992 presidential election. For a discussion on presidential use of radio, see Han, "New Strategies for an Old Medium," 25–45.

46. The weekly radio address was also continued during the George W. Bush administration, with a complete transcript of each address available on the White House webpage. The weekly radio address has now evolved into the weekly video address in the Barack Obama administration and is available for viewing on the White House webpage.

47. Kernell, *Going Public*, 91.

48. Memo from Kristin Clark Taylor to John Sununu, Feb. 15, 1990, John Sununu Files, Office of the Chief of Staff to the President, Formerly Withheld, NLGB Control Number 12130, GBPL.

49. Memo from Kristin Clark Taylor to John Sununu and Andy Card, "On-the-Road Regional Media Coverage," Feb. 13, 1990, David Demarest Files, White House Office of Communications, Freedom of Information Act Request 2003–1478-F, GBPL.

50. Ibid.

51. Memo from Andy Card to David Demarest, Feb. 21, 1990, David Demarest Files, White House Office of Communications, Freedom of Information Act Request 2003–1478-F, GBPL.

52. Memo from Marlin Fitzwater to Andy Card and Dave Demarest, Feb. 23, 1990, Marlin Fitzwater Files, Press Office/Alpha Files, Box 25, GBPL.

53. Memo from Marlin Fitzwater to George Bush, Mar. 14, 1989, Marlin Fitzwater Files, Press Office/Subject Files, Box 3, GBPL.

54. Memo from Kirstin Clark Taylor to George Bush, Mar. 31, 1989, Marlin Fitzwater Files, Press Office/Subject Files, Box 4, GBPL.

55. Memo from Marlin Fitzwater to Joseph Hagin, Mar. 6, 1990, Marlin Fitzwater Files, Press Office/Subject Files, Box 4, GBPL.

56. Memo from Kristin Clark Taylor to George Bush, Feb. 20, 1990, Marlin Fitzwater Files, Press Office/Subject Files, Box 4, GBPL.

57. Memo from Kristin Clark Taylor to George Bush, June 8, 1989, Marlin Fitzwater Files, Press Office/Subject Files, Box 4, GBPL. Those cartoonists in attendance included: Tony Auth, *Philadelphia Inquirer*, Linda Francis Boileau, *State Journal* (Frankfort, Kentucky), Paul Conrad, *Los Angeles Times*, Bill Garner, *Washington Times*, Mike Lane, *Baltimore Sun*, Jeff MacNelly, *Chicago Tribune*, Patrick Oliphant, Universal Press Syndicate, David Seavey, *USA Today*, Dana Summers, *Orlando Sentinel*, and Dick Wright, *Providence Journal-Bulletin*.

58. Memo from Kristin Clark Taylor to George Bush, "Disabled Media Articles from Roundtable Interview of May 1, 1990," July 12, 1990, David Demarest Files, White House Office of Communications, Freedom of Information Act Request 2003–1478-F, GBPL.

59. Memo from Kristin Clark Taylor to George Bush, "Resulting Articles from Interview with Health and Fitness Writers," June 11, 1990, David Demarest Files, White House Office of Communications, Freedom of Information Act Request 2003–1478-F, GBPL.

60. See memo from Deb Amend to John Sununu, Brent Scowcroft, Richard Darman, Roger Porter, and Marlin Fitzwater, "Pre-Brief for Hispanic Media Executives Luncheon," Feb. 25, 1991, David Demarest Files, White House Office of Communications, Freedom of Information Act Request 2003–1478-F, GBPL, and memo from Mary Sladek to George Bush, "Hispanic Business Magazine," Mar. 1, 1991, David Demarest Files, White House Office of Communications, Freedom of Information Act Request 2003–1478-F, GBPL.

61. Memo from Kristin Clark Taylor to George Bush, "*BusinessWeek* Article on the Environment," July 23, 1990, David Demarest Files, White House Office of Communications, Freedom of Information Act Request 2003–1478-F, GBPL.

62. Memo from Kristin Clark Taylor/Cheryl Kienel to George Bush, "Times Mirror Editorials," July 30, 1990, David Demarest Files, White House Office of Communications, Freedom of Information Act Request 2003–1478-F, GBPL.

63. Memo from Kristin Clark Taylor to George Bush, "Clip Package of Recent Roundtable Interviews," Aug. 3, 1990, David Demarest Files, White House Office of Communications, Freedom of Information Act Request 2003–1478-F, GBPL.

64. Memo from Kristin Clark Taylor to George Bush, "Press Coverage of Interview with Economic Writers/Letter to the Editor Concerning Regional Press Conference," June 22, 1990, David Demarest Files, White House Office of Communications, Freedom of Information Act Request 2003–1478-F, GBPL.

65. Memo from Kristin Clark Taylor to George Bush, "Article on Your Participation in Regional Press Conference," June 14, 1990, David Demarest Files, White House Office of Communications, Freedom of Information Act Request 2003–1478-F, GBPL.

66. Memo from Kristin Clark Taylor to George Bush, "Press Coverage of Interview with Economic Writers/Letter to the Editor Concerning Regional Press Conference," June 22, 1990, David Demarest Files, White House Office of Communications, Freedom of Information Act Request 2003–1478-F, GBPL.

67. Memo from Roman Popadiuk to Marlin Fitzwater, Mar. 9, 1990, Press Office, Daily Guidance File, Formerly Withheld, NLGB Control Number 9667, GBPL.

68. Ibid.

69. Memo from Leigh Ann Metzger to John Sununu, Nov. 5, 1990, John Sununu Files, Office of the Chief of Staff to the President, Formerly Withheld, NLGB Control Number 12122, GBPL.

70. Memo from David Demarest to Assistants to the President, "Guidelines for Video Messages," Oct. 26, 1989, Rose Zamaria Files, White House Office of Management and Administration, Freedom of Information Act Request 2003–1478-F, GBPL.

71. Memo from Kristen Clark Taylor to John Sununu, "Satellite Interviews," May 9, 1990, David Demarest Files, White House Office of Communications, Freedom of Information Act Request 2003–1478-F, GBPL.

72. Memo from Maria Eitel Sheehan to George Bush, "Your Appearance with Mrs. Bush in Public Service Announcements for the 'Cartoon All-Stars to the Rescue' Program," Apr. 25, 1990, David Demarest Files, White House Office of Communications, Freedom of Information Act Request 2003–1478-F, GBPL.

73. Edwards, "George Bush and the Public Presidency," 145.

74. Bush's dislike for most aspects of the public presidency was evident even in regards to photographers with whom he did not have to communicate directly. While he got along with press photographers personally, he was bothered by the act of being photographed itself, which he viewed as getting away from the "serious business" of being president. See Kumar, *Managing the President's Message*, 132–33.

75. It should be noted, however, that the total number of Reagan's public activities might have been higher during his first term, particularly in 1981, had it not been for the injuries he sustained during the assassination attempt in March 1981. The number of public activities for Bill Clinton during his first four years in office also increased over the totals for George H. W. Bush. See Han, "Rose Garden Strategy Revisited," 170–73. See also Han, *Governing from Center Stage*, 209–12.

76. Kolb, *White House Daze*, 3–4.

77. Demarest, "Bush Presidency and Communications," 84.

78. For a discussion of Bush's relationship with his speechwriters, see Kolb, *White House Daze*, and Podhoretz, *Hell of a Ride*.

79. Noonan, *What I Saw at the Revolution*, 336.

80. Greene, *Presidency of George Bush*, 145.

81. Gelderman, *All the President's Words*, 146.

82. Medhurst, preface to *Rhetorical Presidency*.

83. Medhurst, "Why Rhetoric Matters: George H. W. Bush in the White House," in *Rhetorical Presidency*, 4.

84. Tony Snow quoted in Kumar, *Managing the President's Message*, 132.

85. Wicker, *George Herbert Walker Bush, 128.*

86. See Schlesinger, *White House Ghosts*, 368–69, and Bush, *All the Best*, 423–24. Bush would also become emotional in several post-presidency addresses, including remarks he gave on behalf of his son, Jeb, at the end of his two terms as governor of Florida in December 2006.

87. "Memo from George Bush to David Demarest and Speechwriters," June 15, 1991, Rose Zamaria Files, White House Office of Management and Administration, Freedom of Information Act Request 2003–1478-F, GBPL.

88. As an outside contractor, Gamble was paid $3,000 per month by the Bush-Quayle '88 campaign and, when used by the White House, would receive $1,500 per month (as he did in May 1989 for the "writing of humorous material for use by President Bush"). Several memos in the Rose Zamaria files at the Bush Library detail this relationship. See "Invoice from Doug Gamble," May 31, 1991; memo from David Demarest to Bonnie Newman, "Doug Gamble," June 1, 1989; memo from Drucie Scaling to Betty Ubbens, "Doug Gamble," Nov. 23, 1992; and letter from Doug Gamble to Drucie Scaling, Nov. 24, 1992, Rose Zamaria Files, White House Office of Management and Administration, Freedom of Information Act Request 2003–1478-F, GBPL.

89. Smith, "George Herbert Walker Bush," 349.

90. James Gerstenzang, "Bush Needs the Speech of His Career, Again," *Los Angeles Times*, Aug. 20, 1992, A6.

91. Demarest, "Bush Presidency and Communications," 87–88.

92. Pfiffner, *Strategic Presidency*, 141–43.

93. Memo from Dorrance Smith to Andy Card, David Demarest, Marlin Fitzwater, and Gregg Petersmeyer, "June 12–13 Speech," May 20, 1991, Andrew Card Files, White House Office of Chief of Staff, Freedom of Information Act Request 2003–1478-F, GBPL.

94. For table 1, see Han, *Governing from Center Stage*, 209–12. To determine the frequency with which Bush discussed policy issues, each major presidential address, as listed in the *Public Papers of the Presidents*, was content analyzed. Major presidential addresses were considered national addresses (inaugurals, state of the union or other addresses to a joint session of Congress, addresses to the nation that are broadcast live on television and radio); policy addresses (other major addresses that presidents use to outline policy goals, including addresses to business, labor, or other interest groups, or university commencement addresses); news conferences (the prepared opening statement given by the president); and radio addresses. A total of twelve specific policy subcategories were developed for coding, which were then categorized by international, domestic, or economic policy issues. Each reference to a particular policy within a speech was then counted to measure the frequency with which Bush discussed issues on the agendas. Policy topics for the speeches were then rank-ordered based on how often each was mentioned.

95. Gray, "The President as Leader," 10.

96. Gelderman, *All the President's Words*, 143.

97. Rozell, *The Press and the Bush Presidency*, 165.

98. Victor Gold, "George Bush Speaks Out," *Washingtonian* magazine, Feb. 1994.

Chapter 3. External Factors

1. George H. W. Bush, "Austin College Leadership Institute Convocation Address," Sherman, Texas, Nov. 1, 2002.

2. See Baum and Kernell, "Has Cable Ended the Golden Age?" 99–114.

3. See Cohen, *Presidency in the Era of 24-Hour News.*

4. Cook, Gomery, and Lichty, eds., introduction to *Future of News*, xvii.

5. "Meet the New Media Monsters," *Economist*, Mar. 11, 1989, p. 65.

6. Bagdikian, *Media Monopoly*, ix–xvii; Bagdikian, *New Media Monopoly*, 3.

7. Underwood, "Newspapers' Identity Crisis," 24.

8. Kipling, "Lost Generation," 28.

9. See Emery and Emery, *Press and America*, 545.

10. Collins, "What's Missing on Sunday," 9.

11. Tozzi, "Salary Watch," 15; Garneau, "Average Pay for Reporters Declines," 12.

12. Katz, "Reinventing the Media," 19.

13. Kerbel, *Remote and Controlled*, 52.

14. Graber, *Processing Politics*, 161–62.

15. Downie and Kaiser, *News about the News*, 9.

16. Ibid., 10.

17. Cronin and Genovese, *Paradoxes of the American Presidency*, 121–22.

18. Kumar, discussant comments for "The Media and Public Opinion."

19. Demarest, "Bush Presidency and Communications," 87; Barilleaux and Rozell, *Power and Prudence*, 73.

20. Demarest, "Bush Presidency and Communications," 87–89, 94.

21. Memo from Marlin Fitzwater to George Bush and John Sununu, Apr. 14, 1989, Marlin Fitzwater Files, Press Office/Alpha Files, Box 25, GBPL.

22. Memo from Marlin Fitzwater to Andy Card and David Demarest, Feb. 23, 1990, Marlin Fitzwater Files, Press Office/Alpha Files, Box 25, GBPL.

23. Memo from Marlin Fitzwater to John Sununu and David Demarest, Oct. 12, 1989, Marlin Fitzwater Files, Press Office, Formerly Withheld, NLGB Control Number 6170, GBPL.

24. Memo from Marlin Fitzwater to John Sununu, July, 21, 1989, John Sununu Files, Office of the Chief of Staff to the President, Formerly Withheld, NLGB Control Number 13441, GBPL.

25. Memo from Joseph W. Hagin II to David Bates, David Demarest, Marlin Fitzwater, and Brent Scowcroft, July 17, 1989, Marlin Fitzwater Files, Press Office/Alpha Files, Box 26, GBPL.

26. Memo from Joseph W. Hagin II to Andrew Card Jr. and Marlin Fitzwater, Feb. 7, 1989, Marlin Fitzwater Files, Press Office/Alpha Files, Box 26, GBPL.

27. Written comments on memo from Joseph W. Hagin II to Marlin Fitzwater, Feb. 21, 1989, Marlin Fitzwater Files, Press Office/Alpha Files, Box 26, GBPL; memo from Joseph W. Hagin II to Stephen Studdert, Marlin Fitzwater, and C. Boyden Gray, Feb. 21, 1989, Marlin Fitzwater Files, Press Office/Alpha Files, Box 26, GBPL.

28. Written comments on memo from Marlin Fitzwater to George Bush, Nov. 14, 1990, Press Office/Subject Files, Box 4, GBPL.

29. Fitzwater, *Call the Briefing!* 211–12.

30. Note from George Bush to Marlin Fitzwater, Mar. 14, 1990, Marlin Fitzwater Files, Press Office, Formerly Withheld, NLBG Control Number 6168, GBPL.

31. Unsent letter from Fitzwater to Barbara Cohen, Washington bureau chief of CBS News, Mar. 14, 1990, Marlin Fitzwater Files, Press Office/Alpha Files, Box 4, GBPL.

32. Note from Alixe Glen to Marlin Fitzwater, undated, Press Office, Daily Guidance File, Formerly Withheld, NLGB Control Number 9655, GBPL.

33. Memo from Roman Popadiuk to John Sununu, "Dan Rather Transcripts," Sept. 5, 1991, Marlin Fitzwater Files, Press Office, Formerly Withheld, NLGB Control Number 6169, GBPL.

34. See Han, *Governing from Center Stage*, 82.

35. For example, see memo from Mary Kate Grant to John Sununu, "Weekly Editorial Round-Up," Aug. 17, 1989, Mary Kate Grant Files, Speech Office, Box 8, GBPL.

36. Memo from Mary Kate Grant to John Sununu, "Regional Newspapers," Mar. 12, 1989, Mary Kate Grant Files, Speech Office, Box 8, GBPL.

37. Memo from Maria Eitel Sheehan to Dorrance Smith, May 22, 1991, Project Files, White House Office of Media Affairs, Freedom of Information Act Request 2003–1478-F, GBPL.

38. Note from Marlin Fitzwater to James M. Hildreth, Feb. 4, 1992, Marlin Fitzwater Files, Press Office/Correspondence Files, Box 40, GBPL.

39. Fitzwater, *Call the Briefing!* 97.

40. Thomas, *Front Row at the White House*, 150–51.

41. Personal note from Marlin Fitzwater to Maureen Dowd and Andrew Rosenthal, *New York Times*, Apr. 25, 1991, Marlin Fitzwater Files, Press Office/Correspondence Files, Box 37, GBPL.

42. Letter from Marlin Fitzwater to Juan Williams, *Washington Post*, Mar, 19, 1991, Press Office/Correspondence Files, Box 39, GBPL.

43. Note from George Bush to Marlin Fitzwater, Jan. 6, 1990, Marlin Fitzwater Files, Press Office, Formerly Withheld, NLGB Control Number 6119, GBPL.

44. Note from George Bush to Jim Baker, Marlin Fitzwater, and Kathy Super, Aug. 26, 1992, Marlin Fitzwater Files, Press Office, Formerly Withheld, NLGB Control Number 6125, GBPL.

45. Letter from Marlin Fitzwater to Peter Jennings, ABC News, Feb. 12, 1991, Marlin Fitzwater Files, Press Office/Correspondence Files, Box 38, GBPL.

46. Letter to Marlin Fitzwater from Albert Hunt, *Wall Street Journal*, Jan. 22, 1992, Marlin Fitzwater Files, Press Office/Correspondence Files, Box 40, GBPL.

47. Letter to Marlin Fitzwater from Douglas A. Harbrecht, *Business Week*, Feb. 3, 1992, Marlin Fitzwater Files, Press Office/Correspondence Files, Box 40, GBPL.

48. Memo from Marlin Fitzwater to request presidential visit to the Washington Bureau of Hearst Newspapers, Mar. 29, 1989, Marlin Fitzwater Files, Press Office/Alpha Files, Box 26, GBPL; request for scheduling recommendation, Feb. 24, 1989, Marlin Fitzwater Files, Press Office/Alpha Files, Box 26, GBPL; request for participation in a *Frontline* documentary, June 15, 1992, Marlin Fitzwater Files, Press Office/Correspondence Files, Box 44, GBPL; note to David Demarest from Margaret Tutweiler, Aug. 25, 1992, Marlin Fitzwater Files, Press Office, Formerly Withheld, NLGB Control Number 6152, GBPL.

49. Personal note from Marlin Fitzwater to John McWethy, ABC News, undated, Marlin Fitzwater Files, Press Office/Correspondence Files, Box 35, GBPL.

50. Letter from Marlin Fitzwater to Tom Johnson, CNN, Mar. 20, 1992, Marlin Fitzwater Files, Press Office/Correspondence Files, Box 40, GBPL.

51. Letter from Marlin Fitzwater to Lorne Michaels, NBC, July 19, 1989, Marlin Fitzwater Files, Press Office/Correspondence Files, Box 35, GBPL.

52. Letter from Marlin Fitzwater to Tim Russert, NBC News, Aug. 8, 1989, Marlin Fitzwater Files, Press Office/Correspondence Files, Box 35, GBPL.

53. Vice Pres. Dan Quayle appeared alone on the September 20, 1992, broadcast of *Meet the Press.* Regarding a request for Bush to appear on NBC's *The Today Show*, Fitzwater wrote in a memo to Margaret Tutweiler, who took over as director of communications in the summer of 1992: "Tim Russert has been very aggressive in pursuing 'an' interview with NBC, he would ultimately like the President to do *Meet the Press.* Undated memo, week of Aug. 25 to Aug. 31, 1992, Marlin Fitzwater Files, Press Office, Formerly Withheld, NLGB Control Number 6153, GBPL.

All correspondence between Fitzwater and Russert from the Marlin Fitzwater Files, Press Office/Correspondence Files, Box 41, GBPL.

54. List of media activities from spring 1992, undated, Marlin Fitzwater Files, Press Office, Formerly Withheld, NLGB Control Number 6142, GBPL.

55. Memo outlining media opportunities, May 22, 1992, Marlin Fitzwater Files, Press Office/Alpha Files, Box 6, GBPL.

56. Rozell, *The Press and the Bush Presidency*, 3–4.

57. Liebovich, *Press and the Modern Presidency*, 151.

58. Fitzwater, *Call the Briefing!* 11–12.

59. Edwards, "George Bush and the Public Presidency," 149.

60. Gray, "President as Leader," 6–7.

61. Letter from Christopher Matthews to Marlin Fitzwater, Jan. 4, 1993, with Fitzwater response, Jan. 5, 1993, Marlin Fitzwater Files, Press Office/Correspondence Files, Box 40, GBPL.

62. Rosenstiel, *Beat Goes On*, 7.

63. Ibid., 18.

64. Patterson, "Doing Well and Doing Good."

65. Kenski, "A Man for All Seasons?" 95.

66. Maltese, *Spin Control*, and Han, *Governing from Center Stage*, 220–21.

67. Ragsdale, *Vital Statistics on the Presidency*, 184.

68. For a discussion of the news media environment during the early 1990s, see David Shaw, "Not Even Getting a First Chance, *Los Angeles Times*, Sept. 15, 1993.

69. Edwards, "George Bush and the Public Presidency," 149.

70. Ibid., 133–35.

71. Stuckey and Antczak, "Governance as Political Theater," 30.

72. Brace and Hinckley, *Follow the Leader*, 147.

73. Sidey, "Some Personal Reflections," 35.

74. Heith, *Polling to Govern*, xi.

75. Ibid., 3.

76. For example, the October 19, 1990, Opinion Digest provided a seven-page analysis of the latest polling data from the *Times Mirror* poll, the ABC News/*Washington Post* poll, the CBS News/*New York Times* poll, the Hotline/KRC poll, as well as polls from Gallup and the Wirthlin Group on issues such as presidential approval, the budget, the savings and loan scandal, the 1990 midterm elections, Congress, party images, and the direction of the country. See memo from David M. Carney to John Sununu, "Opinion Digest," Oct. 19, 1990, White House Office of Records Management, PL327215 Political Affairs, Freedom of Information Act Request 2003–1478-F, GBPL.

77. Memo from Ed Rogers to George Bush, July 12, 1990, White House Office of Records Management, PR014 Public Opinion Polls, Box 156, GBPL. The memo was marked "The President Has Seen."

78. Heith, *Polling to Govern*, 16–23.

79. Memo from Roger B. Porter to George Bush, Oct. 29, 1990, White House Office of Records Management, PR014 Public Opinion Polls, Box 156, GBPL. Bush wrote the response "Good!" on the memo on October 30, 1990.

80. Memo from Richard B. Wirthlin to John Sununu, Oct. 20, 1990, John Sununu Files, Office of the Chief of Staff to the President, Box 83, GBPL.

81. Memo from Marlin Fitzwater to George Bush, Nov. 17, 1991, White House Office of Records Management, PR014 Public Opinion Polls, Box 157, GBPL.

82. Memo from Judy Smith to George Bush, Jan. 23, 1992, White House Office of Records Management, PR014 Public Opinion Polls, Box 157, GBPL. The memo was marked "The President Has Seen."

83. Heith, *Polling to Govern*, 112–16.

84. Thomas, *Front Row at the White House*, 92–93.

85. Greene, *Presidency of George Bush*, 147–48.

86. Liebovich, *Press and the Modern Presidency*, 171.

Chapter 4. Bush's Major Public Addresses

1. Campbell and Jamieson, *Deeds Done in Words*, 14–27.

2. One electoral vote came from a faithless elector in West Virginia, who voted for Dukakis's running mate, Sen. Lloyd Bentsen of Texas, as president and Dukakis as vice president.

3. As discussed by Elisabeth Bumiller in a story about George W. Bush in 2004, "It was in a moment of irritation during the 1988 campaign that the Republican presidential candidate, Vice President George Bush, first derided 'the vision thing,' as he called it, thus employing an ungainly piece of Bush-speak to describe a leader's ability to set forth inspiring national goals. Mr. Bush, who may have been one of the most self- effacing presidents in recent American history, went on to become a one-term incrementalist with little taste for big schemes." See Bumiller, "Bush Gets 'Vision Thing' and Embraces Big Risks," *New York Times*, Jan. 12, 2004, accessed Jan. 18, 2009 at http://www.nytimes.com/2004/01/12/politics/12LETT.html?ex=1389243600&en=72a6159980245012&ei=5007&partner=USERLAND.

4. "Inaugural Address," Jan. 20, 1989, *The Public Papers of the Presidents of the United States: George Bush, 1989.*

5. Noonan, *What I Saw at the Revolution*, 337.

6. Naftali, *George H. W. Bush*, 69.

7. Catherine L. Langford, "George Bush's Struggle with the 'Vision Thing,'" in *Rhetorical Presidency*, ed. Medhurst, 25–26.

8. Rozell, *The Press and the Bush Presidency*, 29–30.

9. "President Bush's Breeze of Decency," *New York Times*, Jan. 21, 1989, sec. 1, p. 26.

10. "A New Breeze Is Blowing, *Boston Globe*, Jan. 21, 1989, p. 14.

11. "The Inaugural," *Washington Post*, Jan. 21, 1989, p. A24.

12. "A Subtle Change," *Los Angeles Times*, Jan. 21, 1989, p. 8.

13. David Broder, "Speech Mixes a Pinch of Carter, Dash of FDR; President Rebukes Partisanship, Materialism and Vietnam Era's Divisiveness," *Washington Post*, Jan. 21, 1989, p. A1.

14. David R. Gergen, "George Bush's Balky Start," *U.S. News and World Report*, Jan. 30, 1989, p. 34.

15. Stephen Kurkjian, "The Inauguration of George Bush/News Analysis: Soft, Homespun Notes Color Inaugural Speech," *Boston Globe*, Jan. 21, 1989, p. 1.

16. Robert Shogan, "Analysis Bush Speech: Time to 'Talk as Neighbors,'" *Los Angeles Times*, Jan. 21, 1989, p. 1.

17. Paul A. Gigot, "Bush Must Beat the Odds to Make His Tenure Work," *Wall Street Journal*, Jan. 21, 1989, p. 1.

18. Robert L. Bartley, "Scripts for a New President," *Wall Street Journal*, Jan. 21, 1989, p. 1.

19. Rozell, *The Press and the Bush Presidency*, 32.

20. Wilson did not address Congress in 1919 and 1920 due to health reasons. Warren Harding's two messages in 1921 and 1922, along with Calvin Coolidge's first in 1923, were oral addresses to Congress. However, Coolidge's remaining state of the unions between 1924 and 1928 and all four of Herbert Hoover's (1929–33) were written messages.

Franklin D. Roosevelt delivered an oral state of the union with his first in 1934. Exceptions during the modern era include Harry Truman in 1946 and 1953, Dwight Eisenhower in 1961, Richard Nixon in 1973, and Jimmy Carter in 1981. See Gerhard Peters, "State of the Union Messages," the American Presidency Project, http://www.presidency.ucsb.edu/sou.php, accessed Jan. 26, 2009.

21. Ibid.

22. Campbell and Jamieson, *Deeds Done in Words*, 52–53.

23. "Proposed Communications Plan for the President's Address to a Joint Session of the Congress, Thursday, February 9, 1989," Barbara G. Kilberg Files, Office of Public Liaison, Formerly Withheld, NLGB Control Number 4656, GBPL.

24. Ibid.

25. Ibid.

26. Memo from Marlin Fitzwater to John Sununu, "Updated Budget Speech Media Plan," Feb. 7, 1989, Marlin Fitzwater Files, Press Office/Alpha Files, Box 27, GBPL.

27. "Address on Administration Goals before a Joint Session of Congress," Feb. 9, 1989, *The Public Papers of the Presidents of the United States: George Bush, 1989.*

28. A total of twelve policy categories were used for coding, as well as a category for nonpolicy remarks (including introductory, closing, and ceremonial remarks). The policy categories closely match those used in my previous research on White House communication strategies. See Han, *Governing from Center Stage.*

29. David R. Gergen, "Bush's Second Inaugural Speech," *U.S. News and World Report*, Feb. 13, 1989, p. 87.

30. "Bush: Strong Symbolism," *Los Angeles Times*, Feb. 10, 1989, p. 6.

31. Robin Goldstein, "Speech: OC Lawmakers React Enthusiastically," *Orange County Register*, Feb. 10, 1989, p. A24.

32. John W. Mashek, "Bush's Agenda: A Gentler Approach to Capitol Hill," *Boston Globe*, Feb. 10, 1989, p. 9.

33. Donald M. Rothberg, "It's Bush's Ball Game Now," Associated Press, Feb. 10, 1989.

34. "Good Start on the Environment," *Los Angeles Times*, Feb. 10, 1989, p. 6.

35. Maureen Dowd, "Bush Bids Congress Join Him in Mission of U.S. 'Greatness,'" *New York Times*, Feb. 10, 1989, p. A1.

36. E. J. Dionne Jr., "Something Borrowed, Nothing Blue," *New York Times*, Feb. 10, 1989, p. A16.

37. Walter Shapiro, "Reaganomics with a Human Face," *Time*, Feb. 20, 1989.

38. Bush, *All the Best*, 413.

39. Peter B. Gemma Jr., "Bush's New Direction Is the Wrong Way to Go," *USA Today*, Feb. 10, 1989, p. 10A.

40. Tom Shales, "The Yawn of an Era; President Bush's Ho-Hum Presentation and the Pauses for Applause," *Washington Post*, Feb. 10, 1989, p. D1.

41. See Han, *Governing from Center Stage*, 212–15.

42. Rozell, *The Press and the Bush Presidency*, 65–67.

43. Memo from Edward McNally to David Demarest, "The 'T' Word Is Over," Nov. 10, 1989, Backup Speech Files, White House Office of Speechwriting, Formerly Withheld, NLGB Control Number 6291, GBPL.

44. Memo from David M. Carney to Roger B. Porter, "Some Early Thoughts on the Upcoming State of the Union Address," Dec. 12, 1989, Chris Dube Files, White House Office of Political Affairs, Freedom of Information Act Request 2003–1478-F, GBPL.

45. Memo from James W. Cicconi to John Sununu, "Competitiveness Package for State of the Union," Jan. 10, 1990, Backup Speech Files, White House Office of Speechwriting, Formerly Withheld, NLGB Control Number 6292, GBPL.

46. Memo from Evan J. Kemp Jr. to John Sununu, "State of the Union Address," Jan. 9, 1990, General Subject Files, Office of White House Records Management, Formerly Withheld, NLGB Control Number 2222, GBPL.

47. Memo from Amy L. Schwartz to Nelson Lund, "Thoughts for the State of the Union Address," Dec. 19, 1989, Amy Schwartz Files, Office of Counsel to the President, Formerly Withheld, NLGB Control Number 18830, GBPL.

48. Memo from Andrew Carpendale to Jim Cicconi, "State of the Union Points," Jan. 26, 1990, General Subject Files, Office of White House Records Management, Formerly Withheld, NLGB Control Number 2225, GBPL.

49. Note from James A. Baker III to Brent Scowcroft, Jan. 25, 1990, Virginia Lampley Files, National Security Council, Formerly Withheld, NLGB Control Number 17211, GBPL.

50. See memo from Andy Foster to David M. Carney, "State of the Union Comments," Jan. 15, 1990, and memo from Sally Simon to David M. Carney, "Suggested Comments for State of the Union Address," Jan. 16, 1990, Chris Dube Files, White House Office of Political Affairs, Freedom of Information Act Request 2003–1478-F, GBPL.

51. "Address before a Joint Session of the Congress on the State of the Union," Jan. 31, 1990, *The Public Papers of the Presidents of the United States: George Bush, 1990.*

52. "Reax to State of Union," *The Hotline*, Feb. 1, 1990, accessed on Lexis/Nexis Academic Universe.

53. David R. Gergen, "The Rush to Glory of 'Crazy Legs' Bush," *U.S. News and World Report*, 12 Feb. 1990, p. 30.

54. Andrew Rosenthal, "Bush is Cautious on Domestic Goals," *New York Times*, Feb. 1, 1990, p. A1.

55. James Gerstenzang and David Lauter, "Troop Plan Shows that Bush Knows How to Seize Moment," *Los Angeles Times*, Feb. 1, 1990, p. 18.

56. William H. Freivogel, "Bush Address Lacked Reagan's Flourishes," *St. Louis Post-Dispatch*, Feb. 1, 1990, p. 1C.

57. William Schneider, "A Year Later, Still No Bush Agenda," *National Journal*, Feb. 10, 1990, p. 362.

58. Walter V. Robinson, "Bush Proposes Deeper Troop Cuts; State of Union Talk a Reflection of the Public Mood," *Boston Globe*, Feb. 1, 1990, p. 1.

59. Tom Shales, "The Understatement of the Union; From George Bush, Something Borrowed, Something Bland," *Washington Post*, Feb. 1, 1990, p. C1.

60. Rozell, *The Press and the Bush Presidency*, 67.

61. Michael Duffy, "At Home: A Case of Doing Nothing," *Time*, Jan. 2, 1991.

62. Memo from Charles E. M. Kolb to Roger B. Porter, "State of the Union Themes," Dec. 4, 1990, General Subject Files, Office of White House Records Management, Formerly Withheld, NLGB Control Number 2228, GBPL.

63. Ibid.

64. Memo from Roger B. Porter to John Sununu, "State of the Union Address: Themes," Dec. 30, 1990, Draft Files, Office of Speechwriting, Box 81, GBPL.

65. Ibid.

66. Ibid.

67. Memo from Jennifer Grossman to Mark Lange, "Today's Meeting with Porter, Demarest," Jan. 9, 1991, Draft Files, Office of Speechwriting, Box 81, GBPL.

68. Memo from Michael L. Williams to Chino Chapa, "State of the Union," Nov. 29, 1990, John Schmitz Files, Office of Counsel to the President, Formerly Withheld, NLGB Control Number 10184, GBPL.

69. Memo from Hanns Kuttner to Roger B. Porter, "Health and the State of the Union: Shifting the Health Care Focus" Jan. 5, 1991, Johannes Kuttner Files, Office of Policy Development, Formerly Withheld, NLGB Control Number 14616, GBPL.

70. Memo from Mark Albrecht to Roger Porter, "State of the Union Address," Jan. 15, 1991, Mark Albrecht Files, National Space Council, Formerly Withheld, NLGB Control Number 42453, GBPL.

71. Memo from Marlin Fitzwater to John Sununu, "State of the Union Media Plan," Jan. 25, 1991, Marlin Fitzwater Files, Press Office/Alpha Files, Box 27, GBPL.

72. "Address before a Joint Session of the Congress on the State of the Union," Jan. 29, 1991, *The Public Papers of the Presidents of the United States: George Bush, 1991.*

73. Richard Morin, "War Boosts President's Popularity; Poll Finds Public Troubled by Bush's Handling of Economy at Home," *Washington Post*, Jan. 29, 1991, p. A1.

74. Alan Brinkley, "Bush Surrenders at Home," *New York Times*, Jan. 29, 1991, p. A21.

75. Margaret Carlson, "The State of the Union: So Who's Minding the Store?" *Time*, Feb. 11, 1991.

76. David Dahl, "Bush: "We will succeed'; Iraq: Bombs Killed POW," *St. Petersburg Times*, Jan. 30, 1991, p. 1A.

77. "The State of Bush's Union," *Boston Globe*, Jan. 30, 1991, p. 14.

78. John E. Yang, "Bush's Modest Domestic Proposals Contrast with Expansive World Role," *Washington Post*, Jan. 30, 1991, p. A12.

79. Richard Wolf, "Congress United on War, Divided on Domestic Front," *USA Today*, Jan. 30, 1991, p. 7A.

80. Kenneth T. Walsh, "A President's True Mission," *U.S. News and World Report*, Feb. 11, 1991, p. 46.

81. Maureen Dowd, "President, in State of Union Talk, Dwells on War and the Economy," *New York Times*, Jan. 30, 1991, p. 1.

82. Stephen Kurkjian and John W. Mashek, "Bush Calls War Effort 'on Course'; State of the Union Gives No Promise of a Quick Victory," *Boston Globe*, Jan. 30, 1991, p. 1.

83. Tom Shales, "George Bush, Stating It Smoothly," *Washington Post*, Jan. 30, 1991, p. B1.

84. Rozell, *The Press and the Bush Presidency*, 87.

85. Schlesinger, *White House Ghosts*, 395.

86. Rozell, *The Press and the Bush Presidency*, 116.

87. Tom Morganthau, "Decoding Bush," *Newsweek*, Feb. 10, 1992, p. 22.

88. Schlesinger, *White House Ghosts,* 388–89.

89. Memo from Tony Snow to Speechwriters and Researchers, "State of the Union and Other Stuff," Jan. 8, 1992, Backup Speech Files, White House Office of Speechwriting, Formerly Withheld, NLGB Control Number 6310, GBPL.

90. Memorandum, "Selected State of the Union Agenda Items," Dec. 10, 1991, Nelson Lund Files, Office of Counsel to the President, Formerly Withheld, NLGB Control Number 10751, GBPL.

91. Memo from Bobbie Kilberg to Sam Skinner, "NFIB and NAWD Business Coalition Building for the State of the Union," Jan. 20, 1992, Samuel Skinner Files, Office of the Chief of Staff to the President, Formerly Withheld, NLGB Control Number 6074, GBPL.

92. Memo from Charles Kolb to Tony Snow, undated, General Subject Files, Office of White House Records Management, Formerly Withheld, NLGB Control Number 2234, GBPL.

93. Memo from Marlin Fitzwater to Sam Skinner, "State of the Union Press Activities," Jan. 21, 1992, Marlin Fitzwater Files, Press Office/Alpha Files, Box 27, GBPL.

94. Memo from Dorrance Smith to Sam Skinner, "State of the Union Activities," Jan. 28, 1992, Katherine Holt Files, White House Office of Media Affairs, Freedom of Information Act Request 2003–1478-F, GBPL.

95. "Address before a Joint Session of the Congress on the State of the Union," Jan. 28, 1992, *The Public Papers of the Presidents of the United States: George Bush, 1992–93.*

96. For example, see Judy Keen, "Awaiting 'State of the Union,' Bush Aides Downplay Expectations," *USA Today,* Jan. 28, 1992, p. 1A, and "Speech Hopes Lowered, 'Damage Control' Begins," *St. Louis Post-Dispatch,* Jan. 28, 1992, p. 1A.

97. Michael Duffy, "State of the Union," *Time,* Feb. 10, 1992.

98. Tom Morganthau, "Decoding Bush," *Newsweek,* Feb. 10, 1992, p. 22.

99. Kenneth T. Walsh and David Gergen, "Blowin' in the Wind," *U.S. News and World Report,* Feb. 10, 1992, p. 24.

100. Marci McDonald, "Facing the Union; Bush's State of the Union Address Gets a Cool Reception in Recession-Torn New Hampshire," *Maclean's,* Feb. 10, 1992, p. 20.

101. "The Tinkerer; Mr. Bush's New War, and Paper Sword," *New York Times,* Jan. 30, 1992, p. A20.

102. "The State of the Union," *Washington Post,* Jan. 29, 29 1992, p. A20.

103. Ann Devroy, "A Declaration of Political War on the Democrats," *Washington Post,* Jan. 29, 1992, p. A1.

104. Tom Baxter, "Politics Verdict on Speech Must Wait," *Atlanta Journal and Constitution,* Jan. 29, 1992, p. A7.

105. Walter V. Robinson, "'Status Quo-Plus' Plan For Recovery," *Boston Globe,* Jan. 29, 1992, p. 17.

106. Tom Shales, "The Main Event: Bush vs. Recession," *Washington Post,* Jan. 29, 1992, p. B1.

107. Naftali, *George H. W. Bush,* 140.

108. Scott Williams, "Comedy Central Lampoons President Bush's Speech," Associated Press, Jan. 29, 1992.

109. Schlesinger, *White House Ghosts,* 395.

Chapter 5. Bush's Public Activities

1. Bush, *Speaking of Freedom*, 3.

2. Memo from Rae Nelson to Roger Porter, "Mobilizing Support for Administration Policies," Feb. 23, 1989, Doreen Torgerson Files, White House Office of Policy Development, Freedom of Information Act Request 2003–1478-F, GBPL.

3. Han, "Rose Garden Strategy Revisited," 169–71.

4. Ragsdale, *Vital Statistics on the Presidency*, 175. Note, however, that Ragsdale categorizes these speeches as "minor policy addresses," while I categorize them as major policy addresses, separate from the inaugural and state of the union addresses.

5. Totals for other contemporary presidents during their first (or only) terms include Richard Nixon—107, Jimmy Carter—119, Ronald Reagan—89, and Bill Clinton—224. See Han, "Rose Garden Strategy Revisited," 172–73.

6. "Advanced Text of Remarks upon Departure for Europe," July 8, 1989, *The Public Papers of the Presidents of the United States: George Bush, 1989.*

7. Other activities included presenting the press with an advance text of remarks upon departure for Europe and remarks at the welcoming ceremony in Warsaw on July 9, 1989; a statement by Fitzwater on Bush's meeting with Polish Chairman Wojceich Jaruzelski in Warsaw, toasts at a luncheon at the U.S. ambassador's residence in Warsaw, remarks to the Polish National Assembly in Warsaw, the distribution of a White House fact sheet on proposed assistance for Poland and Hungary, remarks to the Polish Little League baseball players in Warsaw, and a toast at the state dinner in Warsaw on July 10, 1989; remarks to U.S. embassy employees and their families in Warsaw, a question-and-answer session with reporters following a luncheon with Walesa in Gdansk, a statement by Fitzwater on U.S. technical assistance for Poland, and distribution of an advance text of remarks at the departure ceremony in Gdansk on July 11, 1989. See *The Public Papers of the Presidents of the United States: George Bush, 1989.*

8. Schlesinger, *White House Ghosts*, 370–71.

9. Naftali, *George H. W. Bush*, 82.

10. Bush, *All the Best*, 433.

11. Rozell, *The Press and the Bush Presidency*, 42–43.

12. Memo from Bob Simon to Ed McNally, "Gdansk Speech," June 26, 1989, Backup Speech Files, White House Office of Speechwriting, Formerly Withheld, NLGB Control Number 6248, GBPL.

13. Memo from Edward E. McNally to George Bush, "Address at the Lenin Shipyard Gates in Gdansk—and 'Comments' on the Four 'Major' Speeches for Poland and Hungary," July 1, 1989, Draft Speech Files, White House Office of Speechwriting, Box 22, GBPL.

14. Handwritten note on speech draft, "Solidarity Workers Monument Lenin Shipyard Gates, Gdansk, Tuesday, July 11, 1989, 2:10 P.M.," undated, Draft Speech Files, White House Office of Speechwriting, Box 22, GBPL.

15. The lines of "Let them look at Poland" are similar to Kennedy's remarks in his Berlin speech in which he repeated the phrase "Let them come to Berlin."

16. "Remarks at the Solidarity Workers Monument in Gdansk," July 11, 1989, The *Public Papers of the Presidents of the United States: George Bush, 1989.*

17. James Gerstenzang and Jack Nelson, "'Time of Destiny,' Bush Tells Poland President,

Delivers Emotional Plea for Democracy at Birthplace of Solidarity," *Los Angeles Times*, July 12, 1989, p. 1.

18. Stephen Kurkjian, "Bush Asks Poles' Patience with Reform; With Walesa at His Side in Gdansk, President Offers Vision of a New Life," *Boston Globe*, July 12, 1989, p. 1.

19. Maureen Dowd, "Bush Urges Poles to Pull Together," *New York Times*, July 12, 1989, p. A1.

20. "Mr. Bush and the Other 10 Percent," *New York Times*, July 12, 1989, p. A22.

21. "Aid for Poland," *Washington Post*, July 12, 1989, p. A22.

22. R. W. Apple Jr., "A Polish Journey; Bush Escapes Pitfalls in Weathering Tough Economic and Political Climate," *New York Times*, July 12, 1989, p. A8.

23. Hugh Sidey, "High-Wire Act," *Time*, July 24, 1989.

24. Larry Martz et al., "The Green Summit," *Newsweek*, July 24, 1989, p. 12.

25. Douglas Stanglin et al., "Unquiet on the Eastern Front," *U.S. News and World Report*, July 17, 1989, p. 31.

26. Schlesinger, *White House Ghosts*, 372.

27. Bush, *Speaking of Freedom*, 81–82.

28. Memo from Edward E. McNally to Chriss Winston, "Sound Bite 'Theme' For Drug Speech," Aug. 31, 1989, Backup Speech Files, White House Office of Speechwriting, Formerly Withheld, NLGB Control Number 6211, GBPL.

29. See memo from Barrie Tron to David Demarest, "Drug Policy Communications Plan—Satellite Media Tours and Network Programs," Aug. 11, 1989, and "Cabinet Participation in Announcement and Promotion of the National Drug Control Strategy," undated, Barrie Tron Files, White House Office of Public Affairs, Freedom of Information Act Request 2003–1478-F, GBPL.

30. Memo from David Demarest to Interested Parties, "Communications Plan for Drug Control Strategy Activities for the Months of August and September," Aug. 16, 1989, Barrie Tron Files, White House Office of Public Affairs, Freedom of Information Act Request 2003–1478-F, GBPL. The magazines targeted for articles included *Modern Maturity, Readers Digest, American Health, Ebony, Foreign Affairs, Parenting, ABA Journal, Chronicle of Higher Education, Education Week, Ladies Home Journal, Guideposts, Prevention, Sports Illustrated, Law and Order, Police, Hispanic Business, Forbes,* and *Boys Life.*

31. "Address to the Nation on the National Drug Control Strategy," Sept. 5, 1989, *The Public Papers of the Presidents of the United States: George Bush, 1989.*

32. David Lauter and Douglas Jehl, "Today's Drug Speech Key Part of Bush Agenda," *Los Angeles Times*, Sept. 5, 1989, p. 1.

33. James Barron, "Democrats Criticize the Drug Plan as Lacking Toughness and Money," *New York Times*, Sept. 6, 1989, p. 1.

34. Stephen Kurkjian, "Risky Political Gamble without New Funding; The President's Drug Plan," *Boston Globe*, Sept. 6, 1989, p. 3.

35. Ann Devroy and Helen Dewar, "Bush Sets Coordinated Attack on Drug Trade; Nation Already Has 'Basic Weapons,'" *Washington Post*, Sept. 6, 1989, p. A1.

36. Randolph Ryan, "For Bush, a Test of Leadership in the War on Drugs," *Boston Globe*, Sept. 6, 1989, p. 19.

37. John Podhoretz, "Staging of Speech Spoiled Emotion," *Washington Times*, Sept. 6, 1989, p. A6.

38. Tom Morganthau, Mark Miller, and Joseph Contreras, "Now It's Bush's War," *Newsweek*, Sept. 18, 1989, p. 22.

39. David Gergen and Kenneth T. Walsh, "The Rise and Rise of George Bush," *U.S. News and World Report*, Sept. 18, 1989, p. 25.

40. Anthony Lewis, "Abroad at Home; The Phony War," *New York Times*, Sept. 10, 1989, sec. 4, p. 31.

41. Schlesinger, *White House Ghosts*, 373.

42. Rozell, *The Press and the Bush Presidency*, 38–39.

43. Memo from Marlin Fitzwater to John Sununu and Brent Scowcroft, "Public Appearances by the President on Foreign Policy," May 1, 1989, Backup Speech Files, White House Office of Speechwriting, Formerly Withheld, NLGB Control Number 6218, GBPL.

44. "Remarks at the University of Texas Commencement Ceremony in Austin, Texas," May, 19, 1990, *The Public Papers of the Presidents of the United States: George Bush, 1990.*

45. Memo from Dan McGroarty to George Bush, "University of South Carolina Commencement," May 8, 1990, Speech Draft Files, White House Office of Speechwriting, Box 58, GBPL. Bush returned the memo to McGroarty with the following handwritten comments: "1) Front end needs a little tightening. 2) I like specific 4 points. 3) Needs about 1 page less. 4) 1 humorous anecdote around p. 3."

46. Ibid.

47. Memo from Jim Pinkerton to Chriss Winston, "University of South Carolina Commencement Draft," May 7, 1990, Speech Draft Files, White House Office of Speechwriting, Box 58, GBPL.

48. "Remarks at the University of South Carolina Commencement Ceremony in Columbia," May, 12, 1990, *The Public Papers of the Presidents of the United States: George Bush, 1990.*

49. Ann Devroy, "Bush Backs E. Europe Aid 'Corps'; New Program to Seek Money and Volunteers from Private Sector," *Washington Post*, May 13, 1990, p. A1.

50. Maureen Dowd, "Volunteer Corps for East Europe," *New York Times*, May 13, 1990, sec. 1, p. 10.

51. Stephen Kurkjian, "Bush Condemns Past East Europe Regimes on Rights Abuses," *Boston Globe*, May 13, 1990, p. 20.

52. "Bush Tells 'Slovenly' Press to Shape Up; President Gets Testy When Reporters Fail to Join Him on Early Jog," *Washington Post*, May 13, 1990, p. A25.

53. Rachel Martin Harlow, "Agency and Agent in George Bush's Gulf War Rhetoric," in *Rhetorical Presidency*, ed. Medhurst, 57.

54. Rozell, *The Press and the Bush Presidency*, 91–93.

55. Memo from David Demarest to George Bush, "Communications Plan for Operation Desert Shield," Nov. 14, 1990, Daily Guidance File, Press Office, Formerly Withheld, NLGB Control Number 20032, GBPL. Bush wrote the following remarks on the memo: "Brent/John: How much of this has been done. What more can be done. Let's discuss next week."

56. Memo from David Demarest to John Sununu, Brent Scowcroft, and Marlin Fitzwater, "Gulf Communications Strategy," Dec. 21, 90, John Sununu Files, Office of the Chief of Staff to the President, Formerly Withheld, NLGB Control Number 12525, GBPL.

57. Memo outlining "Gulf Strategy January Themes and Messages," undated, Carol Aarhus Files, White House Office of Speechwriting, Formerly Withheld, NLGB Control Number 6374, GBPL.

58. Demarest explained the concept of "communications task forces" in a memo to White House Senior Staff: "The office of communications has established ten task forces to draft communications strategies for the issues as stake this fall. . . . The task forces provide a more formal vehicle to manage a broad spectrum of activities. Specifically, they will be responsible for: 1. Developing communications plans for targeted issues; 2. Organizing necessary events and activities to get our messages across; and 3. Creating material for appropriate interest and constituent groups, as well as media, such as regional and specialty press and editorial boards." The ten groups developed during the fall of 1990 included education, crime and drugs, environment, foreign policy/defense, savings and loan, economy, Judge Souter, family issues, civil rights, and misc. issues/potential vetoes. See memo from David Demarest to White House Senior Staff, "Communication Task Forces," Sept. 4, 1990, Sig Rogich Files, White House Office of Public Events and Initiatives, Freedom of Information Act Request 2003–1478-F, GBPL.

59. Harlow, "Agency and Agent," 63.

60. Bush also wrote an "Open Letter to College Students" that was sent to 460 colleges and universities on January 9, 1991. See *The Public Papers of the Presidents of the United States: George Bush, 1991.*

61. "Address to the Nation Announcing Allied Military Action in the Persian Gulf," Jan. 16, 1991, *The Public Papers of the Presidents of the United States: George Bush, 1991.*

62. Bush, *Speaking of Freedom*, 504.

63. Bush and Scowcroft, *A World Transformed*, 451.

64. For a thorough analysis of media coverage and public opinion during the Gulf War, see Bennett and Paletz, eds., *Taken by Storm.*

65. See *The Public Papers of the Presidents of the United States: George Bush, 1991.*

66. Marvin Kalb, "A View From the Press," in *Taken by Storm*, 4.

67. James Gerstenzang, "Had 'No Choice' Other Than War, Bush Says," *Los Angeles Times*, Jan. 17, 1991, p. 1.

68. Stephen Kurkjian and John W. Mashek, "Bush, in Speech, Pledges US 'Will Not Fail,'" *Boston Globe*, Jan. 17, 1991, p. 8.

69. James Barron, "War in the Gulf: America's Reaction," *New York Times*, Jan. 17, 1991, p. 1.

70. Walter Mears, "Bush Stakes His Presidency on Swift, Clear Victory," Associated Press, Jan. 17, 1991.

71. Adam Nagourney, "Calm, Decisive Bush Wins Backers with Top TV Form," *USA Today*, Jan. 17, 1991, p. 4A.

72. John Podhoretz, "War Speech to Nation Rated as Bush's Best," *Washington Times*, Jan. 17, 1991, p. A4.

73. Tom Shales, "Television, Eyewitness on the Front Line," *Washington Post*, Jan. 17, 1991, p. C1.

74. Evan Thomas, "Strong and Steady," *Newsweek*, Jan. 28, 1991, p. 34.

75. "George Bush's Critics," *Economist*, Jan. 26, 1991, p. 46.

76. Strobe Talbott, "A Storm Erupts," *Time*, Jan. 28, 1991.

77. Memo from David Demarest to George Bush, "Gulf Communications Plan," Feb. 6, 1991, Philip D. Brady Files, Office of the Chief of Staff to the President, Formerly Withheld, NLGB Control Number 5578, GBPL.

78. Holly G. McIntush, "Political Truancy: George Bush's Claim to the Mantle of 'Education President,'" in *Rhetorical Presidency*, ed. Medhurst, 106–107.

79. Memo from Roger B. Porter to John Sununu, "Education Policy Advisory Committee," June 1, 1989, Backup Speech Files, White House Office of Speechwriting, Formerly Withheld, NLGB Control Number 6227, GBPL.

80. Memo from Barrie Tron to David Demarest, "Communications/Marketing Plan for the Administration's Education Initiatives," July 19, 1990, Barrie Tron Files, White House Office of Public Affairs, Freedom of Information Act Request 2003–1478-F, GBPL.

81. Memo From Barrie Tron to David Demarest and Chriss Winston, "Communications Plan and Timeline for the Administration's Education Initiatives," Oct. 22, 1990, Doreen Dorgerson Files, White House Office of Policy Development, Freedom of Information Act Request 2003–1478-F, GBPL.

82. States' Impact on Federal Education Policy Project, "The George H. W. Bush Years," accessed May 15, 2009 at http://www.archives.nysed.gov/edpolicy/research/res_essay_bush_ghw_outline.shtml.

83. Memo from David Demarest to George Bush and John Sununu, "Three Month Plan," Mar. 21, 1991, John Sununu Files, Office of the Chief of Staff to the President, Formerly Withheld, NLGB Control Number 12517, GBPL.

84. McIntush, "Political Truancy," 112.

85. "Address to the Nation on the National Education Strategy," Apr. 18, 1991, *The Public Papers of the Presidents of the United States: George Bush, 1991.*

86. Barbara Kantrowitz, "Playing Catch-Up," *Newsweek*, Apr. 22, 1991, pg. 28.

87. Paul Richter, "Bush Details Sweeping Plan to 'Reinvent' U.S. Education," *Los Angeles Times*, Apr. 19, 1991, p. 1.

88. John E. Yang, "Bush Unveils Education Plan; Local Innovation, Parental Involvement Stressed in Setting Goals for '90s," *Washington Post*, Apr. 19, 1991, p. A1.

89. Richard Benedetto, "Critics See Politics in Education Plan," *USA Today*, Apr. 19, 1991, p. 4A.

90. John W. Mashek, "School Proposal Unveiled by Bush," *Boston Globe*, Apr. 19, 1991, p. 1.

91. Kevin Leary and John Wildermuth, "State Educators React to Bush 'Revolution,'" *San Francisco Chronicle*, Apr. 19, 1991, p. A15.

92. "An Education President for All?" *New York Times*, Apr. 19, 1991, p. A26.

93. "Education: Bush Is Learning," *Business Week*, Apr. 29, 1991, p. 106.

94. Richard N. Ostling, et al., "A Revolution Hoping for a Miracle," Time, Apr. 29, 1991.

95. McIntush, "Political Truancy," 113.

96. Memo written by Lamar Alexander to undisclosed recipients, "30-Day Strategy: Education," undated, Backup Speech Files, White House Office of Speechwriting, Formerly Withheld, NLGB Control Number 6306, GBPL.

97. Memo from Charles E. M. Kolb to Roger B. Porter, "Health Care Speech," Jan. 30, 1992, General Subject Files, White House Office of Records Management, Formerly Withheld, NLGB Control Number 2204, GBPL.

98. "Cleveland Speech: Announcing the President's Health Plan," undated memo, Speech Backup Files, White House Office of Speechwriting, Formerly Withheld, NLGB Control Number 6317, GBPL.

99. Memo from Marlin Fitzwater to Samuel Skinner, "Health Care Announcement," Jan. 29, 1992, Marlin Fitzwater Files, Press Office/Subject Files, Box 42, GBPL.

100. "Remarks to the Greater Cleveland Growth Association in Cleveland, Ohio," Feb. 6, 1992, *The Public Papers of the Presidents of the United States: George Bush, 1992–93.*

101. "Bush: TV Reception for Health Care Plan," *The Hotline*, Feb. 7, 1992.

102. Ann Devroy, "President Unveils Health Care Plan; 'Preserve' but 'Reform' Existing System," *Washington Post*, Feb. 7, 1992, p. A1.

103. Douglas Jehl, "Bush Health Plan Cost: $100 Billion Insurance," *Los Angeles Times*, Feb. 7, 1992, p. 1.

104. Charlotte Grimes, "President Campaigns for His Health Plan," *St. Louis Post-Dispatch*, Feb. 7, 1992, p. 1A.

105. Michael Kranish and Richard A. Knos, "Bush Offers Cost-Control Health Plan; Eyes Tax Breaks on Insurance," *Boston Globe*, Feb. 7, 1992, p. 1.

106. "The President's Health Care Plan," *Washington Post*, Feb. 7, 1992, p. A24.

107. David S. Broder, "The Race for President: A Daily Digest," *Washington Post*, Feb. 7, 1992, p. A4.

108. David Ellis, et al., "Social Policy: Rx Band-Aids to Patch Up Health Care," *Time*, Feb. 17, 1992.

109. Steven V. Roberts and Gloria Borger, "A Time of Fury and Despair," *U.S. News and World Report*, Feb. 17, 1992, p. 22.

110. Bill Turque, et al., "Northern Exposure," *Newsweek*, Feb. 17, 1992, p. 20.

Chapter 6. Conclusion

1. "Remarks at Texas A&M University in College Station, Texas," Dec. 15, 1992, *The Public Papers of the Presidents of the United States: George Bush, 1992–93.*

2. Catherine L. Langford, "George Bush's Struggle with the 'Vision Thing,'" in *Rhetorical Presidency*, ed. Medhurst, 20.

3. Ibid., 22–23.

4. Greene, *Presidency of George Bush*, 148.

5. Ibid., 185.

6. Martin J. Medhurst, "Afterword: Evaluating the Rhetorical Presidency of George H. W. Bush," in *Rhetorical Presidency*, ed. Medhurst, 197. Medhurst goes on to explain that he witnessed Bush's skills as an orator firsthand when they shared a stage at Texas A&M University at a forum in 1996: "George Bush rose to the occasion magnificently, speaking for over an hour and holding his audience in rapt attention from beginning to end. As a speaker, he was funny, using a self-deprecating humor, as well as informative, insightful, slightly profane, clear, and persuasive. He successfully identified with those students and made one of the better speeches of his entire career." I had a similar reaction when meeting President Bush and hearing him give both an informal address to students followed by a formal address at Austin College in Sherman, Texas, in November 2002. He was fully engaged with both audiences, articulate, and funny and self-deprecating in a Reaganesque

manner. As I was in the early stages of outlining this manuscript, I came away wondering how the President Bush I had witnessed that day had not emerged more often during his time in the White House.

7. See Langford, "George Bush's Struggle," 34.

8. Ibid.

9. Cohen, *Presidential Responsiveness and Public Policy-making*, 18.

10. For a discussion of Bush's governing style, see Naftali, *George H. W. Bush*, chapter 4.

11. Kumar, *Managing the President's Message*, 150–51.

12. C-SPAN 2009 Historians Presidential Leadership Survey, accessed May 24, 2009 at http://www.c-span.org/PresidentialSurvey/Overall-Ranking.aspx. Reagan's overall ranking improved from eleventh to tenth, while his rating for "Public Persuasion" increased from fourth to third, as well as his rating for "Vision/Setting an Agenda," which increased from eighth to seventh.

13. Steve Roberts, quoted in "Presidential Lessons Learned in Working with the New Media," in *Dialogues on Presidential Leadership, Selected Remarks From: Annual Awards Dinner and Spring Symposium* (Washington, D.C.: Center for the Study of the Presidency, spring 2000), 76.

14. Rozell, *The Press and the Bush Presidency*, 7.

15. "Internet Sapping Broadcast News Audience," Pew Research Center for the People and the Press, June 11, 2000.

16. Sunstein, *republic.com*, 3.

17. "Bottom-Line Pressures Now Hurting Coverage, Say Journalists," Pew Research Center for the People and the Press, May 23, 2004.

18. Graber, *Processing Politics*, 1.

19. Downie and Kaiser, *News about the News*, 10–11.

Bibliography

Bagdikian, Ben H. *The Media Monopoly*. 4th ed. Boston: Beacon Press, 1992.

———. *The New Media Monopoly*. Boston: Beacon Press, 2004.

Barilleaux, Ryan J. "George Bush and the Changing Context of Presidential Leadership." In *Leadership and the Bush Presidency: Prudence or Drift in an Era of Change?* Edited by Ryan J. Barilleaux and Mary E. Stuckey. Westport, Conn.: Praeger, 1992.

Barilleaux, Ryan J., and Mark J. Rozell. *Power and Prudence: The Presidency of George H. W. Bush*. College Station: Texas A&M University Press, 2004.

Baum, Matthew A., and Samuel Kernell. "Has Cable Ended the Golden Age of Presidential Television?" *The American Political Science Review* 93, no. 1 (March 1999): 99–114.

Bennett, W. Lance, and David L. Paletz, eds. *Taken by Storm: The Media, Public Opinion, and U.S. Foreign Policy in the Gulf War*. Chicago: University of Chicago Press, 1994.

Brace, Paul, and Barbara Hinckley. *Follow the Leader: Opinion Polls and the Modern Presidents*. New York: HarperCollins Publishers, 1992.

Brody, Richard A. *Assessing the President: The Media, Elite Opinion, and Public Support*. Stanford: Stanford University Press, 1991.

Burke, John. *The Institutional Presidency*. Baltimore: Johns Hopkins University Press, 1992.

Bush, George. *All the Best, George Bush: My Life in Letters and Other Writings*. New York: Scribner, 1999.

Bush, George H. W. *Speaking of Freedom: The Collected Speeches*. New York: Scribner, 2009.

Bush, George, and Brent Scowcroft. *A World Transformed*. New York: Alfred A. Knopf, 1998.

Campbell, Karlyn Kohrs, and Kathleen Hall Jamieson. *Deeds Done in Words: Presidential Rhetoric and the Genres of Governance*. Chicago: University of Chicago Press, 1990.

Canes-Wrone, Brandice. *Who Leads Whom? Presidents, Policy, and the Public*. Chicago, University of Chicago Press, 2006.

Cohen, Jeffrey E. *The Presidency in the Era of 24-Hour News*. Princeton, N.J.: Princeton University Press, 2008.

———. *Presidential Responsiveness and Public Policy-making: The Public and the Policies that Presidents Choose*. Ann Arbor: University of Michigan Press, 1997.

Collins, Mary. "What's Missing on Sunday." *Columbia Journalism Review* (March/April 1992): 9.

Cook, Philip S., Douglas Gomery, and Lawrence W. Lichty, eds. *The Future of News: Television-Newspapers-Wire Services-Newsmagazines*. Baltimore: Johns Hopkins University Press, 1992.

Cornwell, Elmer E., Jr. *Presidential Leadership of Public Opinion*. Westport, Conn.: Greenwood Press, 1965.

Cronin, Thomas E., and Michael A. Genovese. *The Paradoxes of the American Presidency.* 2d ed. New York: Oxford University Press, 2004.

Demarest, David F., Jr. "The Bush Presidency and Communications." In *The Bush Presidency, Part Two: Ten Intimate Perspectives of George Bush.* Edited by Kenneth W. Thompson. Lanham, Md.: University Press of America, 1998.

Downie, Leonard, Jr., and Robert G. Kaiser. *The News about the News: American Journalism in Peril.* New York: Alfred A. Knopf, 2002.

Duerst-Lahti, Georgia, and Rita Mae Kelly. "On Governance, Leadership, and Gender." In *Gender Power, Leadership, and Governance.* Edited by Georgia Duerst-Lahti and Rita Mae Kelly. Ann Arbor: University of Michigan Press, 1995.

Duffy, Michael, and Dan Goodgame. *Marching in Place: The Status Quo Presidency of George Bush.* New York: Simon and Schuster, 1992.

Edwards, George C., III. *At The Margins: Presidential Leadership of Congress.* New Haven: Yale University Press, 1989.

———. "George Bush and the Public Presidency: The Politics of Inclusion." In *The Bush Presidency: First Appraisals.* Edited by Colin Campbell and Bert A. Rockman. Chatham, N.J.: Chatham House Publishers.

———. *On Deaf Ears: The Limits of the Bully Pulpit.* New Haven: Yale University Press, 2003.

———. *The Public Presidency: The Pursuit of Popular Support.* New York: St. Martin's Press, 1983.

Edwards, George C., III, and Stephen J. Wayne. *Presidential Leadership: Politics and Policy Making.* 5th ed. New York: St. Martin's Press, 1999.

Emery, Michael, and Edwin Emery. *The Press and America: An Interpretive History of the Mass Media.* 8th ed. Boston: Allyn and Bacon, 1996.

Eshbaugh-Soha, Matthew. *The President's Speeches: Beyond "Going Public."* Boulder: Lynne Rienner Publishers, 2006.

Fitzwater, Marlin. *Call the Briefing! Bush and Reagan, Sam and Helen: A Decade with Presidents and the Press.* New York: Random House, 1995.

Gelderman, Carol. *All the President's Words: The Bully Pulpit and the Creation of the Virtual Presidency.* New York: Walker and Company, 1997.

Genovese, Michael A. *The Power of the American Presidency 1789–2000.* New York: Oxford, 2001.

Graber, Doris A. *Processing Politics: Learning from Television in the Internet Age.* Chicago: University of Chicago Press, 2001.

Gray, C. Boyden. "The President as Leader." Presented in a Forum at the Miller Center of Public Affairs on February 17, 1994. In *The Bush Presidency: Ten Intimate Perspectives of George Bush.* Edited by Kenneth W. Thompson. Lanham, Md.: University Press of America, 1997.

Greene, John Robert. *The Presidency of George Bush.* Lawrence: University Press of Kansas, 2000.

Greenstein, Fred I. *The Presidential Difference: Leadership Style from FDR to Clinton.* Princeton, N.J.: Princeton University Press, 2000.

Griscom, Tom. "The Great Communicator: The Reagan Presidency." In *The Reagan Presi-*

dency: Ten Intimate Perspectives of Ronald Reagan. Edited by Kenneth W. Thompson. Lanham, Md.: University Press of America, 1997.

Grossman, Michael Baruch, and Martha Joynt Kumar. *Portraying the President: The White House and the News Media.* Baltimore: Johns Hopkins University Press, 1981.

Han, Lori Cox, *Governing from Center Stage: White House Communication Strategies during the Television Age of Politics.* Cresskill, N.J.: Hampton Press, 2001.

———. "New Strategies for an Old Medium: The Weekly Radio Addresses of Reagan and Clinton." *Congress and the Presidency* 33, no. 1 (spring 2006): 25–45.

———. "The President over the Public: The Plebiscitary Presidency at Center Stage." In *The Presidency and the Challenge of Democracy.* Edited by Michael A. Genovese and Lori Cox Han. New York: Palgrave Macmillan, 2006.

———. "Public Leadership in the Political Arena." In *Leadership and Politics, Vol. 2 of Leadership at the Crossroads.* Edited by Michael A. Genovese and Lori Cox Han. Westport, Conn.: Praeger Publishers, 2008.

———. "The Rose Garden Strategy Revisited: How Presidents Use Public Activities." In *In the Public Domain: Presidents and the Challenges of Public Leadership.* Edited by Lori Cox Han and Diane J. Heith. Albany: SUNY Press, 2005.

Hargrove, Erwin C. *The President as Leader: Appealing to the Better Angels of Our Nature.* Lawrence: University Press of Kansas, 1998.

Hart, Roderick P. *The Sound of Leadership: Presidential Communication in the Modern Age.* Chicago: University of Chicago Press, 1987.

Heith, Diane J. *Polling to Govern: Public Opinion and Presidential Leadership.* Stanford: Stanford University Press, 2003.

Hess, Stephen. *Presidents and the Presidency.* Washington, D.C.: Brookings Institution, 1996.

Hill, Dilys M., and Phil Williams, eds. *The Bush Presidency: Triumphs and Adversities.* New York: St. Martin's Press, 1994.

Jacobs, Lawrence R., and Robert Y. Shapiro. *Politicians Don't Pander: Political Manipulation and the Loss of Democratic Responsiveness.* Chicago: University of Chicago Press, 2000.

Jones, Charles O. *Separate but Equal Branches: Congress and the Presidency.* 2d ed. New York: Chatham House Publishers, 1999.

Katz, Jon. "Reinventing the Media." *Columbia Journalism Review* (March/April 1992): 19.

Kenski, Henry C. "A Man for All Seasons? The Guardian President and His Public." In *Leadership and the Bush Presidency: Prudence or Drift in an Era of Change?* Edited by Ryan J. Barilleaux and Mary E. Stuckey. Westport, Conn.: Praeger, 1992.

Kerbel, Matthew Robert. *Remote and Controlled: Media Politics in a Cynical Age.* 2d ed. Boulder: Westview Press, 1999.

Kernell, Samuel. *Going Public: New Strategies of Presidential Leadership.* 4th ed. Washington, D.C.: CQ Press, 2007.

Kessel, John H. *Presidents, the Presidency, and the Political Environment.* Washington, D.C.: CQ Press, 2001.

Kipling, Richard E. "A Lost Generation." *Columbia Journalism Review* (September/October 1991): 28.

Kolb, Charles. *White House Daze: The Unmaking of Domestic Policy in the Bush Years.* New York: Free Press, 1994.

Kumar, Martha Joynt. Discussant Comments for "The Media and Public Opinion." In *Honor and Loyalty: Inside the Politics of the George H. W. Bush White House.* Edited by Leslie D. Feldman and Rosanna Perotti. Westport, Conn.: Greenwood Press, 2002.

———. *Managing the President's Message: The White House Communications Operation.* Baltimore: Johns Hopkins University Press, 2007.

Lammers, William W., and Michael A. Genovese. *The Presidency and Domestic Policy: Comparing Leadership Styles, FDR to Clinton.* Washington, D.C.: CQ Press, 2000.

Lang, Kurt, and Gladys Engel Lang. *Politics and Television.* Chicago: Quadrangle Books, 1968.

Liebovich, Louis W. *The Press and the Modern Presidency: Myths and Mindsets from Kennedy to Election 2000.* Rev. 2d. ed. Westport, Conn.: Praeger, 2001.

Lowi, Theodore J. *The Personal President: Power Invested, Promise Unfulfilled.* Ithaca, N.Y.: Cornell University Press, 1985.

Maltese, John Anthony. *Spin Control: The White House Office of Communications and the Management of Presidential News.* 2d ed. rev. Chapel Hill: University of North Carolina Press, 1994.

———. "Spin Control in the White House" In *Understanding the Presidency.* Edited by James P. Pfiffner and Roger H. Davidson. New York: Longman, 1997.

Medhurst, Martin J., ed. *The Rhetorical Presidency of George H. W. Bush.* College Station: Texas A&M University Press, 2006.

Mervin, David. *George Bush and the Guardianship Presidency.* New York: St. Martin's Press, 1996.

Naftali, Timothy. *George H. W. Bush.* New York: Henry Holt and Company, 2007.

Nelson, W. Dale. *Who Speaks for the President? The White House Press Secretary from Cleveland to Clinton.* Syracuse, N.Y.: Syracuse University Press, 1998.

Neustadt, Richard E. "Looking Back: Meanings and Puzzles." In *Looking Back on the Reagan Presidency.* Edited by Larry Berman. Baltimore: Johns Hopkins University Press, 1990.

———. *Presidential Power.* New York: Wiley, 1960.

Noonan, Peggy. *What I Saw at the Revolution: A Political Life in the Reagan Era.* New York: Random House, 1990.

Northouse, Peter G. *Leadership: Theory and Practice.* Thousand Oaks, Calif.: Sage Publications, 1997.

Pfiffner, James P. *The Strategic Presidency: Hitting the Ground Running.* 2d ed. rev. Lawrence: University of Kansas Press, 1996.

Podhoretz, John. *Hell of a Ride: Backstage at the White House Follies 1989–1993.* New York: Simon and Schuster, 1993.

The Public Papers of the Presidents of the United States: George Bush, 1989–1993. Washington, D.C.: Government Printing Office, 1990–93.

Ragsdale, Lyn. *Vital Statistics on the Presidency: George Washington to George W. Bush.* 3d ed. Washington, D.C.: CQ Press, 2009.

Reston, James. *Deadline: A Memoir.* New York: Random House, 1991.

Rockman, Bert A. "The Leadership Style of George Bush." In *The Bush Presidency: First*

Appraisals. Edited by Colin Campbell and Bert A. Rockman. Chatham, N.J.: Chatham House, 1991.

Rose, Richard. *The Postmodern President.* 2d ed. Chatham, N.J.: Chatham House Publishers, 1991.

Rosenstiel, Tom. *The Beat Goes On: President Clinton's First Year with the Media.* New York: Twentieth Century Fund Press, 1994.

Rossiter, Clinton. "The Presidency—Focus of Leadership." *New York Times,* November 11, 1963. Reprinted in *The Dynamics of the American Presidency.* Edited by Donald Bruce Johnson and Jack L. Walker. New York: John Wiley and Sons, 1964.

Rozell, Mark J. *The Press and the Bush Presidency.* Westport, Conn.: Praeger Publishers, 1996.

Sabato, Larry. *Feeding Frenzy: How Attack Journalism Has Transformed American Politics.* New York: Free Press, 1991.

Schlesinger, Robert. *White House Ghosts: Presidents and Their Speechwriters.* New York: Simon and Shuster, 2008.

Shogan, Colleen J. *The Moral Rhetoric of American Presidents.* College Station: Texas A&M University Press, 2006.

Sidey, Hugh. "Some Personal Reflections." In *The Bush Presidency, Part Two: Ten Intimate Perspectives of George Bush.* Edited by Kenneth W. Thompson. Lanham, Md.: University Press of America, 1998.

Skowronek, Stephen. *The Politics Presidents Make: Leadership from John Adams to George Bush.* Cambridge: Belknap/Harvard Press, 1993.

Smith, Craig R. "George Herbert Walker Bush." In *U.S. Presidents as Orators: A Bio-Critical Sourcebook.* Edited by Halford Ryan. Westport, Conn.: Greenwood Press, 1995.

Stuckey, Mary E. *The President as Interpreter-in-Chief.* Chatham, N.J.: Chatham House, 1991.

Stuckey, Mary E., and Frederick J. Antczak. "Governance as Political Theater: George Bush and the MTV Presidency." In *Leadership and the Bush Presidency: Prudence or Drift in an Era of Change?* Edited by Ryan J. Barilleaux and Mary E. Stuckey. Westport: Praeger, 1992.

Sunstein, Cass R. *Democracy and the Problem of Free Speech.* New York: Free Press, 1993.

———. *republic.com.* Princeton, N.J.: Princeton University Press, 2001.

Tebbel, John, and Sarah Miles Watts. *The Press and the Presidency: From George Washington to Ronald Reagan.* New York: Oxford University Press, 1985.

Thomas, Helen. *Front Row at the White House: My Life and Times.* New York: Touchstone, 1999.

Tiefer, Charles. *The Semi-Sovereign Presidency: The Bush Administration's Strategy for Governing without Congress.* Boulder: Westview Press, 1994.

Tozzi, Lisa. "Salary Watch: The TV Story." *Columbia Journalism Review* (November/December 1992): 15.

Tulis, Jeffrey K. *The Rhetorical Presidency.* Princeton: Princeton University Press, 1987.

Underwood, Doug. "The Newspapers' Identity Crisis." *Columbia Journalism Review* (March/April 1992): 24.

Warshaw, Shirley Anne. *The Keys to Power: Managing the Presidency.* New York: Longman, 2000.

Waterman, Richard W., Robert Wright, and Gilbert St. Clair. *The Image-Is-Everything Presidency: Dilemmas in American Leadership.* Boulder: Westview Press, 1999.

Weko, Thomas J. *The Politicizing Presidency: The White House Personnel Office, 1948–1994.* Lawrence: University of Kansas Press, 1995.

Wicker, Tom. *George Herbert Walker Bush.* New York: Viking, 2004.

Yeutter, Clayton. "Accomplishments and Setbacks." Presented in a Forum at the Miller Center of Public Affairs on April 30, 1993. In *The Bush Presidency: Ten Intimate Perspectives of George Bush.* Edited by Kenneth W. Thompson. Lanham, Md.: University Press of America, 1997.

Index

Other titles in the Joseph V. Hughes Jr. and Holly O. Hughes Series on the Presidency and Leadership:

Politics of Shared Power	Louis Fisher
Shaping and Signaling Presidential Policy	Meena Bose
Games Advisors Play	Jean A. Garrison
Managerial Presidency, Second Edition	James P. Pfiffner
The American Campaign	James E. Campbell
Good Advice: Information and Policy Making in the White House	Daniel E. Ponder
Congressional Abdication on War and Spending	Louis Fisher
Presidents and the People	Mel Laracey
The Opposition Presidency	David A. Crockett
Presidency, Congress, and Divided Government	Richard S. Conley
The White House World	Kumar and Sullivan
Between Law and Politics	Richard Pacelle Jr.
The Presidency and Women	Janet M. Martin
The Character Factor	James P. Pfiffner
Out of Touch	Michael J.Towle
Power and Prudence	Barilleaux and Rozell
The Nerve Center	Sullivan and Baker
Saving the Reagan Presidency	Abshire and Neustadt
Nixon's Business	Nigel Bowles
Policy by Other Means	Steven A. Shull
Institutionalizing Congress and the Presidency	Mordecai Lee
Scripted for Change	Victoria A. Farrar-Myers
Running against the Grain	David A. Crockett
Intelligence and National Security Policymaking on Iraq	Pfiffner and Phythian
Honest Broker? The National Security Advisor and Presidential Decision Making	John P. Burke
The Leadership of George Bush	Roman Popadiuk
The Unitary Executive and the Modern Presidency	Barilleaux and Kelley
The Provisional Pulpit	Brandon Rottinghaus
Bridging the Constitutional Divide	Russell L. Riley
White House Politics and the Environment	Daynes and Sussman
Nixon's Super-Secretaries	Mordecai Lee